Development in Latin America

Víctor Ramiro Fernández
Gabriel Brondino
Editors

Development in Latin America

Critical Discussions from the Periphery

palgrave
macmillan

Editors
Víctor Ramiro Fernández
Institute of the Humanities and Social Sciences of Litoral
National Scientific and Technical Research Council (CONICET) and National University of Litoral (UNL)
Santa Fe, Argentina

Gabriel Brondino
Institute of the Humanities and Social Sciences of Litoral
National Scientific and Technical Research Council (CONICET) and National University of Litoral (UNL)
Santa Fe, Argentina

ISBN 978-3-030-06380-1 ISBN 978-3-319-92183-9 (eBook)
https://doi.org/10.1007/978-3-319-92183-9

Cover image © EduLeite
Cover design: Akihiro Nakayama

Printed on acid-free paper

This Palgrave Macmillan imprint is published by the registered company Springer International Publishing AG part of Springer Nature.
The registered company address is: Gewerbestrasse 11, 6330 Cham, Switzerland

Preface

This book is part of an ambitious project that attempts to cross the borders of the Spanish and Portuguese speaking worlds and take to the Anglo-Saxon world a proposal oriented at recovering in a creative, non-dogmatic, and critical way the contributions of Latin American structuralism. From this, we expect to promote a novel lecture about the transformations that are taking place in the global economy and, especially, in its periphery.

The origins of the project can be traced back to a workshop held in March 2015 at the Institute of Economic Research of the National Autonomous University of Mexico (UNAM) with financial assistance from the Antipode Foundation. The workshop was coordinated by the Globalization, Knowledge, and Development Program (PROGLOCLODE) of UNAM, the Institute of Humanities and Social Sciences of the National University of Litoral and CONICET (Argentina), and the Institute of Urban and Regional Research and Planning of the Federal University of Rio de Janeiro, and a large group of researchers from different parts of Latin America participated.

One of the main conclusions in several discussions and debates of the workshop—especially but not exclusively about the fate of national political projects of the governments that were part of the "Pink Tide"—was about the necessity to strategically recover the contributions that Latin American structuralism made to development theory during the first decades after World War II. Such recovery ought to be dynamic, in the sense of recovering the most original elements of this school and interpellate them to the new global context.

This inspired the editors to organize and promote a new round of debates in another workshop with scholars belonging to different Latin American academic centers that eventually contributed to this volume. This time the workshop was held at Santa Fe, Argentina, in July 2017. There, the idea of revising central aspects of the evolution of structuralist thought was strengthened. Specifically, the need to recover the notion of power and domination as crucial categories of the analysis of development. Also, to critically revise other elements of the analysis as well as introduce absent ones. All these tasks were (and still are) in order to make structuralism fruitful again for analyzing peripheral development from the periphery.

This revision and update distance us from that followed by neo-structuralism in the early nineties. Neo-structuralism revision downplays precisely those elements we highlight: the conflict dimension of the analysis. Such dilution, in our opinion, has limited this school to understand, precisely, the *structural* factors that explain why the periphery, although it has been transformed into a dynamic space of accumulation, has generated inside its space new asymmetries and new forms of subalternity, and what measures should be taken to reverse them.

Alternatively, by following a different path, this book intends to recover Latin America's critical thinking tradition and contribute to think novel strategies of development. Although each chapter of this book has a different disciplinary background, it pursues a constructive dialogue among several disciplines belonging to the Social Sciences and tries to offer a holistic view of development.

We hope with this book to have advanced one step forward (as little as it may be) in recovering Latin America's capacity to think for itself, developing its own tools, and implementing its own policy. Even more, in building consciousness of the acritical and colonial assimilation of theories from the North in Latin American academic centers, particularly since the advent of the Washington Consensus.

Santa Fe, Argentina
March 2018

Víctor Ramiro Fernández
Gabriel Brondino

Acknowledgments

This book is not an exclusive work of the authors who participate in it, but also of many people who helped during the process of elaboration. We are deeply grateful to Joel Sidler for his patient and careful editing assistance. We thank Andrea Galeotti, Budi Akmal Djafar, and Marion Werner for reading parts of the manuscript and making thoughtful suggestions, as well as improving the English. We also thank our colleagues of the Research Group on Development, State, and Public Policy of the Institute of Humanities and Social Sciences of Litoral (Santa Fe, Argentina) for support during all the endeavor. Special thanks go to Andrés Cammisi and the State's Workers Association (*Asociación de Trabajadores del Estado*). Alina Yurova also deserves special thanks for being interested in this project and opening the doors at Palgrave for publishing. Finally, we would like to thank the National University of Litoral and the National Scientific and Technical Research Council of Argentina and congratulate them for their joint effort of creating the Institute of Humanities and Social Sciences of Litoral, the brand-new institute where this project took place.

Víctor Ramiro Fernández
Gabriel Brondino

Contents

Notes on Contributors

Carlos Antônio Brandão is Professor of Urban and Regional Planning in the Institute of Urban and Regional Research and Planning at Federal University of Rio de Janeiro (IPPUR/UFRJ). After receiving his PhD in Economics from the Unicamp, he focused on Urban and Regional Planning, acting on the following subjects: Latin American underdevelopment, regional development, and urban and regional planning.

Gabriel Brondino is Lecturer of Political Economy at The School of Social and Juridical Sciences of the National University of Litoral and Doctoral Fellow of Argentina's National Scientific and Technical Research Council. He received his MSc in Economic Development in 2016 from the University of San Martin and is a PhD candidate at the University of Buenos Aires.

Víctor Ramiro Fernández is Professor of Economic Geography and State Theory in the School of Humanities and Sciences at the National University of Litoral, Argentina. After receiving his PhD in Political Science in 1999 from the Autonomous University of Madrid, Spain, he was appointed researcher in Argentina's National Technical and Scientific Research Council (CONICET). He is the Director of the Institute of Humanities and Social Sciences of the Litoral (CONICET and UNL).

Armando Di Filippo is an Argentine economist, graduated from the National University of Litoral Argentina (1965), and Master in Economic Sciences from the University of Chile (1971). He worked as an international civil servant in UN ECLAC during the period (1970–2000). He has been a visiting professor at several universities in Europe and America, including the Universities of Barcelona (1997–2000), Paris (2001), and Stanford California (2005). He is the author among other books of *Desarrollo y desigualdad social en América Latina* (1981 Fondo de Cultura Económica) and of *Poder Capitalismo y Democracia* (2012 Editorial RIL).

Numa Mazat is Professor of Development Economics in the Institute of Economics at Federal University of Rio de Janeiro, Brazil. He received his PhD in 2013 from the Federal University of Rio de Janeiro. He was a visiting scholar at Columbia University (2013/2014) and an external consultant to the Brazilian Institute for Applied Economic Research (IPEA) and the CGEE/ECLAC.

Carlos Aguiar de Medeiros is Professor of Development Economics in the Institute of Economics at Federal University of Rio de Janeiro, Brazil and a CNPq researcher. He received his PhD in 1992 from the University of Campinas, Brazil. He was a visiting scholar at Cambridge University (2006) and an external consultant to the Brazilian Institute for Applied Economic Research (IPEA) and several United Nations organizations.

Margarita Olivera is Assistant Professor of Economic Development at the Institute of Economics (IE), Federal University of Rio de Janeiro, Brazil. After receiving her PhD in Economics in 2009 from the Sapienza University of Rome, Italy, she has been a post-doctoral researcher and Lecturer of Trade at the Masters' Programs of Economic Development and International Cooperation at National University of San Martin, Argentina from 2011 to 2014. She has been a visiting scholar at the JNIAS Institute of the Jawaharlal Nehru University, New Delhi, India in 2010, and a post-doctoral researcher and Lecturer of Economic Policy at the University of Pavia, Italy (2009–2010). Her areas of research are regional integration, trade and geopolitics in Latin America, and theories of growth and economic development.

Emilia Ormaechea is Lecturer of Globalization and Development at The School of Social and Juridical Sciences of the National University of Litoral and Doctoral Fellow of Argentina's National Scientific and Technical Research Council. She received her MSc in Social Science in 2018 from the National University of Litoral and is a PhD candidate in Economic Development at the National University of Quilmes.

Sebastián Sztulwark is a researcher at the Institute of Industry, National University of General Sarmiento, and at the National Scientific and Technical Research Council of Argentina (CONICET). He obtained his PhD in Economics from the National Autonomous University of México (UNAM). His fields of specialization are knowledge economics and development economics.

Davide Villani is a PhD candidate at the Open University, UK, and associate lecturer at Goldsmiths College. His research interest ranges from financialization, structural change, and economic development. His PhD thesis focuses on the increasing corporate lending of the corporate sector among developed countries.

Nicolás Hernán Zeolla holds an MSc in Economic Development from the University of San Martin and is a PhD candidate at the University of Buenos Aires. He is a doctoral fellow at the Centre for Studies on Economics and Development, Institute of High Social Studies, UNSAM, and CONICET. His research fields are international macroeconomics and finance, especially international capital flow regulation, corporate debt issuance, and asset structure. He is lecturer in the University of Buenos Aires, the National University of Avellaneda, and the National University of Lomas de Zamora.

List of Figures

List of Tables

CHAPTER 1

Introduction

Víctor Ramiro Fernández and Gabriel Brondino

There are two sentences written by Raúl Prebisch (1901–1986) in two milestone moments of his intellectual career and, simultaneously, of the situation of Latin America in the global capitalist economy that are worth noticing. The first one was formulated in the context of an enormous restructuring of global capitalism at the beginnings of the second post-war, where the new established architecture of international institutions led to the Golden Age of central capitalism, a unique phase of growth and industrialization:

> Why not search for our own principles when even traditional principles are suffering a severe process of critical revision? (Prebisch 1944, quoted in Mallorquín 2005, 384; authors' own translation)

It reflects Prebisch's ambition of setting up an original theoretical framework that accounts for the specificities of Latin American economies and what development strategy should follow. This was a task that he carried on tirelessly forward over the next four decades.

V. R. Fernández (✉) • G. Brondino
Institute of the Humanities and Social Sciences of Litoral, National Scientific and Technical Research Council (CONICET) and National University of Litoral (UNL), Santa Fe, Argentina
e-mail: rfernand@fcjs.unl.edu.ar

V. R. Fernández, G. Brondino (eds.), *Development in Latin America*,
https://doi.org/10.1007/978-3-319-92183-9_1

When he wrote the second sentence, it had been well over a decade since capitalism had suffered the crisis that ended the Golden Age, while Latin America arrived at a situation of fragility—that dragged long ago—inaugurating what was later known as the 'Lost Decade':

> Although in recent years I have tried to critically review my own thinking, to renew it to response for the changes that have taken place and collect the thought of others, I have not been able to dispense the center-periphery concept in which my first ideas of theoretical renovation materialized. I believe that it continues to be valid even when it is necessary to continue efforts to incorporate new elements, give it greater coherence, and gather the disperse fragments in a systematic presentation. (Prebisch 1981, 29; authors' own translation)

Both sentences share, however, the same nature: the challenge of building an analytical framework to interpret and orient development strategies for Latin America in the global capitalist economy, recognizing the center-periphery relations implied in its functioning.

From this challenge, Prebisch and an important group of intellectuals nucleated in the United Nations' Economic Commission for Latin America (and the Caribbean; henceforth ECLAC) gave birth to an original theoretical contribution, not limited to economic development and policy, but also to the social sciences in general, denominated as Latin American Structuralism. According to one of its major exponents, it was the only effort of creating a body of thought on economic policy that had emerged within the developing world (Furtado 2003).

Even when not all its members considered themselves as 'structuralists', the origin of the concept lies in the effort of analyzing the dynamics of capitalism and of Latin America from a structural perspective. Such perspective did not deny the theoretical frameworks imported from the center, but rather creatively rearticulate them to generate a novel interpretation of the opportunities and challenges to development in Latin America within the global structure of center-periphery relations.

An 'originality of the copy', as denominated by Cardoso (1977), that did not appeal to the notion of structure as an abstract field of static logical relations, as in European structuralism—particularly, as in Levi Strauss' structuralism, but rather attempted to understand the peripheral condition through a methodological apparatus that recognized the diachrony and the historical specificity of the region and the way in which non-economic factors affected economic models. Hence, differently from

French Marxist structuralism, Latin American structuralism was idiosyncratic and 'historical', even when one can recognize different sources of inspiration in each member of the school in the combination of structure and process (Boianovsky 2015).

The introduction of historical trajectories and the proper combination of structure-process in the analysis also distinguishes the approach from Anglo-Saxon structuralism. In the latter, the analysis of underdevelopment consists of identifying structural 'rigidities' that impede the proper functioning of free markets (Arndt 1985). Its point of departure was to revisit the assumptions of neoclassical theory that were inadequate to understand backward economies and modify them to adapt the general theory to that peculiar cases (Arndt 1988).

From such structural-historical analysis of Latin American development emerged the need to promote structural change, based on what the center had and the periphery lacked, that is, on an industrialization capable of mitigating internal social and productive inequalities, and simultaneously accomplish a better international insertion.

The possibility of structuralism to advance the theoretical and empirical arguments that grounded the necessity and the form of structural change in a peripheral context became the cause of the temporal distance between the two challenges launched by Prebisch. The first challenge may be interpreted as the trigger of what eventually was an invaluable collection of knowledge for understanding the obstacles and tasks for the development of the periphery in the world-system. The second challenge continues to weigh like a dagger among Latin American social scientists, a challenge that is today even more relevant considering the last 20 years of political and economic variations in the region.

Latin America inaugurated the twenty-first century with big expectations given non-minor political changes that started in Venezuela with the ascent of Hugo Chavez and the Bolivarian revolution, the election of Lula da Silva of the Worker's Party in Brazil in 2002, together with the rise of left or center-left governments in Argentina, Uruguay, Bolivia, Nicaragua, Ecuador, Chile, and Paraguay. Although variegated in origins and forms, such experiences coped a great part of the region and formed what has been denominated as the 'Pink Tide' (Chodor 2015).

Such governments pushed forward the creation of macro-regional institutions such as the Bolivarian Alliance for the Peoples of Our America (ALBA), the Union of South American Nations (UNASUR), the Bank of the South, and reinforced the Southern Common Market (MERCOSUR).

These institutions reflected the will to construct an autonomous space associated with the need to promote an alternative project beyond the neoliberal hegemony that dominated in the nineties.

The governments of the pink tide attempted to recover several principles widely promoted but hardly accomplished, such as equality in the most unequal region of the world, the deepening of democracy after fragile transitions from military regimes, and the expansion of civil and social rights to ethnic and minority groups historically relegated. And it did so by opposing the omnipotent free-market ideology that the Washington Consensus imposed.

The inspiring Latin American setting, accompanied by sustained output growth and reduction of poverty and inequality, began progressively to crumble at the beginning of the second decade of this century. Brazil experienced a singular coupe d'état by parliamentary ways, Argentina moved from a neo-developmentalist project to a conservative one, while Venezuela has gone through external and internal deterioration that weakens its government against the opponents of the Chavist legacy. Such stage of regression broke the institutional support of the main representatives of the Latin American pink tide.

Notwithstanding the causes that have given rise to the retreat of the pink tide, which are still a matter of discussion among scholars, it is interesting to stand out this institutional regression as a manifestation of the historical difficulties that the region has had to constitute a political bloc with a regional integration mode alternative to that promoted by central countries, specifically the United States. Indeed, it is important to highlight that the main regional institution of South America, MERCOSUR, has now been transformed, under the leadership of Brazil and Argentina, into an operating center to dismantle neo-developmentalist projects, to weaken and isolate the political projects that resist the current neoliberal turn, and to reorient the integration process toward a complementation with the Pacific Alliance. And this retreat is within a context of uncertainty awakened by the undefined strategy of President Trump and the expansion of China in the region.

This new setting of Latin America resumes the discourse of the Washington Consensus, associated with the need and benefits of integrating to the international market and the avoidance of populist management, but still contains the same historical unresolved problems: primary or semi-industrialized economic structures, fragile positions in global value chains, social and spatial heterogeneities, that in conjunction reproduce income and wealth inequality and low long-run growth.

The vertiginous changes experimented in the region in the last 40 years or so must be understood within the context of a larger transformation scenario. We are referring to the process of global restructuring of capitalism by the end of the sixties and beginning of the seventies. Such restructuring implied a qualitative change of the links between global processes and national trajectories. Enabled by technological progress, a new temporal-spatial logic of reproduction of capitalism emerged, based on increasing financialization and fragmentation of production. However, this new logic left unaltered the hierarchical center-periphery structure of the capitalist system, notwithstanding the evidence of some cases of development within the periphery, specifically in East Asia, and the recent rise of China as a contesting power to US hegemony.

Within this complex setting, the following questions are in order: what are the factors that weaken the development of the periphery? What is the relevance of center-periphery categories for the analysis of development? What role do geopolitics and geoeconomics have in understanding the different trajectories of the periphery? What is the role of the State and in what form it must be implicated? What are the possibilities of building a consistent and enduring development policy within the periphery, specifically Latin America? What is the importance of industrialization and industrial policy for development in the periphery? How does financialization impact in the periphery and what types of financial policies are required? Such questions demand, in turn, an enveloping question: which analytical tools are required for a proper answer?

Neither Prebisch's thought, his founding idea of center-periphery and Latin American structuralism in general, nor the reality in which such ideas took place have been static. Indeed, in the mid-seventies, there was a process of crisis and restructuring of capitalist accumulation on a global scale, whose mutations are still under discussion today. Prebisch's second sentence consequently invites us to reflect on the validity of structuralist thought and the center-periphery analysis. Hence, it demands to ask: in what way has structuralism responded to the changes of its dynamic reality?

As a general answer, we sustain that the theoretical heritage of structuralism is of great relevance to reflect on Latin American development in the current vertiginous process of capitalist transformation. Despite the passage of time, and considering the criticism and rejection received, center-periphery analysis is still relevant, especially when combined with the notion of structural heterogeneity. Such articulation allows a proper analysis of the limits and distortions of the 'peripheral' accumulation process, based on the study of internal socio-productive structures, the international insertion, and how different actors (and their interests) are embedded in power relations both inside and outside the peripheral national spaces.

On the internal side, structuralism identified a heterogeneous social structure that enhances, contrary to the center, a heterogeneous productive structure associated, in turn, with an imitative and exclusive consumption pattern. Such dynamic was the cause of the inability to transform the pattern of accumulation that would, on the external side, allow a change in the traditional specialization pattern based on exports of primary goods, as well as avoid a passive assimilation of foreign technology and capital imposed by transnational companies.

Both internal and external processes cannot be understood if not properly located within a framework of power and conflictive relations, commanded by domestic oligarchies in alliance with transnational companies.

Based on this theoretical framework, during the seventies, a leading group of structuralists opened a rich debate about 'development styles'. Such debate was intended to delve with the Latin American style, especially focusing on what type of structural change was required and what was the political viability to pursue it.

However, as warned by Prebisch in the second sentence cited above, the durability and usefulness of the approach ultimately depend on its ability to incorporate 'new elements' that allow to understand those aspects that, at the time, were not visible in the Golden Age of capitalism. That is, it depends on its capacity to incorporate elements that allow to understand the great transformations operated in capitalism in the last 40 years or so.

To what extent has progress been made in this direction? After the great crisis of the seventies, structuralism sought to adequate its framework in face of two convergent processes. On the one hand, the globalization process led by central capital as an attempt to overcome distributive conflicts within their national spaces and to avoid domestic control and regulations, on the other hand, the crisis of industrialization strategies in some countries of Latin America. At the level of ideas, the revitalization of liberal thinking in the field of development associated the failures of industrialization with structuralist thinking.

In such context, and after Prebisch's last work (Prebisch 1981), ECLAC inaugurated a new research program, called neo-structuralism, that aspired to bring up to date his predecessors' ideas in order to made them consistent with the new global and regional reality.

However, the contributions of neo-structuralism by the end of the eighties and up to date, self-proclaimed as a part of the theoretical heterodoxy, led to a displacement of the role of power relations associated with conflict and domination. Such concepts had acquired increasing relevance over time in structuralist thought, in part due to the interaction of the approach with other theories such as dependency analysis (*dependentismo*). They also had a clear presence in Prebisch's last work, where it is in fact reflected a transition from strict economic analysis toward a multidisciplinary perspective.

Through the conceptual displacing of power and the contradictory and conflictive relations implied in it, the new analytical perspective developed by neo-structuralism has upset in a risky way substantial theoretical elements of their predecessors, which affect both the type of diagnosis made and the development strategies suggested. In another sense, the displacement leads to the 'functionalization' of the neo-structuralist framework to the new forms of center-periphery reproduction. Indeed, it is important to understand that the 'center' neither transfers nor grants changes in the forms of accumulation, but rather seeks to couple the periphery to its own accumulation process, and one way of doing it is by imposing their rules of the game (theories as well as political and administrative tools that are concretely implemented in decision-making) correlated to their interests.

In sum, the recent economic and political oscillations of Latin America and the restrictions and weaknesses of neo-structuralism demand a 'return forwards', a 'back to the future': a revision to recover the forgotten and submerged analytical categories of structuralism that give account of the peripheral condition, as well as the obstacles and limitations which are to be faced to overcome it.

It is in the context of such recovery that this book accepts Prebisch's challenge of incorporating new and rich elements that strengthen and qualify Latin American critical thought of development. Such acceptance must discourage any attempt of returning to structuralism as an historical story in a determinate moment of Latin American history. The invitation repels the idea of going back to it as a sarcophagus that is opened and the valuable remains are extracted to be exhibit in a sort of open museum of ideas. We propose, rather, to show structuralism as an inspiring platform to interpret the positioning and the alternatives of the region in face of the profound transformations of global capitalism in the last decades. Our aim is to update it in an alternative way as proposed by neo-structuralism.

What are, then, the novel elements that should be introduced to answer Prebisch's challenge? In this book, we will focus on seven interrelated dimensions:

1. Given the relevance of center and periphery, an analysis of the transformation that such concepts underwent in face of the crisis and restructuring of capitalism in late seventies.
2. An understanding of the multiple spatial scales (regional, national, subnational) in which the process of capitalist restructuring is deployed.
3. An understanding of the current action margins and past conditionings within the geopolitics and geoeconomics of capitalism; aspects often implicit but basically absent in structuralist analysis.
4. The paradoxical place given to State in structuralist analysis, where it has an increasing importance in the analysis but simultaneously has increasing limitations to act or influence in the structural transformation of the economies.
5. Based on the last point, a discussion of the alternatives for industrialization in the periphery and the new modes of industrial policy in face of the current context of internationalization of production.
6. Linked to previous items, an analysis of the role of finance capital and the current process of financialization in peripheral strategies of development, as well as the nexus between finance and productive investment.
7. Finally, a discussion of alternative ways of regional integration to deploy strategic development policies (based on the previous discussion) in Latin America.

The acknowledgments and recoveries proposed run in parallel of pointing out a series of absences, weaknesses, and due updates required by structuralism in the different dimensions analyzed in this book. At the same time, in addressing these dimensions, the restrictions and necessary reformulations of neo-structuralism are stand out.

As a final remark, this book intends to promote from the periphery and toward the center, but specially within the periphery, an intensive research program that recovers and updates the contributions to development analysis made from the periphery to face the complex and changing nature of global capitalism and its impact on these areas in the new century.

References

Arndt, Heinz W. 1985. The Origins of Structuralism. *World Development* 13 (2). Pergamon: 151–159. https://doi.org/10.1016/0305-750X(85)90001-4.

———. 1988. 'Market Failure' and Underdevelopment. *World Development* 16 (2). Pergamon: 219–229. https://doi.org/10.1016/0305-750X(88)90137-4.

Arrighi, Giovanni, and Jessica Drangel. 1986. The Stratification of the World-Economy: An Exploration of the Semiperipheral Zone. *Review (Fernand Braudel Center)* 10 (1). Research Foundation of SUNY for and on behalf of the Fernand Braudel Center: 9–74. https://doi.org/10.2307/40241047.

Boianovsky, Mauro. 2015. Between Lévi-Strauss and Braudel: Furtado and the Historical-Structural Method in Latin American Political Economy. *Journal of Economic Methodology* 22 (4). Routledge: 413–438. https://doi.org/10.1080/1350178X.2015.1024879.

Cardoso, Fernando Henrique. 1977. The Originality of a Copy: CEPAL and the Idea of Development. *CEPAL Review* 4: 7–40.

Chodor, Tom. 2015. *Neoliberal Hegemony and the Pink Tide in Latin America*. London: Palgrave Macmillan UK. https://doi.org/10.1057/9781137444684.

Furtado, Celso. 2003. *En Busca de un Nuevo Modelo: Reflexiones sobre la Crisis Contemporánea*. Buenos Aires: Fondo de Cultura Económica.

Mallorquín, Carlos. 2005. Raúl Prebisch y el Deterioro de la Tesis de los Términos de Intercambio. *Revista Mexicana de Sociología* 67 (2): 379–426. http://www.scielo.org.mx/scielo.php?script=sci_arttext&pid=S0188-25032005000200005&nrm=iso.

Prebisch, Raúl. 1981. *El Capitalismo Periférico: Crisis y Transformación*. México, D.F.: Fondo de Cultura Económica.

CHAPTER 2

Why Does Structuralism Return to the Forefront?

Víctor Ramiro Fernández and Gabriel Brondino

Introduction

In this chapter, we discuss Latin American structuralist thought and the transformations it underwent after the neo-structuralist renewal.[1] The initial analysis of the United Nations' Economic Commission for Latin America[2] (ECLAC), during the fifties, was biased (or focused almost strictly) toward the economic aspects of development. The malformations associated with the industrialization process evidenced in the sixties, in a regional context of increasing tension due to social conflict and revolutionary movements, led to a review of the initial propositions and to the introduction of sociological and political elements into the picture. Specifically, contributions in this period highlighted the role of power and domination in defining the structure of both domestic and international social relations in peripheral capitalism.

The structural crisis of capitalism on a global scale in the seventies deepened the crisis of industrialization in Latin America. Successive restructuring

V. R. Fernández (✉) • G. Brondino
Institute of the Humanities and Social Sciences of Litoral, National Scientific and Technical Research Council (CONICET) and National University of Litoral (UNL), Santa Fe, Argentina
e-mail: rfernand@fcjs.unl.edu.ar

V. R. Fernández, G. Brondino (eds.), *Development in Latin America*,
https://doi.org/10.1007/978-3-319-92183-9_2

obliged Latin American economies to adjust their productive structures to the new global regime of accumulation and international order of rules and regulation. The transition was not an easy process, as was evidenced in the eighties. Eventually, large-scale reform took place under the sign of neo-liberalism. Under neo-liberal hegemony, ECLAC revised its theoretical framework to offer an alternative policy vision to the Washington Consensus (WC) in the nineties, denominated *neo-structuralism*.

This revision, nonetheless, led to important theoretical transformations of its predecessor. In this chapter, we focus on showing that the neo-structuralist renewal implied a dilution or simply exclusion of the analysis of power and domination relations, and discuss the consequences of such absence for the analysis and formulation of development strategies. Such consequences lead us to revisit structuralism precisely on this abandoned aspect. However, such revisiting demands both to attend the transformations in capitalism in the last 40 years and to introduce some other elements that were weakly theorized.

We organize this chapter into four sections. The first section discusses how development thinking in Latin America evolved during the golden age of capitalism (from post-World War II to mid-seventies). This section has, in turn, three subsections. The first one analyzes the essential aspects of the emergence and development of structuralism. The second one discusses the origins of dependency analysis and its criticism to structuralism. The third one highlights how this criticism impacts later elaborations of structuralism, based mainly on introducing political and sociological elements into the analysis, then dominated by an economic perspective.

The second section analyzes the convergence of the global crisis of capitalism and the Latin American crisis of industrialization during the seventies. The crisis, along with substantial lobbying of right-wing circles, enables the emergence of neo-liberal development policy in the region and weakens the structuralist development program. Neo-structuralism emerged as a renewed approach of structuralism, and as an alternative to neo-liberal thinking. Such a shift, as we have said, brings forward substantial changes in the theoretical conceptualization of peripheral societies.

In the third section, we pretend to go "back to the future" and recover the contributions of the "last" Prebisch and link them to "late" structuralism. Prebisch's last writings provided an alternative solution—and formulated answers—to deal with the emerging regional crisis of the seventies and eighties.

The fourth and last section focuses on the elements that are necessary to be reconsidered, introduced, and articulated to recover structuralism as a theoretical platform for discussing development in the periphery in the new century and for promoting development policies. In this way, we anticipate how each element will be discussed in the following chapters.

Post-World War II Global Order and Latin American Structuralism

A Fertile Context for the Birth of Latin American Structuralism

Toward the end of the forties, Raúl Prebisch, together with a group of intellectuals working in the recently created ECLAC, advanced the hypothesis that the development problems of Latin America were caused mainly by the effects of the international trade pattern (and division of labor) until then in force. Contrary to the traditional vision that free trade and specialization would lead to a convergence of incomes, Prebisch held that international economic relations were not between equal nations, but between hierarchically structured central and peripheral countries, and that this structural difference led to divergence. The main form in which this divergence manifested was in the observed phenomenon of a deterioration in the terms of trade of peripheral economies (Prebisch 1949).[3] Although international relations in trade and finance were the main vehicle for transmission, at the root of the problem layed the asymmetrical distribution of the fruits of technical progress.

To break with this unequal development dynamic, it was necessary to promote autonomously a process of industrialization. Industrialization was believed to be the main driver of growth and technical progress, and an important source of employment (Prebisch 1952). Thus, ECLAC's analysis constituted the ideological support of the Import Substitution Industrialization (ISI) policies that were being promoted by many countries in the region. If, as Love (1995, 305) says, reality had preceded politics, and politics had preceded theory, it was now the job of the theory to set the foundation for a strategy that was gaining ground in the region and other undeveloped spaces during the interwar period, especially after the crisis of the thirties.

After World War II, the objective of economic and social security was as important as political and military security, given the experience of the Great Depression in the thirties and its association with the emergence of totalitarian regimes (Polanyi 2001). Although the United States affirmed its global hegemony in the fifties, the upsurge of decolonization processes and the nationalist empowerment linked to self-determination of new countries made the United Nations (UN) a truly global entity and its institutions more independent of the American guidance (Toye and Toye 2004). ECLAC and structuralism conformed, respectively, the institutional and conceptual platforms to back up industrial policies oriented to promote the structural change required to overcome the peripheral condition. Industrialization represented the inevitable road toward development and, according to Prebisch, it was the main mean of expansion for the region.

Failed Expectations and the Emergence of Dependency Analysis

Throughout the fifties, the global context and the policies implemented favored the expansion and consolidation of an industrialization process that was the basis for sustained growth in the region. However, toward the end of that decade, bottlenecks related to the process became apparent and the conditions were not reached to face the "difficult" phase of substitution (Baer 1972). The evidence raised the alarm that industrialization did not linearly imply development. As stated by Hirschman (1968, 32), "industrialization was expected to change the social order and all it did was to supply manufactures." There was a consensus that ISI had reached its limits. Furtado (1966, 375), for example, claimed that:

> In Latin America ... there is a general consciousness of living through a period of decline ... The phase of 'easy' development, through increased exports of primary products or through import substitution, has everywhere been exhausted.

"Actually existing" industrialization was very different from the one conceptualized by ECLAC, and this was aptly reflected in the notion of "structural heterogeneity" (Pinto 1970). Peripheral economies manifested substantial disparities at social (income), economic (productivity), and spatial (regions) levels (see the next subsection).

Additional to this regional economic context, a process of social resistance and revolution (Gunder Frank 1969) contributed to an increasingly complex and inhospitable scenario for the certification of ECLAC's proposals. Critics both within and out of ECLAC emphasized the bias toward internal markets, the excessive state intervention, and the strong tariff protection of ISI; on the other hand, they recommended the need for rationalization of imports combined with an active export promotion of manufactures and regional integration (Bielschowsky 2016).

At the beginning of the sixties, Prebisch left the executive secretariat of ECLAC and assumed first the direction of the Latin American Institute for Economic and Social Planning (ILPES), and later the United Nations Conference on Trade and Development (UNCTAD) (Gabay 2008). Prebisch's departure and the power loss of the institution "to explain the economic stagnation and aggravation of social problems in Latin America during the 1960's" (Bodenheimer 1970, 124) further consolidated the critics' position of their growing dissatisfaction with ECLAC's posture.

A great deal of criticism came from left-wing scholars who, departing from Prebisch's analysis, opened a debate about dependency relations of the periphery with the center in global capitalism. Dependency analysis was clearly more complex and radical than its structuralist precursor, as well as wider in its sources, since many of its promoters came from Marxist circles outside Latin America (Paul Baran, André Gunder Frank, Samir Amin, among others), as well as inside (Ruy Mauro Marini, Theotônio dos Santos, Vania Bambirra, among others). Even though it emerged at the beginnings of the sixties, it was in the second half of that decade that the approach reached its culminating point. Discussions about dependency continued during the seventies as well.[4]

Despite specificities in the different contributions of dependency analysis (Kay 1989), one can identify two common elements. First, the idea that the peripheral condition can only be understood by studying the functioning of the global structure of capitalism. The dependency analysis was particularly concerned with how the general structure of capitalism conditioned the dynamics of the periphery (Cardoso 1980). Second, the dependency analysis introduced sociological and political insight to the study of peripheral capitalism and its development.

However, the mechanic-formal analysis with a lack of historical rigor of dependency analysis left a vacuum to explain national and regional specificities of the relations of production (Laclau 1971). In this sense, dependency analyses encouraged a view in which, as long as capitalism existed, the periphery would continue to reproduce in conditions of super-exploitation led by transnational capital in connivance with imperialist nations; development of the core produced underdevelopment of the periphery (Gunder Frank 1966). Therefore, the action margin of the latter to develop an autonomous and endogenous space of accumulation within capitalism was inexistent. Dependency analysis not only questioned the unfeasibility of developing the periphery under capitalism, but also the faith of the latter.

This vision showed that the distance with structuralism was widening. In the middle of the seventies, Gunder Frank (1977, 358) claimed that in face of "the attendant critical problems in Latin America and elsewhere, the developmentist old dependence theory (sic) [structuralism], and indeed ideology, appears to be entirely bankrupt". Such verdict was not unlinked from the general idea that ECLAC's view was "a way to put blinkers on the consciousness of the peoples, showing them just a straight path ahead towards a prosperous future through industrialization and the strengthening of the State" (Cardoso 1977, 14).

Dependency analysts were not in agreement with structuralism's state-led reformist strategy and considered it naïve to call for foreign investments to complement domestic efforts of industrialization. On the contrary, for them, foreign capital, materialized in the increasing relevance of transnational companies, was a necessary movement of the new and increasing needs of central capitalism to exploit the periphery (Marini 1977).

While the cold war was sharpening, political revolutions in the region consolidated and threatened to spread together with the growing insurrectional imaginary. In this context, capitalism began to be judged for its loss of dynamism and its propensity to stagnate. Even though such pessimism was objectionable in facts (Palma 1978), dependency analysis encouraged scholars and political activists to think that there was no sense to continue to develop within a "dying" system, rather, detach from such dependency completely, thereby transcending capitalism and building socialism.

However, "history built up a trap against the wave of pessimism" and this was very much so for capitalism (Cardoso 1977, 32). Capitalism was not heading to its collapse, but, on the contrary, it experienced a profound restructuring of its regime of accumulation and mode of regulation that recreated its dynamism (see the next section). On the other hand, in other peripheral spaces, a handful of development experiences belied the deterministic view of dependency analysis and laid the foundations for discussing the exit of the peripheral condition through industrialization directed by the state (Evans and Deyo 1987).

The Contributions of Political Science and Sociology to the "Economics" of Structuralism: "Late" Structuralism

Structuralism did not remain static in face of the criticism by dependency analysis and the convoluted regional scenario of the sixties and seventies. Structuralism in general and ECLAC, in particular, were compelled to break with a perspective that was exclusively focused on economics (Rodríguez 1980). This process of conceptual openness gave birth to contributions that incorporated the sociological and political dimension to center-periphery analysis and highlighted the role of power and domination in social relations.

Such a multidisciplinary approach enriched the analysis of the forms that the process of accumulation and distribution adopted in the periphery. Differently from dependency analysis, "late" structuralism did not depart from a deterministic view where the global system absorbed and diluted national and regional particularities, but rather it identified an amalgam of historically constructed actors and institutions that shaped a complex matrix of classes and interests that gave place to specific socio-economic formations in the region (Cardoso and Faletto 1969).[5]

From the analysis of the feedback between the impact of Latin American external insertion, and its internal socio-political configuration, the notion of "structural heterogeneity" was born, developed by Anibal Pinto (1919–1996). Such a concept attempted to highlight the specificity of the Latin American development process, by showing how the combination of industrialization by substitution, the traditional specialization pattern, and the internal power structure tended to shape a socio-productive structure with dissimilar productivity and income levels among sectors and strata. Such a structure promoted a process of accumulation where heterogeneity was accentuated rather than reduced. In Pinto's own words:

> The pace of development has been far from accelerating, consolidating and becoming "self-sustained"; Dependency on the exterior has changed in outward appearance, but in many cases it has become just as influential as in the past [chronic indebtedness, alienation of economic policy decisions, technological subordination, foreignization (*extranjerización*) of basic activities, etc.]; Large segments of the population, the productive structure and the "economic space" have been totally or substantially excluded from the progress made in the "modern pole". In other words, the fruits of technical progress have been concentrated in three ways: at the social level, in terms of economic "strata", and at the regional level. Lastly—and more importantly—there is no real sign

> that the trend in question will correct itself spontaneously. On the contrary, it seems reasonable to assume—and there are arguments to support this hypothesis—that it could or ought to accentuate. (Pinto in Bielschowsky 2016, 307)

In such a framework, there was a skeptical and critical view of the role of foreign capital and its links with national (dis)integration and (the lack of) autonomy. The presence of transnational companies progressively transformed the center-periphery relationship, breaking the contradictory logic of industrialization and dependency, making possible a "path of 'dependent development'" (Palma 1978, 909).

ECLAC's initial analysis was not so critical but optimist with the potential role of foreign capital.[6] For example, Prebisch (1963, 5–6), worried about "the marked failure of capital formation to reach the levels demanded by contemporary technology", believed that

> foreign enterprise has a very important part to play, both because of its knowledge of export practices and external markets, and on account of its level of technical and economic know-how, which domestic firms cannot usually attain in a short time. (Prebisch 1963, 56)

However, as the negative effects of foreign enterprises began to be apparent, structuralists argued that transnational companies settled with the elitist and constrained demand of protected internal markets, with a higher propensity to import and a reluctance to export (Marinho 1981). It thus reinforced the dependent productive structure, inhibited the possibility to develop an autonomous space of accumulation, and aggravated the processes of social and spatial disintegration and inequality. Foreign penetration, in fact, manifested not only at the productive level, but also culturally and ideologically through the system of advertising and mass media, and politically through the pressure of private international and national organizations to favor their interests (Sunkel 1971, 58–60).

Another subject of major revision was the role of the state in peripheral economies. Initially, the state was considered an active promoter of development, responsible for planning the allocation of resources for industrialization and structural change. The state demanded by ECLAC was even more "interventionist" than a central state, given that it had to develop the economy in a period shorter than what it took in central nations (Gurrieri 1987). In the original position, however, there was not a thorough analysis of the socio-political restrictions peripheral states had to carry on this task.

Contributions in the sixties added more realism to this initial technocratic vision of the state. Among these, those of Jorge Graciarena, Marcos Kaplan, Octavio Ianni, and Guillermo O'Donnell stand out.[7] The introduction of sociological and political elements into the analysis displaced the imaginary full of assumptions about the state's capabilities to act upon the society and its economy. On the contrary, the state was caught in between a complex framework of actors, where dominant classes and foreign corporations limited structural changes and sought to capture the state and prevent developmental projects that could turn the balance of power against them. Based on a conflictual class-based schema, it was argued that the state reproduced, while it was limited to modify, structural heterogeneity.

The given levels of inequality and exclusion in the region explained part of the insurrectional turmoil, triggered by the Cuban revolution and the proliferation of social movements and resistance against capitalism and imperialism. Since the Alliance for Progress program was unable to overcome such confrontation, the United States changed its geopolitical strategy in the region and attempted more direct ways to intervene through the promotion of authoritative regimes (O'Donnell 1978a).

In this context, a discussion of the "development styles" in the region was underway. The initial efforts were carried forward by the Mathematical Models Group (*Grupo de Modelos Matemáticos*) of the Center of Development Studies (*Centro de Estudios del Desarrollo*, CENDES), under the leadership of Oscar Varsavsky (CENDES 1969; Varsavsky 1971). There was an increasing nonconformity not only about the process of development in Latin America but also about the concept of development itself. They considered the association of development with high-income levels per capita a quantitative fallacy.

> Development is a relative concept, but relative to the goals that a country poses itself; to its own National Project ... If the current state of our country is not like we—not the IDB or the IMF—want it to be, then we are underdeveloped. When we reach our objectives, we will be developed ... We should not care less if this happy time comes, that the United States or the economists continue to call us underdeveloped because we do not have a maximum income per capita. (Varsavsky, quoted in Pinto 1978, 564; translation by the authors)

How could development be pursued and for whom? What was the development style necessary and feasible for Latin America? Can we really find alternative styles with respect to those followed by central countries? What are the structural constraints to such alternative paths? Graciarena (1976, 186) defined a development style as the "specific and dynamic modality adopted by a social system within a particular context and at a particular moment in history". Such modality, then, should be understood within a structurally conflictive system, as well as within the historically shaped structures inside that system. Hence, "the style's viability depends on the social forces it can mobilize to overcome obstacles and resistance to its implementation or continuity" (Graciarena 1976, 181). Note the importance of introducing the notion of power into the analysis, since:

> the agents, in order to be effective and to be able to make their styles viable, must necessarily be a power elite, a dominating group, coalition or class, an "Establishment", or some other similar entity which controls the State apparatus. (Graciarena 1976, 182)

Through the introduction of socio-political elements (the role of power, conflictive dynamics, etc.) into "pure" economic analysis, a proper understanding of peripheral development was reached. In such understanding, structural heterogeneity, the impact of foreign capital, and the nature of peripheral states and its implication played a major role in the discussion of viable and desirable "development styles". The analysis of "peripheral condition" had reached by then the "age of majority". These contributions were developed, however, in a period in which the Golden Age and Latin American industrialization entered their decline.

Converging Crises in the Seventies and the New Global Scenario for Latin American Periphery

Crisis and Restructuring of Global Capitalism

By the end of the sixties and throughout the next two decades, capitalism underwent a crisis of global magnitudes. The fall in the rate of profit due to an intensification of the distributive conflict within central nations marked the end of the Golden Age of growth, supposedly based on a "collaborative" arrangement between capital and labor, regulated by welfare states (Cavalieri et al. 2004).

The way out of the conflict was through a profound restructuring of the organizational forms of industrial capital and a substantive change in the managerial practices of large enterprises (Duménil and Lévy 2001). The direct effect of the restructuring was the geographic relocation of production, which promoted industrialization in several parts of the periphery and led to the formation of a new international division of labor (Fröbel et al. 1977). Such industrialization, however, did not lead to income-level convergence (Arrighi et al. 2003).

The main vehicles of global productive restructuring were, on the one hand, the technological progress made in connective technologies (transportation and communication), which allowed firms to operate globally in real time (Castells 2009, Chap. 3), and on the other, the increasing process of financialization (Duménil and Lévy 2007).

Transformations, nonetheless, did not stop at the productive and accumulative levels. Profound alterations of the regulatory-institutional apparatus also took place and several global (and more aggressive) institutions started to gain relevance on policy decisions of national states (Kotz and McDonough 2010). The emerging institutional apparatus pressed for a dismantling of national barriers to the free movement of financial capital and deregulation of the economy in general. In this sense, the new context implied a change in the correlation of forces, in which capital took the offensive to restore its power and interests. Global fractions of capital gained more and more conditioning capacity over smaller fractions of capital, labor, and the state, whose action capacity was circumscribed to the national space (Ross and Trachte 1990).

Repercussions in Latin America: Crisis of Industrialization and Structural Adjustment

Global restructuring converged and simultaneously contributed to the growing crisis of the ISI model in Latin America—a model that ECLAC had encouraged but was not necessarily responsible for its distorted translation. National specificities aside, almost all countries in the region showed problems associated with its productive structure. As mentioned above, such problems were related to the difficulties of building capital-goods industries and competitive consumer-goods industries in the international markets. This productive structure led to bottlenecks in the growth phase that put pressure on the trade balance and contributed to its deterioration. Structural deficits aggravated in the second half of the seventies, and this led to a process of growing external indebtedness (Bértola and Ocampo 2012).

The indebtedness was encouraged by financial centers through international banking institutions, holders of an enormous mass of floating capital due to the massive transfer of income from oil-importer countries to oil-exporter countries in the advent of the 1973 Oil Shock. Given the recessive context in the center, such surpluses were channeled to the periphery in the form of loose credits (Thorp 1998, Chap. 7; Devlin and Ffrench-Davis 1995).

Unlike the development experience of European countries at the end of the nineteenth century, or of East Asia after World War II, where states were constituted as coherent power centers, Latin American states were vulnerable against the global crisis and the subsequent capital restructuring and were incapable of implementing ECLAC's proposals. The absence in Latin America of consolidated industrial nuclei and strong states excluded the possibility of building a regional political bloc, capable of resistance or more autonomy with respect to the globalization process (Fiori 1992).

The convergence of the crises also led, as we have stated, to a geopolitical shift of the United States toward the region: from a promotion of aid for development programs to an implicit support of military coups and the implantation of (mostly bloody) authoritarian regimes that interrupted the democratic process. The authoritarian political processes assured the dismantling of social and institutional resistance and adapted the states to the new conditions of indebtedness, sponsored by the financial fraction of transnational enterprises. Such fractions were allies of a great part of the local oligarchies, privileged beneficiaries of the bonds created within the process (Millet and Toussaint 2003). During this process, Latin American debt grew by a factor of ten between beginnings of the seventies and the mid-nineties (Acosta Espinosa 1998).

This debt-led growth process ended abruptly in 1982 with the rise in the interest rates of the Federal Reserve of the United States (Bryan 2013). Such anti-inflationary policy on behalf of the United States aggravated the external fragility of the region, reducing the possibilities of debt renewal and increasing the payments of its services.

Lobby groups and academic circles advocating for economic restructuring capitalized this critical conjuncture to criticize the ISI model and discredit ECLAC and structuralism as their promoters. They argue that the ISI policy was biased toward internal markets and generated misallocation of resources. In other words, the ISI strategy created a large market distortion that favored state enterprises that are often large, inefficient, and potentially corrupt. The elevated protection levels led economic agents to concentrate their efforts on seeking political rents (Krueger 1974), and to an expansion of state expenditures. In the absence of an adequate tax structure, budget deficits increased, and this was—the argument followed—the ultimate cause of high inflation and external disequilibria. Skeptics of the ISI approach argue that to ensure production efficiency, states must dismantle the ISI institutions, liberalize and deregulate markets, reduce expenditures and privatize state-owned enterprise (restructure the state), and reorient the economy toward international markets. These policy recommendations were at the basis of the Structural Adjustment Programs (SAPs) promoted by the international financial institutions (IFIs) (Balassa 1984).

The mainstream prescription for economic growth for the periphery was largely disappointing and the eighties were considered as "the lost decade". The implementation of SAPs did not correct the external disequilibria; rather, heavy restriction to stimulate internal demand generated social deterioration and low activity levels, while inflation persisted (Agarwal and Sengupta 1999; Glassman and Carmody 2001).

The failure of SAP could have marked the end of the IFIs'—such as the World Bank and the International Monetary Fund—role as the instrument to promote the interests of the global capitalist system. Paradoxically, these institutions gained strength and successfully maintained their hegemony. In fact, at the beginnings of the nineties, these Washington-based institutions had gained an unprecedented power not only to impose but also to irradiate the neo-classical paradigm. With notable simplicity, it was installed in the popular imagination that all economic and social problems were due to excessive state intervention and that the solution was pro-market policies.[8] This set of policies were condensed in what Williamson (1990) called the Washington Consensus (WC). Under the WC, international economic institutions had control of the most important political-institutional internal resources of development policies in the region.

A New Theory for the New Scenario: The Emergence of Neo-Structuralism

The neo-classical hegemony that gave theoretical support to SAPs and the WC placed structuralism, in general, and, ECLAC in particular, in a defensive position. Under this position, ECLAC launched neo-structuralism as an alternative to the economic mainstream and as a defense of structuralist postulates. The first task was to demystify ECLAC's responsibility in the failure of ISI and the crisis of the seventies and eighties (Rosales 1988). The defense also acknowledged a new global context, and thus the second task was to revise some outdated structuralist proposals.

The updated or "newly" formed structuralist thought required to overcome a series of analytical limitations. These included

> an excessive confidence in the value of State intervention, an exaggerated and overly prolonged pessimism about external markets, and an incautious management of short-term economic policy which failed to provide timely and practical answers to conjuncture problems, particularly by underestimating the monetary and financial position. (Sunkel and Zuleta 1990, 48)

The criticism of macroeconomic mismanagement was emphasized by most neo-structuralist authors (See Ffrench-Davis 1988; Rosales 1988). Although this led to an emphasis on short-run analysis (Lustig 1991), it also entailed an important theoretical shift from an economic standpoint (see the next subsection).

Although notably like the criticism made by neo-liberals, neo-structuralism highlighted these flaws as the preliminaries of a third task that consisted in the promotion of an alternative development strategy based on the productive transformation that could address simultaneously a dynamic external insertion and the reduction of inequality.

Crucial to this task were the contributions of Fernando Fajnzylber (1940–1991). Standing on the idea of the strategic features of industrialization—and a lucid analysis of the factors that truncated industrialization processes in Latin America (Fajnzylber 1985), Fajnzylber argued in favor of a strategy that focused on raising international competitiveness based on a continuous introduction of technical progress (Fajnzylber 1988) that was compatible with equitable income distribution, given Latin American record of being the most unequal region in the world.

Latin America had, per Fajnzylber, the challenge of fill the "empty box" (growth with equity) and open the "black box" of technical progress. Latin American countries ought to stimulate the development of endogenous nuclei of innovation that enable genuine forms of competitiveness. In other words, increasing participation in international markets should consist in a competitiveness that is not based on wage reductions, subsidies, undervalued exchange rates, or traditional comparative advantages based on the exploitation of natural resources, but on the continuous introduction of innovations in the process of production (Fajnzylber 1990).

The analysis of technical progress also should not be exclusively firm-based since

> it is not only companies which compete in the international market. It is also a field of confrontation between production systems, institutional structures and social organs in which business is an important element but one integrated in a network of relations with the education system, the technological infrastructure, management-labour relations, the public and private institutional apparatus, the financial system, etc. (Fajnzylber 1988, 22)

This aspect took Fajnzylber to introduce education and the scientific and technological system as a fundamental aspect of his proposal, which in the region were not properly developed and integrated. Related to this was the need of the state to have a concerting role and the valorization of public-private cooperation. These features repositioned the state in a constructive place against the neo-liberal attack centered on its responsibility for the backwardness of Latin America (Sunkel and Zuleta 1990).

Fajnzylber's ideas were strongly influential in the platform launched in 1990 by ECLAC through the document "Changing production patterns with social equity" (UN-ECLAC 1990). The document focused on systemic competitiveness with equity as a development strategy alternative to the one biased toward internal markets based on "frivolous" protectionism, and to the one strictly focused on external markets based on indiscriminate openness, promoted by IFIs under the neo-liberal mantra.

The document conceded to neo-classical critics the importance of proper management of short-run macroeconomic disequilibria, mainly through avoiding structural budget deficits. However, differently from neo-liberal thought, ECLAC proposed a perspective oriented to de-ideologize the state and to go beyond the false dilemma of state versus the market. The state should mediate in social conflicts and be an agent of integration of the plurality of actors to reach a "minimum platform of agreements". In the words of Sunkel and Zuleta (1990, 50), "the State must call for concerted action to promote cooperation instead of conflict between the social partners so that they decisively commit themselves to a more equitable and democratic vision of national development". Also, the state should promote an "institutional environment which stimulates the creativity and dynamism of the productive agents (employers and workers) and their capacity for agreement and coordination among themselves" (Sunkel and Zuleta 1990, 43).

Under this new paradigm, ECLAC sought to reassume the importance of structural change to overcome structural heterogeneity and improve income distribution. In fact, income equality has been at the top of the concerns at ECLAC in recent times (ECLAC 2010, 2012, 2014).

From a theoretical and epistemological standpoint, neo-structuralism sought to distance itself from the economic mainstream. It avoids the use of abstract axioms and highlights the importance of historical times to understand development processes. Also, it transcends the realm of rational choice that reduces human action to mere optimizers.

The emphasis given to technical progress, and the importance of an adequate social and institutional environment for its development, allows neo-structuralism to enter into dialogue with a variety of non-orthodox economic approaches, "including the Marxist and radical schools, the regulation school, the post-Keynesians, the institutionalists and the evolutionists" (Pérez Caldentey 2016, 46).

In this respect, evolutionist and institutionalist perspectives have probably been key theoretical frameworks in the dialogue (Hounie et al. 1999). Evolutionism has been important to understand the sources of productivity growth and technological catch-up with central economies through the development of learning capacities (Nelson and Winter 1982). Also, Lundvall's (1992) perspective of systems of innovation has been important for discussing the institutional framework necessary to enhance these capabilities. In this sense, Cimoli and Porcile (2016, 256) have remarked that:

> The cornerstone of industrial policy over the coming decades must be to absorb and accumulate capacities under new paradigms, while building institutions to adapt and generate incremental and even radical innovations within those paradigms. It is capacities (or incapacities) in new technologies

that will determine who is competitive in which branches of economic activity, and who will have a place in the future international division of labour.

The evolutionist perspective dialogues with ECLAC's traditional claim of differences in technology as a factor of divergence with the center, but also about the importance of socio-institutional factors in defining technological trajectories. The emphasis on concerted institutional arrangements based on the interaction of public and private actors has been a priority in neo-structuralism since its inception, given the supposed neglect of its precursors. In this case, it has been Sunkel (1989, 525–526) who has vouched to draw insights from institutionalist theories since:

> Technology is absolutely central to institutionalist thought, so much so that it is the driving force of evolution and change in this approach. Technology is seen as closely related to cultural change, thereby bringing into the picture a dimension of development that is completely absent from structuralism. Technological change is seen as a dynamic, transformation-inducing aspect of culture, deriving from the accumulation of knowledge and transcultural inducements; but cultural patterns, in turn, define the extent and nature of its incorporation into cultural change. This intimate relationship of technology—seen as the cumulative development of ideas, tools, and skills—to the culture from which it derives and to which it contributes is a fundamental element of institutionalism. It is an aspect of development theory that has been badly neglected by structuralism, which has had a more restricted view of technology.

Discontinuities of Neo-Structuralism with Structuralism

In what respect can be claimed that neo-structuralism represents a qualified continuation and update of structuralism? There is an important difference between structuralist thought and economic mainstream that the "last" Prebisch will emphasize and that it is not part of the neo-structuralist discourse. According to Prebisch, neo-classical theory analyzes neither the social structure and its mutations, nor the power relations within it and how they affect income distribution (Prebisch 1979). Neo-structuralism, as mentioned above, attempts to differentiate from neo-classical theory by offering a more plural theoretical framework that emphasizes the relevance of learning and innovation dynamics, as well as the importance of concerting institutions and public-private interaction. By doing this, neo-structuralism

> explicitly characterizes key economic relations as essentially nonantagonistic … [and] radically breaks with its structuralist intellectual origins by postulating, a priori, a mutually beneficial relationship between global flows, the export-oriented regime of accumulation established by neoliberalism, the growth of Latin American economies, and equity and social development of Latin American societies. (Leiva 2008, 12–13)

Since neo-structuralism conceives social relations as mainly non-conflictive, the consideration of power relations, domination, and contradictory interests among social groups or states is absent. This implies a displacement of those elements that, as we highlighted above, were essential to the development of structuralist thought, particularly from the sixties onwards.

Neo-structuralism proposes to analyze national and regional policies based on cooperation networks. This idea displaces the role of hierarchies, in which power and domination are crucial elements to settle conflicts and opposing interests and whose political action are imposed (by discipline) on spaces and actors—either subordinating or excluding them. The idea of networks supposes the possibility of integration without conflict. From this perspective, globalization is not a field of subordination of peripheral spaces, but one of the possibilities in which peripheral actors could profit if properly adapted.

According to neo-structuralism, the main vehicle to attain a competitive external insertion is the development of public-private cooperation networks that enhance learning and innovation processes which improve productivity and reduce the technology gap with the center. This proposal is friendly to the strategy of promoting the upgrade of local actors in the global value chain (Gereffi 2015), but it does not consider an important element to give continuity to structuralist thought, which is that the center controls the strategic functions in the chain and sometimes imposes limits on the qualification of the external insertion.

A closer analysis of the power relations within a global chain reveals the way in which transnational enterprises perform a selective process of exclusion or subordinated inclusion of peripheral spaces and actors (Fernández 2014). This selection is geopolitically supported by central states and the international agencies that promote integration as mutually beneficial, but in reality is a reaffirmation of the hegemony of the center (Werner et al. 2014).

The perspective supposes a sensibility and predisposition on behalf of capitalist agents that occupy the central nodes of the chain and does not reveal their capability to resist and utilize such networks to consolidate its privileges and power (Fernández 2017). In other terms, it ignores the veto power these actors have for blocking development projects destined to revert inequality and promote structural change.

It follows from these considerations that a state that limits itself to promote coordination between actors is insufficient. Rather, what is required is a state with the capacity to revert the behavior of external actors with power and improve its hierarchy to orient the behavior of local actors, both in the productive and financial fields.[9]

The theoretical turn contributed to making neo-structuralist's explanatory profile convergent with that of other international organizations. Such convergence has comprised not only mainly the family of institutions of the UN to which ECLAC belongs, but also the Washington-based organizations, which have progressively revised and introduced into their theoretical framework the institutional dimension, the role of governance, the role of the state, and the analysis of political decentralization and participation (see, e.g., World Bank 1997, 2002; Burki et al. 1999). It also led to a convergence of the language and concepts developed in the center, such as clusters, global value chains, and innovation systems, without a proper analytical re-elaboration that considers the peripheral condition as a specific and structurally contradictory condition (see, e.g., Anlló and Peirano 2005; Ferraro 2010; Padilla Pérez 2014; Hernández et al. 2014).

In this way, neo-structuralism developed a weakness—and a functionality with respect to the center—in the field of ideas. Such weakness translates into the promotion of a subaltern integration to global processes led economically and institutionally from the center. As Leiva points out:

> By accepting the status quo (the export-oriented regime of accumulation) and by rejecting core ideas from its structuralist past—the main one being that transnational corporations and the internationalization of productive structures helped to reproduce Latin America's underdevelopment—neo-structuralism proceeds to hyperbolize the purported harmonious nature of Latin America's actually existing capitalism. (Leiva 2008, 13)

This can also be noted in the criticism of the neglect of structuralism of short-term macroeconomic imbalances and its management. Neo-structuralism will be concerned with keeping the fiscal balance in check and avoid overheating the economy with public spending to prevent inflation and exchange-rate appreciation since this is thought to be one of the causes of balance-of-payments crises.[10]

However, the critique with its following prescription implies a conceptualization of the functioning of markets almost identical to neo-classical theory. The standard model of general equilibrium suggests that a private ownership economy operating through competitive markets will attain optimal resource allocation, optimal meaning, broadly speaking, full employment of the "factors" of production available in the economy.

A wide variety of "imperfectionist" hypotheses can be introduced to explain why markets may not clear and thus full employment not be achieved (Eatwell and Milgate 2011, Chaps. 8 and 10). However, the basic model is not objected and it is considered a true description of how markets should work under perfect competition. We cannot discuss the problems of this conceptualization in depth,[11] neither is it the purpose of the chapter. All we want to stand out is that, by implicitly accepting the basic general equilibrium model, neo-structuralism agrees with the neo-classical vision of society, which considers macro-behavioral (social) phenomena as the result of micro-motivation of self-interested individuals (Schelling 1978). Note the importance of the general equilibrium model, since it proves the *social* rationality of the market outcome—that is, it achieves "optimal" results—as the result of individual rational behavior (Clarke 1991, Chap. 6). Since market prices are rational from a social point of view, the market wage, rent, and rate of interest should not be upset. Power, if exercised, implies a deviation from this level.[12] So, the ideal situation is one where there are no differences in power among the agents of the economy. This is clearly in contradiction with what Prebisch thought about the income distribution process where no arrangement is rational or natural and power relations ultimately define the arrangement.

The "Last" Prebisch and His Linkages with "Late" Structuralism: An Alternative Road to Neo-Structuralism

Overcoming neo-structuralism and its weaknesses demands to observe in depth the discontinuities with structuralism, and at the same time to explore Prebisch's late contributions and the groundwork he left to continue.

As mentioned above, the seventies witnessed successive authoritarian political interruptions in several countries of Latin America. All these regimes, despite their peculiarities, had something in common: they were functional to the new strategy of the United States to maintain hegemony over the region. Differently from the East Asian experience, American geopolitics did not enable those authoritarian experiences to conduct top-down accumulation strategies with social inclusion and dynamic global integration. On the contrary, they promoted such regimes to dismantle, with the connivance of local oligarchies, the institutional infrastructure of ISI, and pushed for deregulation and liberalization of the economies.

In those years, the anteroom of the collapse of Latin American crisis of the eighties and the subsequent prevalence of the WC in the nineties, Prebisch leads a discussion about the challenges that Latin America faced to develop and its theoretical interpretation as director of ECLAC's academic journal (CEPAL Review). He begins with "A critique of peripheral capitalism" (Prebisch 1976), continues with "Socio-economic structure and crisis of peripheral capitalism" (Prebisch 1978), and "The neoclassical theories of economic liberalism" (Prebisch 1979), and closes with "Towards a theory of change" (Prebisch 1980). One should also add the lecture given in London 1986, later published in CEPAL Review as "Dependence, interdependence and development" (Prebisch 1988).

In these papers, Prebisch explicitly acknowledges the relevance of the discussions between "late" structuralism and dependency analysis, and how such debate enriched his center-periphery concept and he asks what is the state of the discussion after the global crisis and restructuring. Prebisch warns about the risks of being co-opted by theories and by concepts developed in the center. The peripheral condition must be understood within a "global theory of capitalist development" (Prebisch 1988, 200).

The major obstacle of the Latin American periphery, per Prebisch, was (and still is) the inconsistent and lack of sufficient capital accumulation, which is manifested in the incapacity to absorb labor force at increasing levels of productivity.

An understanding of such insufficiency demands an analysis of the generation, distribution, and use of the economic surplus. This, in turn, requires a study of the power relations in force in the society. Prebisch highlights three factors that typify peripheral capitalism and in which power relations are manifested, namely the "excessive consumption indulged in the upper strata", the "spurious absorption of labor", and "the disproportionate income the centers extract through the play of power relations at the international level" (Prebisch 1976, 14).

The first two factors encompass the internal dimension. The upper strata—proprietary and dominant classes—introduce new technology and capture the surplus of the productivity gains which are not translated into higher wages of the labor force. A great part of this surplus is then wasted in imitating the consumption pattern of the center, that is, a pattern that does not correspond with the productive structure of the periphery (Prebisch 1978). This deprives surplus for accumulation purposes, and this, in turn, implies that a large part of the labor force remains underemployed or marginalized. The state thus intervenes to absorb and include these segments of the population, but its means of financing also deprive surplus and enhance the limitations to accumulate.

The third factor corresponds to the external dimension. Foreign capital comes in handy to do the job that domestic capital does not perform:

> if the privileged strata earmarked a larger proportion of their income for accumulating more capital, instead of indulging in extravagant consumption, the rate of absorption of the labour force would be speeded up, especially in the lower strata, and distribution would be progressively improved. The system would approach social efficiency. But instead of relying on its own accumulation effort, it resorts to the transnationals, so that others' hands may do what could largely be done by its own, through full utilization of the surplus potential. (Prebisch 1978, 167)

However, this alternative is not the panacea, since foreign capital eventually operates within the internal restrictions to their own benefits and act in connivance with the upper strata of peripheral societies (Prebisch 1976, 60). In conclusion, Prebisch was convinced that the main problem lies in the behavior of the upper strata of peripheral societies, their appropriation of a large part of the surplus and its misuse. The disappearance of foreign capital would not solve the problem of the periphery, but clearly, their presence aggravates the restrictions to accumulate.

These center-periphery relations are not static but are subject to the effects of trends in the center and to social and political changes in the periphery. However, "whatever the nature and intensity of these changes, the center always seeks to defend the aforesaid economic, political and strategic interests, which sometimes coincide and at other times conflict with the interests of the periphery" (Prebisch 1976, 60).

To sum up, the unequal distribution of income and wealth reflected in the heterogeneous social structure, low-productivity employment, and marginalization of the labor force associated with a heterogeneous productive structure together reproduce an asymmetrical distribution; moreover, they promote a form of state implication that boosts the functional anomia and blocks accumulation. On the external front, the power exercised by foreign enterprises and international institutions reinforces the unequal appropriation of the fruits of technical progress.

Central Vectors for New Research Agenda

The production of Prebisch during this period was systematized in a larger work published at the beginning of the eighties (Prebisch 1981). Since then, capitalism has deepened its transformation by configuring a modality of global reproduction based on a technological revolution. Such transformations, however, did not eliminate the center-periphery logic on which Prebisch insisted upon, but invite to a reframing of the forms adopted by the periphery in face of the permanent shifts of capitalism. Prebisch's analysis sat down the foundations to explore the redefinitions of global capitalism and its impact on the periphery.

Now, if those elements inherited from structuralism can be taken as pillars to rethink new viable and sustainable strategies of development, they are not, nonetheless, sufficient. Many of them need to be updated, and other new elements must be introduced to keep alive the structuralist legacy.

The revision of the "last" Prebisch and its links with "late" structuralism allow us to reassume a line of thought that not only relativizes the supposed continuities of neo-structuralism but also identifies the prevalence of some unresolved problems of Latin American economies, as well as the novel limiting factors that have affected the neo-developmentalist experiences commented in Chap. 1.

The first instance of revision is related to the way in which space is introduced in the analysis of development. This is broken down, in turn, into three dimensions.

The first dimension, dealt in Chap. 3 by Sebastián Sztulwark, consists of a revision of the center-periphery concept, a concept that introduces the spatial dimension into the economic analysis. The concept must be revised after the above-mentioned structural crisis of capitalism in the seventies and the subsequent restructuring that gave place to the current phase of globalization. The new forms of exchange and production did not eliminate but rather overlapped with—and recreated—the preterit center-periphery asymmetries that structuralism analyzed in the interwar and postwar periods.

The spatial-temporal restructuring of capitalism consists in the formation of global chains within a process of delocalization of production to the periphery and re-centralization of strategic functions and assets within central countries linked to knowledge activities. This redefines the structural limitations to the generation of surplus in peripheral spaces and its retention by peripheral actors.

The process is also accompanied by changes in the regulation mode, where supra-national institutions (mainly controlled by central states) gain increasing influence over public policy design, while peripheral state institutions have less room for action.

Related to this, the second dimension refers to the role of spatial scales in the analysis of capitalism. This is discussed in Chap. 4 by Carlos Brandão. Different from the center-periphery concept, the notion of a scale was not explicitly addressed in structuralism and neo-structuralism missed such absence. The main concern of scale analysis is how "spatial-scalar arrangements" of the new regulation mode are redefined. Central states and supra-national institutions play a fundamental role in the functional and spatial reorganization of national and subnational institutions of the periphery. Thus, the new forms of scalar articulation promote decentralization and fragment state implication and enable the new logic of power, control, and domination necessary for the deployment of global productive chains.

The last dimension is related to the importance of geo-economics and geopolitics. ECLAC's thought did not explicitly consider geopolitical analysis, mainly because of being an institution that belongs to the UN. The introduction of geopolitics requires considering in a crude way the role of the state's political power and the deployment of strategies that do not discard violence and military force. Such an analysis would have put ECLAC in an awkward position.

The beginning of the twentieth century was marked by a decoupling of growth rates between peripheral and central countries, increasing trade among the periphery, and the formation of political blocs within the periphery that contest the American hegemony. In Chap. 5, Carlos Medeiros and Numa Mazat discuss the evolution of geo-economic and geopolitical strategies followed by the major peripheral countries (Brazil, Russia, India, China, South Africa, and Argentina), the geo-economic and geopolitical response of the United States to these strategies, and the way in which Latin America can, in such a setting, accomplish a dynamic external insertion that overcomes structural heterogeneity.

The second instance of revision starts from recognizing a deficit approach to the role of the state in structuralism. Although the state was considered an important agent in the strategy of industrialization, there was no proper discussion about its peripheral nature and the limits it had in conducting the development strategy. Certainly, the introduction of the sociology of conflict in "late" structuralism, as well as the importance of power in the generation and utilization of surplus in peripheral capitalism of the "last" Prebisch, represented a major contribution to this analysis. However, they lacked a detailed analysis of the way in which state structures are configured through this conflictive dynamic.

This conceptualization of the state was not followed by neo-structuralism. As we have discussed, the change in the analytical perspective from structuralism to neo-structuralism underestimates the importance of conflict and promotes a vision of development based on public-private cooperation. The state is no longer a disciplinarian actor and articulator of counter-strategies, but it joins, as an additional actor, cooperation networks to stimulate learning.

Chapter 6, by Victor Ramiro Fernández and Emilia Ormaechea, situates this lack of a systematic treatment of the state in both structuralism and neo-structuralism in a larger field of problems, related to the difficulties that many theoretical approaches have for considering the specificities of peripheral statehood and their challenges for development. Trying to overcome these limitations, they revalue the complexity of "external" (differentiated combination of geopolitics and geo-economics of the center with the periphery) and "internal" (specificities of social civil societies and their conflicts) factors that act in conformation of the structures and implicative forms of the peripheral states, offering a suggestive way to explain the different development paths followed by Latin America and East Asia, particularly since the second half of the twentieth century. At the same time, they notice the restrictions that both structuralism and neo-structuralism have in recognizing these external and internal logics that operate conforming and conditioning the role of the state for development.

The discussion that derives from this chapter sets a platform to study the implication of the state in two fields crucial for structural change: industrial policy and financing development.

As regards the first camp, the profound changes in capitalism in the last 40 years have not falsified the structuralist hypothesis about the importance of industrialization for structural change and development. Industrialization, however, can take place only through an articulated industrial policy. Chapter 7, by Margarita Olivera, discusses the possibilities for industrial policy in the periphery under the new productive and regulative global setting.

Current conventional visions about industrial policy focus, first, on abandoning the idea of a nationally articulated strategy of industrialization and joining global chains in the segments where countries exhibit comparative advantages (Baldwin 2011). Second, they promote "soft" policies against "hard" ones (tariff protection, subsidies, taxation) that consist of dealing with coordination problems by developing alternative cooperation networks (Harrison and Rodríguez-Clare 2010). These visions are convergent with neo-structuralist ideas on industrial policy.

From a structuralist perspective, however, the definition of industrial policy cannot avoid the dimension of discipline on the part of the state of powerful global actors that propose subordinate forms of integration, and the close linkage of the state with regional and national actors to execute an articulated strategy at the sectoral and spatial levels.

The above-mentioned issues of industrial policy find, however, resistance in the current global regulatory setting, which has substantially reduced the space for industrial policy in peripheral economies given aggressive trade agreements, stronger regulation of intellectual property rights, and several other World Trade Organization regulations.

The second camp is about the role of finance capital and the recent phenomenon of financialization in the process of development, addressed in Chap. 8 by Davide Villani and Nicolás Zeolla. From the seventies onwards, it is evidenced, on the one hand, a process of financial liberalization and deregulation of capital accounts accompanied with increasing international capital mobility, and, on the other, the expansion of the financial sector in the economies.

One of the main problems of financialization is short-termism behavior (Palley 2013, Chap. 2). Firms prefer investments that have sooner payoffs, and thus relegate the long-term strategic investments required for structural change. Given that in peripheral economies most profitable projects are associated with the exploitation of natural resources, financialization dynamics tends to deepen the primarization of the economy. Such a process aggravates structural heterogeneity, labor flexibilization, and precarization, and reinforces traditional specialization patterns of peripheral economies.

Control and state directive and regulatory capacity of the financial system is a fundamental factor for disciplining finance capital that usually has rentier behavior. The capacity to subordinate them for financing productive investment will usually find resistance from a complex of local and international institutions that promote free and unregulated financial markets, and the autonomy of central banks, and avoid any kind of intervention in credit allocation.

Conflict and power relations again become a relevant element in the analysis. Structuralism left open the discussion on this camp, and neo-structuralism did not follow up. The experience of East Asia could be informative. There, the state had important control over the financial-banking system to direct credit flows toward strategic sectors and productive investments. However, the increasing penetration and domination of foreign banks and credit institutions in local financial-banking systems in recent years require an adequate revision to fit the new setting.

Both industrial and financial policy should not be reduced to the national scale and must be thought as part of a geo-economic strategy of Latin American countries to achieve greater economic integration. In Chap. 9, Armando Di Filippo accounts for the evolution of the view in ECLAC about integration and the efforts made by Latin American countries on this camp in the second half of the twentieth century.

In the passing of time, the notion of integration has been narrowed from a multidimensional to a one-dimensional perspective of strict economic integration. Such is the paradigm advocated by the WC and the free trade agreement policy. On the contrary, one can find in Prebisch's reflections a richer notion of integration that transcends the economic aspect of the matter.

All the dimensions discussed in this book constitute the theoretical basis for discussing how such integration may come to reality and, more generally, how development in the periphery can be rethought from a multi-scalar perspective and in the context of newly recreated forms of power and domination.

Notes

1. We do not pretend to offer an extensive review and discussion of the literature. For such matters, we suggest the reader the works of Bielschowsky (2008, 2016), Rodríguez (1980, 2006), Di Filippo (2007), among others.
2. Later to be called Economic Commission for Latin America and the Caribbean.
3. English version: Prebisch (1962).
4. We do not pretend to offer an extensive revision of dependency analysis. For such matters, see Gunder Frank (1977), Palma (1978), Kay (1989), and Love (1990).
5. English version: Cardoso and Faletto (1979).
6. For a study of the role assigned to FDI and transnational corporation in ECLAC's development project throughout its history, see Kerner (2003).
7. See their contributions in Gonzalez Casanova (1990) and O'Donnell (1978b).
8. These ideas are still in force and imposed by the mass media in Latin America.
9. See Chap. 6.
10. See Chap. 8.
11. For such matters see Garegnani (1978, 1979).
12. Curiously enough, neo-classical theory identifies trade unions as an institution with market power, but never central banks, which ought to be independent to set without restrictions the level of the interest rate.

References

Acosta Espinosa, Alberto. 1998. La Deuda Externa en América Latina: Origen, Evolución y Alternativas de Solución. *Revista Ecuador Debate* 45: 64-92.

Agarwal, Manmohan, and Dipankar Sengupta. 1999. Structural Adjustment in Latin America: Policies and Performance. *Economic and Political Weekly* 34 (44): 3129–3136. http://www.jstor.org/stable/4408573.

Anlló, Guillermo, and Fernando Peirano. 2005. *Una Mirada a los Sistemas Nacionales de Innovación en el Mercosur: Análisis y Reflexiones a partir de los Casos de Argentina y Uruguay*. Serie Estudios y Perspectivas. Santiago de Chile: Naciones Unidas.

Arrighi, Giovanni, Beverly J. Silver, and Benjamin D. Brewer. 2003. Industrial Convergence, Globalization, and the Persistence of the North-South Divide. *Studies in Comparative International Development* 38 (1). Springer-Verlag: 3–31. https://doi.org/10.1007/BF02686319.

Baer, Werner. 1972. Import Substitution and Industrialization in Latin America: Experiences and Interpretations. *Latin American Research Review* 7 (1). Latin American Studies Association: 95–122. http://www.jstor.org/stable/2502457.

Balassa, Bela. 1984. Adjustment Policies in Developing Countries: A Reassessment. *World Development* 12 (9): 955–972. https://doi.org/10.1016/0305-750X(84)90053-6.

Baldwin, Richard. 2011. *Trade and Industrialisation after Globalisation's 2nd Unbundling: How Building and Joining a Supply Chain Are Different and Why It Matters.* National Bureau of Economic Research Working Paper No. 17716. http://www.nber.org/papers/w17716.

Bértola, Luis, and José Antonio Ocampo. 2012. *Latin America's Debt Crisis and 'Lost Decade.'* https://goo.gl/W6ej3s.

Bielschowsky, Ricardo. 2008. Sixty Years of ECLAC: Structuralism and Neo-Structuralism. *CEPAL Review*, 97: 171–192. http://repositorio.cepal.org/handle/11362/11325.

———. 2016. Fifty Years of ECLAC Thought: A Review. In *ECLAC Thinking, Selected Texts (1948–1998)*, ed. Ricardo Bielschowsky, 7–43. United Nations.

Bodenheimer, Susanne J. 1970. The Ideology of Developmentalism: American Political Science's Paradigm-Surrogate for Latin American Studies. *Berkeley Journal of Sociology* 15. Regents of the University of California: 95–137. http://www.jstor.org/stable/41035171.

Bryan, Michael. 2013. The Great Inflation. *Federal Reserve History.* https://www.federalreservehistory.org/essays/great_inflation.

Burki, Shahid Javed, Guillermo Perry, and William R. Dillinger. 1999. *Beyond the Center: Decentralizing the State.* Washington, DC: World Bank Publications.

Cardoso, Fernando Henrique. 1977. The Originality of a Copy: CEPAL and the Idea of Development. *CEPAL Review* 4: 7–40.

———. 1980. El Desarrollo en el Banquillo. *Comercio Exterior* 30 (8): 846–860.

Cardoso, Fernando Henrique, and Enzo Faletto. 1969. *Dependencia y Desarrollo en América Latina.* Buenos Aires: Siglo XXI.

———. 1979. *Dependency and Development in Latin America.* University of California Press. https://www.ucpress.edu/book.php?isbn=9780520035270.

Castells, Manuel. 2009. *The Rise of the Network Society: Volume I.* Oxford, UK: Wiley-Blackwell. https://doi.org/10.1002/9781444319514.

Cavalieri, Tiziano, Pierangelo Garegnani, and Meri Lucii. 2004. Anatomia Di Una Sconfitta. *La Rivista Del Manifesto*, no. 48. http://www.larivistadelmanifesto.it/archivio/48/48A20040312.html.

CENDES. 1969. Estilos de Desarrollo. *El Trimestre Económico* 36 (144(4)). Fondo de Cultura Economica: 517–576. http://www.jstor.org/stable/20856097.

Cimoli, Mario, and Gabriel Porcile. 2016. Productivity and Structural Change: Structuralism and Its Dialogue with Other Heterodox Currents. In *Neostructuralism and Heterodox Thinking in Latin America and the Caribbean in the Early Twenty-First Century*, ed. Alicia Bárcena and Antonio Prado, 205–222. Santiago de Chile: United Nations.

Clarke, Simon. 1991. *Marx, Marginalism and Modern Sociology*. London: Palgrave Macmillan UK. https://doi.org/10.1007/978-1-349-21808-0.

Devlin, Robert, and Ricardo Ffrench-Davis. 1995. The Great Latin American Debt Crisis: A Decade of Asymmetric Adjustment. *Revista de Economia Política* 15 (3): 117–142.

Di Filippo, Armando. 2007. La Escuela Latinoamericana del Desarrollo: Tensiones Epistemológicas de un Movimiento Fundacional. *Cinta de Moebio*, no. 29. Universidad de Chile: 124–154. http://www.redalyc.org/html/101/10102901/.

Duménil, G., and D. Lévy. 2001. Periodizing Capitalism: Technology, Institutions and Relations of Production. In *Phases of Capitalist Development*, ed. R. Albritton, M. Itoh, R. Westra, and A. Zuege, 141–162. Springer.

———. 2007. *Crisis y Salida de la Crisis. Orden y Desorden Neoliberales*. México, D.F.: Fondo de Cultura Económica.

Eatwell, John, and Murray Milgate. 2011. *The Fall and Rise of Keynesian Economics*. Oxford University Press. https://doi.org/10.1093/acprof:osobl/9780199777693.001.0001.

ECLAC. 1990. *Changing Production Patterns with Social Equity: The Prime Task of Latin American and Caribbean Development in the 1990s*. Santiago de Chile: United Nations. http://repositorio.cepal.org/handle/11362/37869?show=full.

———. 2010. *Time for Equality: Closing Gaps, Opening Trails*. Santiago de Chile: United Nations. https://www.cepal.org/en/publications/3066-time-equality-closing-gaps-opening-trails-thirty-third-session-eclac.

———. 2012. *Structural Change for Equality: An Integrated Approach to Development*. Santiago de Chile: United Nations. https://www.cepal.org/en/publications/3079-structural-change-equality-integrated-approach-development-thirty-four-session.

———. 2014. *Compacts for Equality: Towards a Sustainable Future*. Santiago de Chile: United Nations. https://www.cepal.org/en/publications/36693-compacts-equality-towards-sustainable-future.

Evans, Peter, and Frederic Deyo. 1987. *The Political Economy of the New Asian Industrialism*. Anthropology of Contemporary Issues. Cornell University Press. https://books.google.com.ar/books?id=GLEClK_3tq4C.

Fajnzylber, Fernando. 1985. *La Industrialización Trunca de América Latina*. Buenos Aires: Grupo Editor Latinoamericano.

———. 1988. International Competitiveness: Agreed Goal, Hard Task. *CEPAL Review* 36: 7–23.

———. 1990. *Industrialization in Latin America: From the "Black Box" to the "Empty Box."* United Nations, Economic Commission for Latin America and the Caribbean. http://repositorio.cepal.org/handle/11362/27811.

Fernández, Víctor Ramiro. 2014. Global Value Chains in Global Political Networks: Tool for Development or Neoliberal Device? *Review of Radical Political Economics* 47 (2): 209–230. https://doi.org/10.1177/0486613414532769.

———. 2017. *La Trilogía del Erizo-Zorro: Redes Globales, Trayectorias Nacionales y Dinámicas Regionales Desde La Periferia*. Barcelona and Santa Fe: Anthropos Editorial and Ediciones UNL.

Ferraro, Carlo, ed. 2010. *Clusters y Políticas de Articulación Productiva en América Latina*. Santiago de Chile: Naciones Unidas.

Ffrench-Davis, Ricardo. 1988. An Outline of a Neo-structuralist Approach. *CEPAL Review* 34: 37–44. https://repositorio.cepal.org/handle/11362/10233.

Fiori, José Luís. 1992. The Political Economy of the Developmentalist State in Brazil. *CEPAL Review* 37: 173–186. http://repositorio.cepal.org/handle/11362/10408.

Fröbel, Folker, Jürgen Heinrichs, and Otto Kreye. 1977. The Tendency Towards a New International Division of Labor: The Utilization of a World-Wide Labor Force for Manufacturing Oriented to the World Market. *Review (Fernand Braudel Center)* 1 (1): 73–88.

Furtado, Celso. 1966. US Hegemony and the Future of Latin America. *The World Today* 22 (9): 375–385.

Gabay, Eliana. 2008. Revisitando a Raúl Prebisch y el Papel de la CEPAL en el Campo de las Ciencias Sociales Latinoamericanas. *Íconos* 12 (2): 103–113. http://www.ingentaconnect.com/content/doaj/13901249/2008/00000012/00000002/art00008.

Garegnani, Pierangelo. 1978. Notes on Consumption, Investment and Effective Demand: I. *Cambridge Journal of Economics* 2 (4). Oxford University Press: 335–353. https://doi.org/10.2307/23596466.

———. 1979. Notes on Consumption, Investment and Effective Demand: II. *Cambridge Journal of Economics* 3 (1). Oxford University Press: 63–82. https://doi.org/10.2307/23596374.

Gereffi, Gary. 2015. *Global Value Chains, Development and Emerging Economies*. Inclusive and Sustainable Industrial Development Working Paper Series WP 18.

Glassman, Jim, and Pádraig Carmody. 2001. Structural Adjustment in East and Southeast Asia: Lessons from Latin America. *Geoforum* 32 (1): 77–90. https://doi.org/10.1016/S0016-7185(00)00039-7.

Gonzalez Casanova, Pablo. 1990. *El Estado en América Latina: Teoría y Práctica*. Biblioteca América Latina. México, D.F.: Siglo XXI. https://books.google.com.ar/books?id=Np1LkHW290YC.
Graciarena, Jorge. 1976. Power and Development Styles. *CEPAL Review* 1: 172–193. http://repositorio.cepal.org/handle/11362/12304.
Gunder Frank, Andre. 1966. The Development of Underdevelopment. *Monthly Review* 18 (4): 17. https://doi.org/10.14452/MR-018-04-1966-08_3.
———. 1969. *Latin America: Underdevelopment or Revolution*. New York: Monthly Review Press.
———. 1977. Dependence Is Dead, Long Live Dependence and the Class Struggle: An Answer to Critics. *World Development* 5 (4): 355–370. https://doi.org/10.1016/0305-750X(77)90041-9.
Gurrieri, Adolfo. 1987. The Validity of the State-as-Planner in the Current Crisis. *CEPAL Review* 31: 193–209. http://repositorio.cepal.org/handle/11362/10203.
Harrison, Ann, and Andres Rodríguez-Clare. 2010. From Hard to Soft Industrial Policies in Developing Countries. *VoxEU.org*. http://voxeu.org/article/hard-soft-industrial-policies-developing-countries.
Hernández, René A., Jorge Mario Martinez-Piva, and Nanno Mulder, eds. 2014. *Global Value Chains and World Trade: Prospects and Challenges for Latin America*. Santiago de Chile: United Nations.
Hirschman, Albert O. 1968. The Political Economy of Import-Substituting Industrialization in Latin America. *The Quarterly Journal of Economics* 82 (1). Oxford University Press: 1–32. https://doi.org/10.2307/1882243.
Hounie, Adela, Lucía Pittaluga, Gabriel Porcile, and Fabio Scatolin. 1999. ECLAC and the New Growth Theories. *CEPAL Review* 68: 7–34. http://repositorio.cepal.org/handle/11362/10684.
Kay, Cristóbal. 1989. *Latin American Theories of Development and Underdevelopment*. London and New York: Routledge.
Kerner, Daniel. 2003. ECLAC, Transnational Corporations and the Quest for a Latin American Development Strategy. *CEPAL Review* 79: 83–95. http://repositorio.cepal.org/handle/11362/10930.
Kotz, David M., and Terrence McDonough. 2010. Global Neoliberalism and the Contemporary Social Structure of Accumulation. In *Contemporary Capitalism and Its Crises: Social Structure of Accumulation Theory for the 21st Century*, ed. Terrence McDonough, Michael Reich, and David M. Kotz, 93–120. New York: Cambridge University Press.
Krueger, Anne O. 1974. The Political Economy of the Rent-Seeking Society. *The American Economic Review* 64 (3). American Economic Association: 291–303. http://www.jstor.org/stable/1808883.
Laclau, Ernesto. 1971. Feudalism and Capitalism in Latin America. *New Left Review* 67 (May-June): 19-38.

Leiva, Fernando Ignacio. 2008. Toward a Critique of Latin American Neostructuralism. *Latin American Politics and Society* 50 (4). Blackwell Publishing Ltd.: 1–25. https://doi.org/10.1111/j.1548-2456.2008.00028.x.

Love, Joseph. 1990. The Origins of Dependency Analysis. *Journal of Latin American Studies* 22 (1–2). Cambridge University Press: 143. https://doi.org/10.1017/S0022216X00015145.

———. 1995. Economic Ideas and Ideologies in Latin America Since 1930. In *The Cambridge History of Latin America: Volume 6: 1930 to the Present*, The Cambridge History of Latin America, ed. Leslie Bethell, vol. 6, 391–460. Cambridge: Cambridge University Press. https://doi.org/10.1017/CHOL9780521232265.008.

Lundvall, Bengt-Ake. 1992. *National Systems of Innovation: An Analytical Framework*. London: Pinter.

Lustig, Nora. 1991. From Structuralism to Neostructuralism: The Search for a Heterodox Paradigm. In *The Latin American Development Debate: Neostructuralism, Neomonetarism, and Adjustment Processes*, ed. Patricio Meller. Boulder, CO: Westview Press.

Marinho, Luiz Cláudio. 1981. The Transnational Corporations and Latin America's Present Form of Economic Growth. *CEPAL Review* 14: 9–34. http://repositorio.cepal.org/handle/11362/12292.

Marini, Ruy Mauro. 1977. La Acumulación Capitalista Mundial y el Subimperialismo. *Cuadernos Políticos* 12. Ediciones Era: 21–39.

Millet, Damien, and Eric Toussaint. 2003. *The Debt Scam: IMF, World Bank, and Third World Debt*. Mumbai: VAK Publication.

Nelson, R., and G. Winter. 1982. *An Evolutionary Theory of Economic Change*. Cambridge, MA: Harvard University Press.

O'Donnell, Guillermo. 1978a. Reflections on the Patterns of Change in the Bureaucratic-Authoritarian State. *Latin American Research Review* 13 (1). Latin American Studies Association: 3–38. http://www.jstor.org/stable/2502640.

———. 1978b. State and Alliances in Argentina, 1956–1976. *The Journal of Development Studies* 15 (1). Taylor & Francis Group: 3–33. https://doi.org/10.1080/00220387808421699.

Padilla Pérez, Ramón. 2014. *Fortalecimiento de las Cadenas de Valor como Instrumento de la Política Industrial: Metodología y Experiencia de la CEPAL en Centroamérica*. Santiago de Chile: Naciones Unidas.

Palley, Thomas. 2013. *Financialization: The Economics of Finance Capital Domination*. New York: Palgrave Macmillan.

Palma, José Gabriel. 1978. Dependency: A Formal Theory of Underdevelopment or a Methodology for the Analysis of Concrete Situations of Underdevelopment? *World Development* 6 (7–8). Elsevier: 881–924.

Pérez Caldentey, Esteban. 2016. A Time to Reflect on Opportunities for Debate and Dialogue Between (Neo)Structuralism and Heterodox Schools of Thought.

In *Neostructuralism and Heterodox Thinking in Latin America and the Caribbean in the Early Twenty-First Century*, ed. Alicia Bárcena and Antonio Prado, 31–84. Santiago de Chile: United Nations.

Pinto, Aníbal. 1970. Naturaleza e Implicaciones de la 'Heterogeneidad Estructural' de la América Latina. *El Trimestre Económico* 37 (145(1)). Fondo de Cultura Económica: 83–100. http://www.jstor.org/stable/20856116.

———. 1978. Estilos de Desarrollo: Conceptos, Opciones, Viabilidad. *El Trimestre Económico* 45 (179(3)). Fondo de Cultura Económica: 557–610. www.jstor.org/stable/23394727.

Polanyi, Karl. 2001. *The Great Transformation: The Political and Economic Origins of Our Time*. Boston: Beacon Press.

Prebisch, Raúl. 1949. El Desarrollo Económico de la América Latina y Algunos de sus Principales Problemas. *El Trimestre Económico* 16 (63(3)). Fondo de Cultura Económica: 347–431. https://doi.org/10.2307/20855070.

———. 1952. Problemas Teóricos y Prácticos del Crecimiento Económico [Theoretical and Practical Problems of Economic Growth]. Santiago de Chile: Naciones Unidas. http://repositorio.cepal.org/handle/11362/13572.

———. 1962. The Economic Development of Latin America and Its Principal Problems. *Economic Bulletin for Latin America* VII (1): 1–22.

———. 1963. *Towards a Dynamic Development Policy for Latin America*. New York: United Nations. http://repositorio.cepal.org/handle/11362/14892.

———. 1976. A Critique of Peripheral Capitalism. *CEPAL Review* 1: 9–76. http://repositorio.cepal.org/handle/11362/12273.

———. 1978. Socio-Economic Structure and Crisis of Peripheral Capitalism. *CEPAL Review* 6: 159–252. http://repositorio.cepal.org/handle/11362/10450.

———. 1979. The Neoclassical Theories of Economic Liberalism. *CEPAL Review* 7: 167–188. http://repositorio.cepal.org/handle/11362/10451.

———. 1980. Towards a Theory of Change. *CEPAL Review* 10: 155–208. http://repositorio.cepal.org/handle/11362/12263.

———. 1981. *El Capitalismo Periférico: Crisis y Transformación*. México, D.F.: Fondo de Cultura Económica.

———. 1988. Dependence, Interdependence and Development. *CEPAL Review* 34: 197–205. http://repositorio.cepal.org/handle/11362/10242.

Rodríguez, Octavio. 1980. La Teoría del Subdesarrollo de la CEPAL: Síntesis y Crítica. *Comercio Exterior* 30 (12): 1346–1362.

———. 2006. *El Estructuralismo Latinoamericano*. Siglo XXI.

Rosales, Osvaldo. 1988. An Assessment of the Structuralist Paradigm in Latin America Development and the Prospects of Its Renovation. *CEPAL Review* 34: 19–36. https://goo.gl/vmjS7f.

Ross, Robert J.S., and Kent C. Trachte. 1990. *Global Capitalism: The New Leviathan*. Albany, NY: SUNY Press.

Schelling, Thomas C. 1978. *Micromotives and Macrobehaviors*. New York: W. W. Norton & Company.

Sunkel, Osvaldo. 1971. Capitalismo Transnacional y Desintegración Nacional en la América Latina. *El Trimestre Económico* 38 (150 (2)). Fondo de Cultura Económica: 571–628.

———. 1989. Structuralism, Dependency and Institutionalism: An Exploration of Common Ground and Disparities. *Journal of Economic Issues* 23 (2). Routledge: 519–533. https://doi.org/10.1080/00213624.1989.11504918.

Sunkel, Osvaldo, and Gustavo Zuleta. 1990. Neo-Structuralism versus Neo-Liberalism in the 1990s. *CEPAL Review* 42: 35–51. https://goo.gl/8zdMnk.

Thorp, Rosemary. 1998. *Progress, Poverty and Exclusion: An Economic History of Latin America in the 20th Century*. IDB.

Toye, John, and Richard Toye. 2004. *The UN and Global Political Economy: Trade, Finance, and Development*. The UN and Global Political Economy. Indiana University Press. https://books.google.com.ar/books?id=dyz07g-NsCIC.

Varsavsky, Oscar. 1971. Largo Plazo: ¿un Sólo Estilo? *El Trimestre Económico* 38 (152(4)). Fondo de Cultura Económica: 1011–1040.

Werner, Marion, Jennifer Bair, and Víctor Ramiro Fernández. 2014. Linking Up to Development? Global Value Chains and the Making of a Post-Washington Consensus. *Development and Change* 45 (6): 1219–1247. https://doi.org/10.1111/dech.12132.

Williamson, John. 1990. What Washington Means by Policy Reform. In *Latin American Adjustment: How Much Has Happened?* ed. John Williamson. Washington, DC: Peterson Institute for International Economics.

World Bank. 1997. *World Development Report 1997: The State in a Changing World*. http://hdl.handle.net/10986/5980.

———. 2002. *World Development Report 2002: Building Institutions for Markets*. http://hdl.handle.net/10986/5984.

CHAPTER 3

The Center and the Periphery in the Structural Logic of the New Capitalism

Sebastián Sztulwark

Introduction

The categories "center" and "periphery" were fundamental components of postwar development theory, particularly Latin American structuralism. They were part of a broader approach that sought to rethink the specific nature of countries that were moving through "late" industrialization processes, in the context of the historic transfer of the leadership of the global economy from Britain to the United States. The rejection of the conventional economic model (and its claim to be universally valid) and the contradictions of postwar industrialization in Latin America prompted early reflections on the very nature of the periphery and the antagonism that is inherent to the dynamics of the global economic system.[1]

The crisis in the Latin American industrialization of the seventies can be read not only in terms of a weakness in power relations but also as the product of a change in the very structural logic of global capitalism. The explanations for this are not necessarily contradictory. During the eighties, a new antistructuralist consensus arose from this crisis, namely that the

S. Sztulwark (✉)
National University of General Sarmiento (UNGS) and National Scientific and Technical Research Council (CONICET), Buenos Aires, Argentina
e-mail: ssztulwa@ungs.edu.ar

V. R. Fernández, G. Brondino (eds.), *Development in Latin America*,
https://doi.org/10.1007/978-3-319-92183-9_3

only possible logic for economic development is a passive adaptation to the decisions of the global market. The difference between the center and the periphery was abolished in the name of a single model of neoliberal globalization.

In response to this dominant vision and the consequences that it brought for development in Latin American countries, recent years have brought a return to the perspective of structural change in the discourse of those economists who have taken up the mantle of postwar structuralism (CEPAL 2012; Ocampo 2011; Cimoli et al. 2005). However, this "neo-structuralist" recovery generally tends to form part of a vision in which the antagonism between the center and the periphery is set aside or watered down in favor of a discourse that emphasizes consensus and cooperation (Leiva 2008).

This chapter, however, assumes that the antagonism between the center and the periphery is a fundamental tool for thinking about the development challenges that Latin America is currently facing. The factors that make this approach relevant cannot be limited to an understanding of the new global context in which it has arisen but must also include a review of the conceptual grounds on which the center-periphery dynamic was established in the postwar period.

This study presents a reflection on the nature of the periphery in the new capitalism, based on the following theoretical and methodological premises: (1) the center and the periphery are two structurally differentiated spaces of accumulation; (2) this differentiation emerged around the position that each occupies within a certain structural logic, in the sense of a specific sequence in which productive activities are articulated, leading to different potentials for accumulation; (3) this structural logic was transformed as part of a more widespread shift in the dynamics of capitalism as a global system; and (4) the change from one structural logic to another took the form of a break with the pre-existing logic.

On that basis, this chapter argues that the structural logic of the new capitalism is chain shaped and differentiates activities that create knowledge from those that reproduce it within different productive sectors. The logic of the chain does not cancel out the idea of structure in the sense of the sector-specific differentiation of production that was typical of postwar capitalism, but it does impose itself on this as the new dominant norm.

The chapter begins by establishing certain conceptual definitions regarding the relationship between spaces of accumulation and structural logic. It goes on to present a stylized representation of the structural logic of postwar capitalism and to describe how the opposition between the center and the periphery was established within this. Next, it attempts to describe the fundamentals of the structural logic of the new capitalism and, therefore, the grounds for a new structural dynamic. The final section contains my conclusions.

Spaces of Accumulation and Structural Logic

From a structuralist point of view, the terms "center" and "periphery" refer to a position in the productive structure of global capitalism—spaces of accumulation that are differentiated according to their function within the dynamics of this structure. The center controls production activities with the greatest potential for accumulation—in other words, those in which complex work predominates.[2] In contrast, the periphery lacks the production capacities needed to dispute the core of global production and instead specializes in activities with less potential for accumulation—in other words, those which are structured around simple work.[3] This issue is not limited to technology-related aspects. Developing and maintaining global technological leadership is something that always comes about in the context of the power relations that characterize global geopolitics.[4]

How is the relationship between simple and complex work represented in the global structure? What categories are used to distinguish between activities with high potential for accumulation and those with limited potential? In postwar Latin American structuralism, that aspect was implicit in the ideal of industrialization that was pursued at the time. However, there was no explicit category to describe the relationship between these two types of activities, no category that could differentiate the theoretical aspect of the problem from its specific historical content. This study sets out to fill that gap using the category "structural logic", which indicates the specific way in which a certain historical stage represents the heterogeneity in the potential for accumulation that exists within the activities that make up the structure of productive global capital. In other words, how the sequence of activities that make up the global economy is defined depending on the level of complexity of the work that each activity entails. From this point of view, spaces of accumulation are defined (and differentiated) in relation to their position with a certain structural logic that changes over time.

In this way, our understanding of the historical nature of spaces of accumulation is always subject to breaks, which come about as a consequence of the rupture in the structural logic that comes with the historical dynamics of global capitalism.[5]

Within this perspective, the distinction between structural change and change in structure is a meaningful one. Structural change, a fundamental point of reference for postwar structuralism, means a change in position within a certain structure. The concept alludes to the internal transformation of production patterns within a space of accumulation that allows this transformation to gradually bring about a transition from peripheral to central functions while a certain structural logic endures, at least within a given period in history. In contrast, a change in structure implies a modification of the dominant structural logic itself and thus of the specific production conditions through which positions within the structure are defined.

Based on these concepts, the rest of this chapter will present an approach to the fundamental elements of change in the structural logic of global capitalism in order to provide a preliminary description of the defining features of the periphery in this new phase in history.

The Structural Logic of Postwar Capitalism

This section begins with a definition of the structural logic of postwar capitalism, which represents the mature phase of industrial capitalism during the Fordist/Keynesian stage,[6] which was the historical context in which classic Latin American structuralism unfolded.

The sequence that expresses the structural logic of this period can be represented through a series of movements: the first and most important is the shift from primary goods to industrial ones. Within this logic, industrialization is seen as a synonym for economic development. But the problem does not end with this first part of the sequence.

Industrialization can be intensified as it advances toward those more capital-intensive branches of activity that are more technologically complex. This implies a transition from consumer goods to producer goods. However, this transition does not complete the sequence, either. Within consumer goods, there may be a growing potential for accumulation that goes from nondurable goods to durable ones, or, within producer goods, from intermediate goods to capital goods, which is the culmination of the entire sequence.

The whole sequence contains a total of four movements, each of which marks a further degree of potential accumulation: (1) from primary goods (PG) to industrial goods (IG); (2) from industrial consumer goods (CG) to producer goods (PdG); (3) from nondurable consumer goods (ND) to durable consumer goods (D); and (4) from intermediate goods (IntG) to capital goods (KG). The structural logic of postwar capitalism (L1) can thus be written as follows:

$$L1 = PG \rightarrow IG\left[CG(ND \rightarrow D) \rightarrow PG(IntG \rightarrow KG)\right]$$

This logic unfolded based on the following properties:

- The existence of a relatively long product lifecycle with low product differentiation. During Fordism, as Corsani (2003) explains, "increases in value essentially rested on controlling the time needed to reproduce standardized merchandise using mechanical technologies". The focus of the innovation process was on adopting technology that was embodied in fixed capital (machinery as a fundamental vehicle for the spread of technology) and on the organizational-type improvements needed to discipline a low-skilled labor force (Rullani 2000). The stars of this show were process innovations, which were oriented toward improvements in the means of production used in the work process and the advances that arose in the wake of the so-called scientific organization of labor (Míguez 2008).
- Those services that were seen as "productive" were ones that performed a specific function in the production process for goods (the direct sphere of validity for L1). These were transportation and distribution services that performed an essential function but that lay outside the production process: moving workers from their homes to the factory and products from the factory to the market. All other services (especially those that take place within the sphere of social reproduction) might have a social value but not a direct function within L1.
- Highly vertically integrated production, which corresponded to an institutional framework of domestic economic regulation. The internationalization of capital and the creation of a global market are not incompatible with the existence of a production model that is articulated within the national sphere (Dicken 2003). One specific feature of the postwar period is the Cold War, and the military and technological hegemony of the United States, which took on a leading role in the structuring of a new international regulatory framework following the Bretton Woods agreements (Stiglitz 2002).

If we start from the premise that the center and the periphery differed during this period as spaces of accumulation due to their role in the global deployment of L1, we can follow the structuralist argument according to which the productive structure of the center is homogenous and diversified, while that of their periphery is heterogeneous and specialized[7] (Rodríguez 1977). Taking this as the point of departure, we can then go on to identify two fundamental aspects of the production structure: (1) the degree of sectoral completeness, which points to the level of productive diversification; and (2) the degree of complexity of the production process, in the sense of how far it is from the global frontline of productivity in any given era.

As stated above, the center represents the dominant space within the system and thus defines the dynamic of the structure. This means that (1) it has sufficient production capacity to cover and dominate the entire range of products defined in L1 (especially in products where there is greater potential for accumulation); and (2) for all these products, it has the highest production capacity of its time (leading-edge global productivity). This is why the structure of the center can be described as diversified and homogenous.

The periphery, in contrast, takes on a subordinate role, which is expressed through an incapacity on two counts: its difficulty in moving through the range of more complex products (due to the absence of deep industrialization) and its inability to achieve the productivity levels found at the center, with the exception of a handful of primary (or basic industrial) export goods. Given these characteristics, the productive structure of the periphery tends to become specialized (low levels of diversification) and heterogeneous (in its productivity levels) in comparison with the standard of the center, which is the central standard in each period.

The dynamic of the structure is subject to spatiotemporal variations that are not changes in the structure itself but rather variations within the same structural logic. They are steps forward and backward within the same logic. In this way, a peripheral country can increase the sectoral completeness of its domestic structure (increased industrialization toward durable goods or producer goods) or bring about variations in productivity (narrowing or expanding the productivity gap as both sides of the relationship change), and these movements can lead to processes of differentiation within the peripheral locations in the structure. This was observed, for example, in the differences in the postwar industrialization patterns of East Asia and Latin America (Fajnzylber 1983; Amsden 2004; Fernández 2017).

From a geographic point of view, the deployment of this structural logic ran parallel to the consolidation of the North Atlantic (north-western Europe and the United States, especially the East Coast) as the space that accounted for most of the cutting-edge industrial production at the time.

In other words, widely used intermediate goods (such as those produced by the petrochemical industry), higher-complexity durable consumer goods (the most emblematic example is the motor vehicle industry), and capital goods ("machines that make machines", which are at the core of L1).

In the late sixties and early seventies, this postwar structural logic came up against concrete limitations to its functioning and deployment. Discussing the reasons for this process is beyond the scope of this paper. However, so as not to leave out a strong factor in the argument, it could be argued that this had to do with a crisis of legitimacy, on the one hand, and of profitability, on the other, in central countries themselves. The fundamental (but not the only) causes for this were (1) increased salaries (associated with the strength of the labor movement at the time) and higher taxes (which supported the welfare state); (2) growing levels of social conflict that was largely expressed through the rejection of industrial work by workers from the center; (3) saturation of a standardized consumption pattern and growing instability in demand; and (4) a crisis in the innovation model, in which only a small fraction of the labor force (those workers that were directly connected to the tasks of "conception") became responsible for increasing the productivity of a huge mass of workers (those who are directly linked to the tasks of "execution"), who played a passive role in this process.[8]

The Structural Logic of the New Capitalism

In the late sixties and early seventies, the largest countries in Latin America—Brazil, Mexico, and Argentina—were expanding their industrialization process, despite certain domestic inconsistencies (Fajnzylber 1983; Katz and Kosacoff 1998). However, this period also marked a serious reversal in the aspiration to a change of position in the global economic structure, not just because of the contradictions that arose within the industrialization process, but also because of a change in the global economic structure. In other words, attempts to change position within the structure coincided with a change in the structure itself.

What this study argues is that the emergence of the structural logic of the new capitalism represented a break with the old logic. This is not a question of a techno-economic paradigm shift (the IT revolution and networked organization) within the same industrial logic of the postwar.[9] Instead, it is a break in the structural conditions in which these technological changes (digitalization) and organizational changes (decentralization) were deployed. The problem is how to understand the nature of this break—the meaning of moving from one logic to another.

So, a new logic was established. New spatiotemporal determinants for accumulation began to emerge in response to this crisis. The structure of the global economy was reconfigured in the form of a global chain: a series of stages in the production process that are divided up into activities that are structurally differentiated but are articulated through the planning power of a leading firm.[10]

What, however, is the nature of this break? Innovation and production are now tied together in a singularly novel way.[11] Let's look at a simple chain model:

Conception stage → Production stage → Commercialization stage

The conception stage consists of developing new production techniques and creating product designs. This is specifically an innovation activity in which new knowledge is produced. Strictly speaking, this does not take place entirely within the company itself. Instead, it is about a link between the company, and the education and research system in a given territory. The strength of labor that is deployed during this stage depends on the degree of complexity of the knowledge system that it rests on[12] and on the company's capacity to exploit the knowledge created in that context for economic ends.

The production stage: at this point, the designs and techniques that were developed during the previous stage are adopted and the task of production itself is carried out—that is, the reproduction, capture, or extraction of natural resources (in the case of primary goods), the physical transformation of raw materials, and the assembly of parts and components (industrial goods), and supply (services[13]). The productive potential of this stage is entirely linked to the capacity to efficiently reproduce existing knowledge. This efficiency should be understood as the relationship between physical productivity and production costs, that is, as the minimization of the unit cost of production of a good or service that embodies a certain production design by adopting the most advanced production techniques of the era. In this case, the speed at which they are adopted plays a critical role in the competition process, which brings to the forefront the technological and institutional barriers to entry that regulate the international dissemination of knowledge.

Commercialization is the last stage in the chain. Although this stage involves a series of relatively simple tasks, one function that is deployed during it may turn out to be decisive to the success or failure of a product on the market. The function in question is the communication between the firm and the consumer and, consequently, the creation of a discourse on the subjective effect that the consumption of specific merchandise has (on the consumer). The efficiency of this communication depends on the construction of a social imaginary that can mobilize consumer's desire (rather than just represent their interests). This is an innovation-intensive activity as its focus is on the production of new knowledge. Although there is a structural continuity between design and communication, it is a different sort of knowledge to that created during the conception stage. The strength of labor for this stage must be sought not so much in the science and technology system or in education and research institutions but rather in the logic that serves to endow merchandise with a cultural "aura". The model for this logic must be sought in the cultural industry itself.[14]

The chain scheme is not universal but it does play a dominant role in the main industries of the new capitalism. Its fundamental properties are:

- Segmentation between innovation-intensive activities (the creation of new knowledge) and production-intensive activities (reproduction of existing knowledge).[15] This segmentation implies that firms that adopt modern production techniques will gradually lose the ability to create their own production techniques (Levín 1997).
- Shortening of the product lifecycle and increasing product differentiation. According to Corsani (2003), this state of affairs entails the transition from a "reproduction regime", in which increasing value essentially rested on control over the time needed to reproduce standardized merchandise, to an "invention regime", in which increasing value is about creating new knowledge. As Vercellone (2011) argues, this implies that it is increasingly far "behind" the sphere of wage labor and the market both in society in general and in the education and research system in particular, which contains the key to productivity and the development of social wealth. These conditions may lead to conflicts in terms of appropriating innovative rents by exercising property rights over intellectual creations.
- The dispersal of production but the centralization of command. The entry of new global actors into the production phase does not imply a growing autonomy in their accumulation process. Leading firms

are being forced to take on governance functions throughout these productive chains as the separation of conception and production entails very high risks for the subcontracting firm—specifically, the risk of the subcontractor not meeting production standards (in terms of quality or delivery times, for example). In this sense, exerting command over the chain implies that if the leading firm wants to guarantee the standard of its product, it cannot extricate itself from the subordinate phases of the chain. It thus must control and punish subcontractors if they do not comply with this standard and should also provide technical assistance to help suppliers develop (Kaplinsky 2000; Humphrey and Schmitz 2001; Sassen 1999).
- The emergence of a new governance structure that is private and global in nature brought the existence of new forms of regulation for global accumulation to the forefront. These pose new challenges to sovereignty in the public domestic sphere, which was the focus of regulation during industrial postwar capitalism. Likewise, the strategies of multinational firms are articulated with global political networks in the construction of new forms of financial, commercial, intellectual property, and environmental regulation, among others, which shape global institutions and have an undeniable center-periphery bias (Sassen 2007; Fernández 2017; Olivera 2018).

So, how should we look at the structural logic of the new capitalism following the emergence of this chain-shaped structure? One option would be suggesting that the break with the previous logic leaves a *tabula rasa*. In this sense, it could be claimed that the growing potential for accumulation (which implies a transition from the simple to the complex) might be sequenced as follows: from the peripheral function of adopting production techniques and designs (which have already been created) to the central function of developing these dominant techniques and designs (adding the term "dominant" implies the inclusion of the commercialization and marketing phase, without which there would be no domination of the subjectivity of the consumer, at least not as a permanent, structural phenomenon). In terms of a cognitive division of labor, this could be expressed as follows: as the transition from activities that reproduce existing knowledge (use and adaptation of knowledge) to others that create new knowledge (cutting-edge global innovation).[16]

However, the structural logic of the new capitalism cannot be described as a *tabula rasa* in comparison with the logic of postwar capitalism. The nature of the rupture is different. The structural differences in sector-specific specialization do not disappear in the course of the transition. The potential for accumulation continues to be heterogeneous within the sector-specific structure of production. However, this heterogeneity is now chain shaped. In this way, forming part of a cutting-edge global sector does not imply taking on the functions of centrality. One example of this would be a worker from the periphery who carries out simple tasks in a high-tech industry.

The core idea to consider, therefore, is that L1 (as the structural logic of postwar capitalism, which is defined according to the degree of complexity of the different goods-producing sectors) remains valid, but is no longer the dominant norm. Instead, it is permeated and given meaning by a new logic that separates activities that create knowledge from those that reproduce it within the different sectors (although not in all of them). That is the nature of the break: a division that is imposed on the previous logic without eliminating it. Consequently, the structural logic of the new capitalism (L2) can be described as follows:

$$L2 = L1/(A \rightarrow D)$$

In other words, in the new capitalism, a chain-shaped structure is imposed on (and divides) the structural logic of postwar capitalism (L1). This new structure expresses a sequence of increasing accumulation that is based on the transition from being an adopter (A) to being a developer (D) of the production techniques and designs that business discourse defines as being dominant.

The structural change in the new capitalism is, therefore, a change in position in the structure in the direction A → D within sectors with increasing potential for accumulation. However, it is worth considering how far L1 is altered (or persists) when it collides with the structural logic of the new capitalism. The fundamental changes are:

- A revaluing of consumer goods in relation to producer goods that derives from the growing importance of esthetics and communication[17]
- The fuller inclusion of services in the structural logic, based on greater innovative potential in both financial services and high-tech services (IT or specialized technical assistance) and in services that are oriented toward mass consumption and tend to be structured as commercial franchise chains with a global reach[18]

- The de-commoditization of primary goods based on increasing product differentiation, be it through advances in the genetic design of living organisms or the certification of designation of origin or of distinctive characteristics in the production process (such as "organic" or "fair trade")[19]

There are some areas where L1 persists: for example, it is noteworthy that it is still not possible to fully separate the conception and execution phases in some parts of the metalworking industry. The existence of complex process technologies functions as a barrier to reaching the level of codification necessary to make process learning independent from product learning (Pisano and Shih 2012). Likewise, mastery of these complex process technologies may function as a complementary asset through which product innovation rents can be appropriated (Teece 1986). In this sense, the metalworking industry expresses certain aspects of the previous logic that are hard for the dominant logic of the new capitalism to assimilate—it is, in other words, an area of resistance to the break in the structural logic.

In this context, being on the periphery takes on new meanings. Although the barriers to entry to innovation-intensive activities are being raised (increasingly complex knowledge systems and the concentration of the capacity to exploit knowledge at a global scale for economic ends), the same is not true of production-intensive stages, the global supply of which is on the rise as new economic actors enter the market (Altenburg et al. 2008). In this way, innovation-intensive activities (the development of production techniques and the creation of dominant design) take on central functions in the new structure, and production-intensive activities (the adopter position) take on a peripheral role in the dynamics of the structure.[20]

In geographic terms, the change in structure has implied a shift in the geographic center of the global economy from the North Atlantic to the Pacific (the West Coast of the United States and East Asia). This region, however, is not a unified space for commanding the global economy. Quite the contrary, it is subject to the chain-shaped segmentation that characterizes the global structure. On one side is the West Coast of the United States, home to the symbolic centers of high-tech innovation (Silicon Valley) and culture (Hollywood). On the other is the east coast of Asia (above all China), where the world's greatest production capacities are now found. The Asian model can also be internally divided into those countries that only dominate the production stage and those that have also made significant advances in second-generation innovation, that is, new developments that complement more fundamental innovation.[21]

In this way, the structural logic of the new capitalism implies a break in what it means to be on the periphery. In line with recent historical changes, the core of capitalist increases in value has shifted toward the sphere of knowledge production, which takes place during the stage that precedes the production of the merchandise itself. It is in relation to this shift that the fundamental antagonisms of the global economy in this new period of history need to be considered.

Conclusions

This study has presented a hypothesis around the emergence of a new structural logic that broke with the one that reigned during postwar capitalism. This break, however, did not imply the disappearance of the antagonism between the center and the periphery. Instead, this antagonism is reproduced and refreshed within the conditions of the new capitalism. This state of affairs is the foundation for new prospects for change.

One such prospect is the deepening of the path followed by the periphery: taking on the role of an early adopter of the dominant techniques and designs that are produced in the center to develop production capacities that can compete with other places on the periphery. This option comes with a policy program of its own: opening up to trade to allow the entry of embodied technology, reinforcing intellectual property rights, developing the capacity for the early adoption of cutting-edge global technology, and so on. The peripheral nature of this option derives from the loss of technological autonomy that is an intrinsic condition of being an adopter. The most significant implication of this is being subjected to the planning strategies of a leading global firm (or several of these), as part of a highly efficient global production scheme, albeit in a subordinate role.

Another option would be to take on the structural change perspective, which would enable a change in position in the structure (in the direction $A \rightarrow D$) within sectors with high potential for accumulation. This implies developing an education and research infrastructure on the basis of which peripheral countries could reach a certain threshold of autonomy in terms of knowledge production. This is the minimum foundation needed for building innovation capacities that would allow such locations to gradually take on certain central functions, at least in sectors that are defined as strategic within a planning process that is independent of global firms and the political networks that support them in order to exercise control over the global economy.

Notes

1. See Prebisch (1962 [1949]) and Hirschman (1980).
2. The relationship between the degree of productive complexity and actual accumulation is not a linear one. It is mediated by the existence of barriers to entry that regulate the conversion of productive knowledge into innovation rents (Rullani 2000; Teece 1986).
3. The existence of land rent as an extraordinary source of accumulation is compatible with a peripheral function in the global economy.
4. For more on this, see Cox (1987), Sassen (2010) and Medeiros and Massat (2018).
5. There are different positions on how to divide up capitalism into stages (Dabat 2006; Pérez 2002). This study draws on the concept of the historical system of accumulation and the transformation within capitalist production that alludes to "the association between a form of production and a logic of accumulation that together guide the long-term trend toward the value of capital increasing, the division of labor, and the reproduction of the most fundamental social relationships" (Dieuaidé et al. 2007: 74). See also Vercellone (2011) and Moulier-Boutang (2004).
6. See Dabat (2006).
7. Strictly speaking, both the center and the periphery have productive substructures that together make up the structure of the global economy.
8. See, among others, Coriat (1991), Gorz (1998), Vercellone (2011), and Piore and Sabel (1984).
9. For more on the concept of techno-economic paradigms, see Freeman and Pérez (1988).
10. It is important to identify the global chain as a historical phenomenon which in the specialist literature is known as the global value chain or global production chain approach, depending on the author. Key examples of approach include Gereffi (1996), Kaplinsky (2000), Humphrey and Schmitz (2001), or Dicken (2003), among others. For a critical perspective on this approach, see Trevignani and Fernández (2017).
11. Production capacities are fundamentally oriented toward the use and adaptation of existing knowledge. According to Bell and Albu (1999) and Bell and Pavitt (1995), these capacities are linked to the replication and circulation of knowledge that has already been established within the production system, with the potential for expanding production capacities using certain methods of production. On the other hand, at the core of the development of innovation capacity lies the acquisition, creation, processing, and accumulation of new knowledge. Innovation and production are intertwined aspects of the valorization process. However, this analytical distinction seeks to differentiate those productive stages that are dominated by

tasks involving the introduction of new knowledge from those that are fundamentally oriented toward the reproduction of existing knowledge (Altenburg et al. 2008).

12. For an analysis of the innovation system from the complexity perspective, see Robert and Yoguel (2010).
13. The conception of a service can be separated from the execution (provision) of it. This is the case, for example, with a large part of mass consumption service chains, in which this fragmentation is expressed in terms of a franchiser (conception) and a franchise (implementation).
14. For more on this, see Lash and Urry (1998), Power and Scott (2004), Bocock (1993), and Lazzarato (2006).
15. This process of productive segmentation is also one of social fragmentation: it entails the spatial separation (at the global level) of skilled workers from unskilled workers, and thus of the organizational unity of workers that were all formerly within the same country (Sassen 1999).
16. Differentiating between first- and second-generation innovations may relativize this trend (Breznitz and Murphree 2011). The first case refers to radically new product innovations, the second, to the development of new attributes for existing products.
17. See Jameson (1991).
18. See Low (2013) and Sztulwark and Girard (2014).
19. See Kaplinsky and Fitter (2004) and Sztulwark and Girard (2016).
20. This structural dynamic cannot be fully understood without taking into account the center-periphery factor in the production of knowledge itself. According to Richard (1997), the hierarchy of the center on this level originates in its "trappings of authority as a hub that endows things with meaning". The function of the center can be as the axis which drives "a system of references around its symbolic authority: establishing standards of meaning or behavior, prescribing uses, legitimizing, decreeing validity" (Richard 1997).
21. For more on this, see Breznitz and Murphree (2011) and Rivera Ríos (2016).

References

Altenburg, Tilman, Hubert Schmitz, and Andreas Stamm. 2008. Breakthrough? China's and India's Transition from Production to Innovation. *World Development* 36 (2): 325–344.

Amsden, Alice. 2004. La sustitución de importaciones en las industrias de alta tecnología: Prebisch renace en Asia. *Revista de la Cepal* 82: 75–90.

Bell, Martin, and Michael Albu. 1999. Knowledge Systems and Technological Dynamism in Industrial Clusters in Developing Countries. *World Development* 27 (9): 1715–1734.

Bell, Martin, and Keith Pavitt. 1995. The Development of Technological Capabilities. In *Trade and International Competitiveness*, ed. Irfan ul Haque, 69–102. Washington: The World Bank.

Bocock, Robert. 1993. *El consumo*. Madrid: Talasa Ediciones.

Breznitz, Dan, and Michael Murphree. 2011. *Run of the Red Queen: Government, Innovation, Globalization and Economic Growth in China*. New Haven: Yale University Press.

CEPAL. 2012. *Cambio estructural para la igualdad: Una visión integrada del desarrollo*. Santiago de Chile: CEPAL.

Cimoli, Mario, Gabriel Porcile, Analissa Primi, and Sebastián Vergara. 2005. Cambio estructural, heterogeneidad productiva y tecnología en América Latina. In *Heterogeneidad estructural, asimetrías tecnológicas y crecimiento en América Latina*, ed. Mario Cimoli, 9–39. Santiago de Chile: CEPAL-BID.

Coriat, Benjamín. 1991. *Pensar al Revés. Trabajo y organización de la empresa japonesa*. Mexico: Siglo Veintiuno Editores.

Corsani, Antonella. 2003. Elementos de uma ruptura: a hipótese do capitalismo cognitivo. In *Capitalismo Cognitivo. Trabalho, Redes e Innovación*, ed. Alexander Galvao, Gerardo Silva, and Giuseppe Cocco, 15–32. Rio de Janeiro: DP&A Editora.

Cox, Robert W. 1987. *Production, Power and World Order: Social Forces in the Making of History*. New York: Columbia University Press.

Dabat, Alejandro. 2006. Capitalismo informático y capitalismo industrial. Acercamiento al perfil histórico del nuevo capitalismo. *Economía Informa* 338: 34–39.

Dicken, Peter. 2003. *Global Shift: Transforming the World Economy*. New York: Guilford Press.

Dieuaidé, Patrick, Bernard Paulré, and Carlo Vercellone. 2007. Introducción al capitalismo cognoscitivo. In *Cambio histórico mundial, conocimiento y desarrollo*, ed. Miguel Angel Rivera Ríos and Alejandro Dabat, 69–91. Mexico: UNAM/Casa Juan Pablos.

Fajnzylberg, Fernando. 1983. *La industrialización trunca de América Latina*. Buenos Aires: Centro Editor de América Latina.

Fernández, Víctor Ramiro. 2017. *La trilogía del erizo-zorro: redes globales, trayectorias nacionales y dinámicas regionales desde la periferia*. Buenos Aires and Santa Fe: Editorial Anthropos and Ediciones de la Universidad Nacional del Litoral.

Freeman, Christopher, and Carlota Pérez. 1988. Structural Crisis of Adjustment, Business Cycles and Investment Behavior. In *Technical Change and Economy Theory*, ed. Giovanni Dosi, Christopher Freeman, Richard Nelson, Gerald Silverberg, and Luc Soete, 38–66. London: Pinter Publisher.

Gereffi, Gary. 1996. Global Commodity Chains: New Forms of Coordination and Control Among Nations and Firms in International Industries. *Competition & Change* 1 (4): 427–439.

Gorz, Andre. 1998. *Miserias del presente, riqueza de lo posible*. Buenos Aires: Paidós.

Hirschman, Albert. 1980. Auge y ocaso de la teoría económica del desarrollo. *El Trimestre Económico* 47 (4), no. 188, October–December: 1055–1077.

Humphrey, John, and Hubert Schmitz. 2001. *Governance and Upgrading: Linking Industrial Cluster and Global Value Chain Research*. IDS WorkingPaper 120.

Jameson, Frederic. 1991. *El posmodernismo o la lógica cultural del capitalismo avanzado*. Buenos Aires: Paidós.

Kaplinsky, Raphael. 2000. Globalization and Unequalization: What Can Be Learned from Value Chain Analysis. *The Journal of Development Studies* 37 (2, December), 117–146.

Kaplinsky, Raphael, and Robert Fitter. 2004. Technology and Globalization: Who Gains When Commodities Are De-Commodified? *International Journal of Technology and Globalisation* 1 (1): 5–28.

Katz, Jorge, and Bernardo Kosacoff. 1998. Aprendizaje tecnológico, desarrollo institucional y la microeconomía de la sustitución de importaciones. *Desarrollo Económico* 37 (148, January–March): 483–502.

Lash, Scott, and John Urry. 1998. *Economías de signo y espacio*. Buenos Aires: Amorrortu Editores.

Lazzarato, Mauricio. 2006. *Políticas del acontecimiento*. Buenos Aires: Tinta Limón Ediciones.

Leiva, Fernando. 2008. *Latin American Neostructuralism. The Contradictions of Post-Neoliberal Development*. Minneapolis: University of Minnesota Press.

Levín, Pablo. 1997. *El capital tecnológico*. Buenos Aires: Catálogos.

Low, Patrick. 2013. The Role of Services in Global Value Chains. In *Global Value Chains in a Changing World*, ed. Debora Elms and Patrick Low, 61–81. Geneva: World Trade Organization.

Medeiros, Carlos Aguiar, and Numa Massat. 2018. *Geopolitics, Geoeconomics and Development Strategies in the New Millennium* (In This Volume).

Míguez, Pablo. 2008. Las transformaciones recientes de los procesos de trabajo: desde la automatización hasta la revolución informática. *Trabajo y sociedad* X (11): 1–20.

Moulier-Boutang, Yann. 2004. Riqueza, propiedad, libertad y renta en el capitalismo cognitivo. In *Capitalismo Cognitivo. Propiedad intelectual y creación colectiva*. Madrid: Traficantes de Sueños.

Ocampo, José Antonio. 2011. Macroeconomía para el desarrollo: políticas anticíclicas y transformación productiva. *Revista de la CEPAL* 104 (August): 7–35.

Olivera, Margarita. 2018. *The Possibilities of Industrialization and Structural Change for the Periphery in the Context of Globalization* (In This Volume).

Pérez, Carlota. 2002. *Technological Revolutions and Financial Capital. The Dynamics of Bubbles and Golden Ages*. Cheltenham: Edgard Elgar.

Piore, Michael, and Charles Sabel. 1984. *The Second Industrial Divide*. New York: Basic Books.
Pisano, Gary, and Willy Shih. 2012. *Producing Prosperity: Why America Needs a Manufacturing Renaissance*. Cambridge, MA: Harvard Business Review Press.
Power, Dominic, and Allen Scott. 2004. *Cultural Industries and the Production of Culture*. London and New York: Routledge.
Prebisch, Raúl. 1962 [1949]. El desarrollo económico de América Latina y algunos de sus principales problemas. *Boletín Económico de la América Latina* VII (1, February).
Richard, Nelly. 1997. La Condición Centro-Marginal Post-Moderna. *Travessia Revista de Literatura* 29 (30): 55–59.
Rivera Ríos, Miguel Angel. 2016. República Popular China: aprendizaje tecnológico y retos del desarrollo exportador. *Economía: teoría y práctica. Nueva Época* 44 (January–June): 83–114.
Robert, Verónica, and Gabriel Yoguel. 2010. La dinámica compleja de la innovación y el desarrollo económico. *Desarrollo Económico* 50 (199): 423–453.
Rodríguez, Octavio. 1977. Sobre la concepción del sistema centro-periferia. *Revista de la CEPAL*, First Semester: 203–248.
Rullani, Enzo. 2000. El capitalismo cognitivo: du déjàvú? *Revista Multitudes* 2: 87–92.
Sassen, Saskia. 1999. *La ciudad global*. Buenos Aires: Eudeba.
———. 2007. *Sociología de la globalización*. Buenos Aires: Katz.
———. 2010. *Territorio, autoridad y derechos. De los ensamblajes medievales a los ensamblajes globales*. Buenos Aires: Katz.
Stiglitz, Joseph. 2002. Globalization and the Logic of International Collective Action: Re-Examining the Bretton Woods Institutions. In *Governing Globalization: Issues and Institutions*, ed. Deepak Nayyar, 238–253. New York: Oxford University Press.
Sztulwark, Sebastián, and Melisa Girard. 2014. Los servicios y el cambio estructural en el nuevo capitalismo. *Realidad Económica* 286: 65–92.
———. 2016. Genetically Modified Seeds and the De-Commodification of Primary Goods. *International Journal of Biotechnology* 14 (2): 132–150.
Teece, David. 1986. Profiting from Technological Innovation. *Research Policy* 15 (6): 285–305.
Trevignani, Manuel, and Víctor Ramiro Fernández. 2017. *Desarrollo y cadenas globales de valor. Una revisión crítica desde la periferia*. Santa Fe: Universidad Nacional del Litoral.
Vercellone, Carlo. 2011. *Capitalismo cognitivo. Renta, saber y valor en la época posfordista*. Buenos Aires: Prometeo.

CHAPTER 4

The Multi-Scalar Articulation of Economic Development

Carlos Antônio Brandão

Introduction

This chapter will attempt to introduce the notion of "multi-scalarity" to enrich structuralist analysis and, at the same time, show a series of limitations of neo-structuralism in order to explain the key spatial dimensions of the remake and reproduction of the center-periphery structures associated with the contradictory dynamics of capitalism.

It is not that Latin American Structuralism (LAS) did not have certain conceptions of spatial scales. Although not fully expressed, these were implied, despite presupposed, and implicit in their creative analysis of the international division of labor, endogenous structural heterogeneities and center-peripheral relations.

Emphasis was placed on the movements of the leading hegemonic cyclical center (first Great Britain, then the United States) (Prebisch 1948; Furtado 1964; Pinto 1970a, 1970b). Primacy has been put on the national scale as an abstract entity, without a differentiated and variegated structural context, although Latin American structuralism also had in its theoretical

C. A. Brandão (✉)
Urban and Regional Research and Planning Institute,
Federal University of Rio de Janeiro, Brazil

V. R. Fernández, G. Brondino (eds.), *Development in Latin America*,
https://doi.org/10.1007/978-3-319-92183-9_4

and strategic horizon the construction of a scale of supranational (continental) dimensions. Thus subnational scales had little or no relevance, although a few of their regional economists have dealt with the intranational inequalities of some Latin American countries (Rofman 1974; Coraggio 1979; De Mattos 1972).

However, in that thought a more dynamic and sophisticated approach to spatial scales has not been developed. Scales were taken as static and exact space unities. But, indeed, as the critical geographic literaturereworked them from the nineties, scales are conflicting, relational, procedural, and contingent social constructs.

Indeed, one of the limitations of Latin American structuralism to understand the current capitalism regards the development of another notion of "multi-scalarity". It will be necessary to comprehend spatial scales not only as a category and unit of analysis, an epistemological and heuristic resource, but also as a type of practice, a discursive and narrative plane, a field and arena of power, a process and an instrument of projects and development strategies that are in dispute. Beyond its perception of national scale as a receptacle, a shelter, a harmonious and passive homogeneous platform of a given geometric plane, it will be needed to take the various scales in which processes and their *loci* are inscribed, sculpted, and erected, materially and symbolically, where social life is organized and reproduced dynamically.

In this regard, a daring research agenda needs to be structured, seeking to overcome its conception of a static scalarity, interpreting scales as closed and self-sufficient entities, or, at best, conceiving a bi-scalarity (national and global).

This chapter intends to propose a more advanced and adherent approach to the reality of the twenty-first century, seeking to grasp the hierarchical, unequal, dynamic, and contradictory development of the capitalist system, its total geo-economic, geo-cultural, and geopolitical redefinition (Wallerstein 1974b, 1979; Braudel 1979; Arrighi 1994), and its particular social production of space (Lefebvre 1974).

Notwithstanding the originality of their reflections on the peripheral condition, neither the structuralism nor the neo-structuralism were able to adequately recover their national trajectories (with their specific processes of accumulation and regulation/legitimation) without incurring some methodological nationalism (Gore 1996; Medeiros 2010; Pendenza 2016).

Neo-structuralism, following international agencies, analyzed and advocated for decentralizing public policy processes (Leyva 2008; Cepal 2012), but maintained a static national scalar conception. The scales are taking as a container, a receptacle of apathetic agents and objects. By understanding them as a harmonious and passive homogeneous platform, in a given geometrical plane, this approach neglects or fails to understand the dynamics of variable geometry. The multiplicity of national and regional spaces, and their respective and peculiar capacity of response, in the face of relentless penetration and reconfiguration made by multi-scale institutional and economic networks and agents, lose their wealth and complexity.

The national spatial scale needs to be understood in a dynamic and relational way that does not neglect the exogenous and conjecturally contextual determinations that come from the hegemonic imperial supranational states in a global context of insertion into the interstate systems in dispute. The challenge nowadays consists in rejecting and overcoming "methodological nationalism", and understanding from its internal dynamics the global behaviors and complexity of the center-periphery relationship.

Therefore, we will try to demonstrate how the notion of "multiscalarity" is necessary to enrich structuralist analysis and capture the scalar complexity of contemporary capitalism from the periphery.

The Wealth (Neglected and Wasted) and the Potentialities of Latin American Critical, Historical-Structural Thinking

Latin America conceived and accumulated for more than half a century, since the late forties (ECLAC 2016), an unusual analytical framework. One that has accumulated by articulating various aspects into a true academic heritage, founding a critical tradition to make a bold and pioneering reflection, which sought to interpret the specificities of the development process in the dependent underdeveloped peripheral condition.

This independent, original, and creative thought was decisively focused on the transformation of the Latin American peripheral situation (Palma 1978; Cardoso 1979; Cardoso and Faletto 1979). However, it became invisible, without the deserved repercussion in world academia, and was politically unfeasible, not raising a sociopolitical force for its effective implementation.

The creative development of a rigorous body of thought occurred in a very pragmatic way, through the appropriation, re-articulation, and self-production of knowledge. It reworked methodologies and concepts, and sought, in a process of successive approximations, to diachronically combine structures, processes in situational and structural contexts, and subjects in action.

Although very heterogeneous, and with hegemony on political economy, this current of thought sought to overcome the only economic determinations by aggregating sociological and political issues of domination and asymmetrical power (without separating the discussion of capital accumulation and the increase in labor productivity, and looking at the problem of surplus distribution). This multidisciplinary and plurimeteorological character should be highlighted in this creative construction. As an example, it adequately composed inductive and deductive methods (Rodríguez 2009).

The center of the program of this theoretical elaboration was a political project based on the awareness and the search for the creation of instruments to generate ruptures in relation to the asymmetric mechanisms of the unequal exchange, by addressing structural heterogeneities and other things, in a deliberate construction of autonomy in a hostile environment. That is, in a singular peripheral context, in the greatest territorial part of the world, which brings together and puts in contradictory coexistence the greatest disparities between underdevelopment and the development of capitalist productive forces.

In addition, like the conservative mainstream in the European and American elaborations, the predominant vision of capitalism neglected and remained oblivious to the situation in which the penetration of factors of modernization, in environments of great underdevelopment, in social relations, and in productive forces, formed *sui-generis* hybrid structures. This fact has not reached the reality of economies and dependent societies, which represents and signifies the peripheral situation and the underdeveloped structural conformation in the general context of evolution and reproduction of world capitalism.

Therefore, unfortunately, the richness, originality, independence, and complexity of the critical thinking in the social sciences developed within this continent did not have proper dissemination, visibility, and influence, especially in the Eurocentric and Anglo-Saxon academic environment. With a few exceptions, its contribution has not been practically translated into English or published in international dissemination vehicles with greater diffusion on a global scale.

The rich and creative Latin American thought was closed in the borders of its national institutions, and even the circulation of the production between the Latin American countries was in a very restricted form. In this context, its unusual and innovative contributions to the nature and specific character of the peripheral situation in the context of world capitalism, which could have not only enriched the debate on the underdevelopment but also shed light on the structure and dynamics of developed countries, was partially lost, wasting substantial fraction of this rich scientific and political experience.

The worst occurred after the so-called lost decade of the eighties, after about five decades of implementing development strategies to some extent oriented by such theoretical conception which promoted some deeper structural transformations in the Latin American continent (Bértola and Ocampo 2012). In this era, the impetus was lost to evolve renewed original thought about the transformations that capitalism was producing to think about a more dynamic and autonomous insertion of Latin America.

If original and autonomous critical thinking has regressed, neoliberal elaborations have advanced. In several rounds of the neoliberalization process, methodological individualism has gained impetus with the sophistication of institutionalist currents that contributed to the loss of power in the analysis of material bases and social processes, of conflicting nature, in historical movement.

The impaired proposal of understanding the peripheral condition as a structural malformation (Furtado 1964) did not advance to elucidate the nature of the obstacles in the truncated capitalist environment, nor to promote an accumulation with another rhythm, but especially with autonomy from the decision centers (Prebisch 1948, 1963).

The analysis of the specific nature of this peripheral part of the whole evolution of capitalism shows that the character of interdependencies and possible dialogues with peripheral-scientific production has been lost, harming both the apprehension of the whole and its various parts.

According to Latin American authors, it is not only a fact that their structures are delayed, but that, over time, the limitations, deprivations, mutilations, and incompleteness of the underdeveloped end up further deforming the structures (productive, occupational, distribution of income and wealth, and the very composition of social classes) (Tavares 1981) that had been diachronically forged throughout the historical constraints placed by the insertion at that national scale in the concert of relations with world dynamics.

Underdevelopment is not seen as a phase, but as a face, which coevolved over time with development. This was the great merit of Latin American thought but was minimally understood by the authors of the North. Underdevelopment should be seen under the distinctive characteristics of the center-periphery relations system and the peculiar nature of the links established with the outside from the subaltern spaces.

The Latin American structuralism had demonstrated how, throughout the various cycles of accumulation, legitimation, and regulation, the reproduction (always in renewed bases) of the properties of the concrete asymmetrical relations between the center and the peripheries operates according to a structural logic over time (Pinto 1970a, 1970b; Bielschowsky 1998).

That is to say, they continue to operate antagonisms, and systemic and hierarchical contradictions. Forming two quite distinct spaces of accumulation (the central and the peripheral), endowed with very particular modes of relation between different spaces, but which depend on the same structural logic and becomes the course of the historical movement, as part of a more general trajectory in the context of the dynamics of capitalism as a world system (see Chap. 3).

This hierarchical and asymmetrical system has been forged throughout history and from the different generation and diffusion of technical progress between central countries and peripheral countries—the first structurally conditioning the development of the later (Fajnzylber 1983). This phenomenon was due both to the asymmetrical exchange relations and the penetration of techniques and large companies in the peripheral national space, which internalizes exogenous forms of consumption and is the passive host of transnational conglomerates that are alien to their internal interests.

Thus, the peripheral, underdeveloped, and dependent situation would conform to, in complex processes of long historical duration, unequal and heterogeneous structures that reproduce truncated and diachronic forms in the varied dimensions: economic, political, cultural, and so on.

The Differences and Plurality of Capitalist Forms and Trajectories Seeking a More Sophisticated Multi-Scaled Analysis of Current Capitalism

It is important to note the original contributions of the available but little-mobilized patrimony and its contribution to the current understanding of the complex process of restructuring global capitalism and the opportunities, constraints, and challenges that Latin America has in the world context. The Latin American School of Critical, Historical, and Structural Thinking can help shed light on the limitations, negligence, and biases of approaches developed in central countries by explaining the particular processes and trajectories that have taken place in peripheral nations (Fernández 2017).

A very illuminating example of possible dialogues that could occur is about the reflections on the diverse "development styles or patterns", elaborated by Anibal Pinto (1970b). This brilliant construction could have discussed the "development paths" in the past with the five "institutional forms" of the French Regulation School (Boyer 1990; Boyer and Saillard 2002), from the late 1970s, or with the "Development Patterns" of the "Campinas' School" (Tavares 1981; Fiori 2014).

Exploring the specificities of nature, coherence, and compatibilization between the structures of the three schools of thought remains a promising and little-explored research agenda for comparing central and peripheral capitalisms (see Table 4.1).

Table 4.1 Three schools of thought and their structure

Development styles (Pinto 1970b)	*Institutional forms (French Regulation School) (Boyer 1990; Boyer and Saillard 2002)*	*Development patterns (School of Campinas, Brazil) (Filgueiras 2013; Brandão 2015a)*
Physical and natural resources		Escape to territorial front of rights and resources
Population: Profiles and aptitudes		Social reproduction of the "bottom" and the labor force
Social structure	Form of salary relationship	Nature and regulation of capital-labor relations
Production organization	Form of competition	Productive structure and competitive oligopoly patterns
External relations	Form of connecting to the international regime	Nature of external insertion
	Forms of the state	Articulation of the state with the process of accumulation
	Form and monetary regime	Method of financing accumulation
		Fractions of capital and leadership in the process of accumulation
		Dominant historical block

Source: Author's own elaboration

The ignorance of the "development styles or patterns" construction was the lack of analysis of world capitalism in its concrete reality. The lack of knowledge about the "development styles or patterns" construction interdicted part of their analytical potential.

However, this contribution from Latin American knowledge produced in Latin America helps recognize that there is no canonical model to be followed in the development process, but a plurality of alternative historical paths and trajectories. Hence, the functioning of the "capitalist machine" must be investigated in its concrete spatial expressions. This poses a challenge for thinking the time-space processes of development: In short, the role of spatial scales (local, regional, national, global, etc.) in these structural processes needs to be urgently and dynamically considered.

These multiple theoretical tasks should lead to better theorizing about decisions (Furtado 1964), contemplating the dynamics of actors, networks, agents, and concrete subjects, social classes and their fractions, the hierarchies of command power, and the actions and chains of reactions of the decisions made (by various agents and social subjects that operate at various spatial scales).

Hegemonic international literature had been proclaiming an inexorable sense of the unification and convergence of the capitalist system toward a kind of Anglo-American "monocultural" capitalist experience, which should guide the adjustments of those who erroneously followed other paths. The existence of an inexorable tendency toward convergence for some "optimal model of capitalism" is defended by denying the reality that confirms daily the diversity of institutional structures, plurality, heterogeneity, and divergence of forms and modes of systemic organization. It thus advocates a pre-established and uniform course of capitalism with similar structures (Crouch 2005).

With a unifying and homogenizing imposition of a scalar tax narrative, it is maintained that there is a sense of unification and confluence of the historical capitalist trajectories toward a kind of meta-type with an excellent "institutional monoculture". This conservative thought believes that there is no power, conflicts, or hierarchies in international or interregional relations. It is not important to see the specific position occupied by peripheral spaces in the system as a whole. Therefore, there is no analytical space to think about the peripheral and complementary position. There are no hegemonies.

Contrary to the conservative view, which advocates a pre-established course toward a uniform composition of capitalism with similar structures, reality demonstrates heteromorphic historical experiences. The capitalist system is by nature polymorphic, following different trajectories and pathways with constant polarization in its structures and repeated conflict of distinct "development styles". There is ongoing competition between the territorial states and the differentiated development experiences; hence, the need to study their particularities and their diverse modes of organization in each historical, institutional, and geographic context.

In fact, no such convergence path exists toward an ideal and superior type of capitalism, as if the more developed regions dictate the agenda and the path that the least developed will follow. There is a polarization between multiple trajectories. There are divergence and plurality of trajectories. The culture, institutions, geography, power structures, and decisions of social class factions count. There is history. It is thus necessary to construct, in the process of successive approximations (upwards and downwards), an approach that simultaneously retains the general determinations and deciphers, and, at the same time, the "real situations", hierarchizing determinations and trying to balance duly determining factors, conditioning factors, and coadjutants in the course of the concrete historical movement, seeking to analyze the conjunctural time, without losing the perspective of the long-lasting structural time.

These investigations discuss the time horizons, beyond the momentary, generating trajectories, possible ways of development, structuring options, and alternatives (diverse and concrete answers to concrete problems). This problem is related to processes, dynamics, structures, subjects, and real-concrete relationships and, therefore, is marked by diversity.

In this context, it becomes indispensable to learn to investigate and to make an adequate balance of the recurrences, persistences, ruptures, and transformations throughout a historical process without linearities, investigating how their pathways, patterns, and development styles were forged and evolved. That is, to understand that each and every capitalism has unique features and explicit general determinations, simultaneously.

Despite having researchers of the stature and erudition of Furtado, Prebisch, and Pinto, the Latin American structuralism did not place at the center of its analysis the triple character of capital accumulation and its distribution or the problematic of conflicts and powers. They had a reading of Marx, Keynes, and Schumpeter, but they did not appropriate the teachings of Kalecki. So, there are limits in its analysis to assume the confliction in all its multiple dimensions and scales.

The Need to Think in Scales and the Theoretical Failure of Neo-Structuralism

The rich tradition of Latin American structuralism here analyzed, unfortunately, did not address the territorial dimension of underdevelopment, which contributed to the lack of scientific investigation of the central questions of power, hierarchies, and hegemonies (from the perspective of spatial scales).

Since the last years of the twentieth century, in the critical field of the social sciences, a huge body of research has placed the issue of scale at the center of reflections. Being a very critical literature, perhaps the only unanimity in this theoretical debate is the taking of scale as a conflictive social construction.

The center-periphery scalar relations have transformed twenty-first-century capitalism and continue to reproduce the conditions of underdevelopment and dependency, but they are of a different nature, requiring a multiplicity of spatial scales. With the advent of neo-structuralism, no progress was made in the debate about the changes in these relations. On the contrary, the debate has regressed.

Unfortunately, in a considerable part of contemporary literature, territory, which should be seen as a politicized environment, conflicting and under construction, is seen as reified, between trade and passivity, mere receptacle, where displacements and movements are inscribed. The consequence of social relations appears as a relation between objects. There is reification, and the territory seems to have decision-making power and is transformed into a collective subject. For example, the endogenous capacity of the community locale is sometimes placed in the foreground, highlighting its high command power. Throughout the world, in the social sciences in general, and particularly in economics, neo-institutionalism has advanced.

In the context of LAS, the incorporation of this theoretical conception also occurred, giving rise to the so-called neo-structuralism (Leyva 2008). The latter, in an attitude opposite of the original LAS, put emphasis on the systems of norms and rules, in the stabilizing instances. That is, in the need to construct contexts that amalgamate divergences, instabilities, and uncertainties through customs and norms that would regulate and co-influence the behavior of agents in social (inter)action, highlighting the role of conventions, co-ordinations, and rationalities. This institutional advance would provide the formation of networks of commitments, loyalties, feelings of belonging, capacities to generate coherences, and social contracts appropriately situated and contextualized.

Part of this intellectual production exaggerates in the endogenous capacity of social actors to self-generate virtuous and germinative processes of dense social identity and cooperative specific to each community. Through mutually beneficial processes of learning and mutual acquisition, reciprocities and solidary relationships would generate interconnected elements that would forge forces that later (without further explanation) would spill over into amplified processes of diffusion of benefits, synergies, and innovations.

More conservative authors of this chain propose a reduction in public regulations, considered as generators of rigidities. For them, the expansion of public-private relations is adequate to make the institutionalcontext more apt to have agility, resilience, and capacity of reaction. They propose strategies of decentralization and participation in search of greater equality.

Alternatively, this research agenda must continually investigate historical realities. Thus, it is crucial to elucidate the structural and enduring issues of the capitalist system in specific contexts, such as: the capitalism intrinsic logics; the social reproduction, which is processed by the permanent struggle of fractions of social classes and their different interests; the central function of the inter-corporate and interstate competition process; the continuous interweaving of the various segments of the productive apparatus; the constitutive nature of the state and of the inter-territorial disputes at a global scale; and the strategic role of the large companies. These are the major theoretical and historical mediations to be developed for the understanding of any structural issues of our reality.

It is necessary to understand the inherent nature and the concrete movement of capitalist regime and its simultaneous character: antagonistic, progressive, and contradictory.

Regarding the complex topic of social reproduction, it is not anachronistic to point out the constant struggle of class factions and the consolidation of hegemonies along with struggles against hegemony. It is impossible to discuss capitalism without an analysis of the multiple fractions of capital (mercantile, agrarian, industrial, banking, etc.). It is impossible not to take into account the fact that the present historical context is ruled, at macro and microeconomic levels, by the political hegemony of mercantile-patrimonial and rent-seeking-financial forms of capital.

It thus becomes necessary to admit the existence of inherent conflict and perennial struggle of multiple interests as well as their varied spaces of unification, the existence of opposing projects and of the coalitions and alliances that build up in every historical and territorial context.

To put the intricate process of inter-capitalist competition and rivalry at the center of the understanding of how the capitalist system works is of great importance to attempt to understand the precise situation of competitive hyper-coercion process. This submit the different modalities of capital to constant struggle, encouraging the use of every possible competitive weapon, including those that are illicit or considered as retrograde (those that could be understood as tools for primitive accumulation) (Harvey 2005; Sassen 2014).

In this context, the concepts of productive apparatus and social system of reproduction are important to understanding the productive coherences and complementarities.

The research agenda should be attentive to the fact that the national scale remains decisive and that disputes for interstate and inter-territorial hegemony as well as regarding state hierarchy, currencies, and weapons still shape the world (Fiori 2014). It should also be attentive to the fact that the world is ruled by the interests of financial power and by the strength of huge corporate structures.

In this sense, the challenge is to promote interpretation in the perspective of developing class fractions which are negotiating a conflictive compromise in a living territory and to elucidate the processes through which struggling social subjects socially produce space and the built environment (Lefebvre 1974; Harvey 1982).

The changes now underway in the times and spaces of capitalist wealth and the social dynamics at a social scale present a series of challenges for the analysis of the spatial expressions of the profound and speedy social, economic, and political transformations in the course.

A critical literature has advocated the need to assume that there is no canonical model to be followed in the process of development, but rather a plurality of possible historical paths and courses; the importance of understanding how the "capitalist machine" works in its spatial expressions; *the challenge of thinking time and space in the process of development*; the urgency to treat the role of (local, regional, national, global, etc.) spatial scales dynamically in these structural processes.

To develop a better theorization of decisions it is central to consider these following issues: the dynamics of concrete actors, networks, agents and subjects; the social classes and their fractions; the hierarchies of power and command; the actions and chains of reactions triggered by decisions made by various social agents and subjects operating at different spatial scales.

The hegemonic international literature announces an inexorable sense of unification and convergence of the capitalist system, in its way to a sort of "monocultural" target Anglo-American capitalist experience, which should be the guideline for correcting the mistaken paths followed by all others. This literature sustains that there is an inexorable tendency of convergence toward some kind of "optimum model" of capitalism, and it thus denies the reality that daily confirms the diversity of institutional structures, the heterogeneity of forms, and modes of systemic organization.

Contrary to the conservative view, which defends the existence of a predetermined course toward a uniform composition of capitalism, with similar structures, reality shows that there is heteromorphy in historical experience. The capitalism system is, by its very nature, polymorphous; it follows different courses (Hall and Soskice 2001), and there is a constant polarization in its structures as well as a constantly renewed struggle between open and diverse "developmental styles". There is a *permanent competition of territorial states and diversified experiences of development*, entailing the need for the study of capitalism's specificities and its diverse modes of organization in each historical, institutional, and geographic context (Wallerstein 1974b, 1979; Braudel 1979; Arrighi 1994; Fiori 2014).

Different political circumstances consolidated the neoliberal options (Harvey 2005; Peck 2017), which ended up reinforcing the discourses of the urgency and depth of the crisis and the imperative of decentralization, of territorial governance, the local interpretation of reality, "suggesting", by means of multilateral agencies, models of behavior and "recommendations" of strategies and "public" actions for development.

The unequal nature of accumulation contradictorily creates a space which is at the same time unified (in the sense of rendering goods uniform and universal) and multiple (unequal, heterogeneous, and generator of asymmetries). "Capital not only produces space in general, but it also produces the real spatial scales which give its coherence to unequal development" (Smith 1984, 19).

In this context, the recent literature on spatial scales produced by the critical geographers, which I will attempt to summarize in the sequence, plays a major role for the elucidation of the hierarchies (and the spatially constructed coherences) that structure the social processes at their various levels, instances, and territories.

The research of the territorial dimension of development must pay attention to the central issues of power, hierarchies, and hegemonies.

In the critical field of the social sciences, a considerable set of works has put the issue of scale at the center of reflections concerning the spatial dimension of capitalist development (Smith 1984; Swyngedouw 1997; Brenner 2001; Marston 2000; Marston et al. 2005, among others). The focus of this debate is the investigation of the nature of spatial scales in capitalism (in general).

Perhaps the only consensus in the theoretical debate is the view that scales are conflictive social constructions. Sallie Marston (2000, 220) explains that "in these recent social theoretical studies, the fundamental point being made is that scale is not necessarily a preordained hierarchical framework for ordering the world—local, regional, national and global. It is instead a contingent outcome of the tensions that exist between structural forces and the practices of human agents".

The scalar approach provides concrete elements to analyze the action of social and political subjects, although not only as supporting a given structure. Structures and subjects are historically and geographically determined and mediated processes. It is necessary to advance the analysis of interactions of decisions that translate structures (with complex mediations), but also metamorphose and renew them.

Collectively and politically constructed, this place of confrontations cannot be defined in itself, but only in its relation to other such places. The scale thus delimits and circumscribes social and political compromises in a contingent and conflictive movement, within a constant process of confrontations and by means of interactions and oppositions. Such movements are repeatedly expressed as empowering and disempowering mechanisms employed by the contenders (in parallel with the upscaling and downscaling processes) (Swyngedouw 2004).

There are re-scaling processes, for example, of the state, capital, and labor, jumping scale games in a constant struggle of scales. In this sense, Neil Smith (1992) wrote that "the scale of struggle and the struggle over scale are two sides of the same coin". In summary, the scale reflects, expresses, and gives spatial concreteness to the answers and confrontations of social subjects in their relationship with the challenges they concretely and contextually face in each moment and each historical and geographic context.

In summary, the socially produced spatial scale must be seen as a privileged angle through which one can apprehend the determinations and conditionings of social phenomena articulated with the territory. At the same time, it is taken as a perspective that enables one to uncover singular social, economic, and territorial processes. But scale also means political arena. The scale as an analytical category and the scale as a category of political praxis are not separated. The analytical selection of the most convenient scale for analyzing the observed phenomena allows one to provide better diagnosis and to suggest coalitions of power and strategic decisions on how to face them. The (simultaneously) scientific and political challenge is, therefore, to attempt to define *what and by what means* each scale can disclose, mobilize, confront, activate, regulate, command, and control.

The scale should be seen as a social and political circumscription that enables contestation. It is thus imperative to develop dynamic and multiscalar strategies—to find the appropriate scale that defines a specific field in which analyses can be conducted, alliances can be built, and strategies for solving the problems identified can be implemented.

Scales are not fixed entities; they are not mere cartographical representations or static relations of proportionality. Scales are inherently dynamic. It is necessary to assume a territorial approach that takes into consideration spatial scales in their movement of transformation.

It is worthwhile bearing in mind that all scales are historically created and politically originated and that they are legitimized by the safeguarding and sheltering of "territorialized"/localized agents which are subject to norms, rules, and parameters defined at these scalar levels. Their distinctive characters define, within a given spatial framework, structures and conjunctures that will shape and mediate the actions and decisions of politically constituted subjects. Factors pertaining to the social, political, and cultural arrangements will impart a certain level of uniformity of purposes to these frameworks. Some communion of future expectations is necessary for the delimitation and circumscription of a given scale.

Building territorialized strategies of development involves discussing decision centers and their mechanisms of legitimization; recognizing the existence of conflict, the dynamic actions of class factions, and analyzing the subjects endowed with transforming decisions; analyzing hegemonies, powers, and hierarchies; and building and ordering diverse mediations (spatial, social, political, monetary, financial, macroeconomic, microeconomic, international, geo-economic, and geopolitical).

Critical reflection on spatial scales should be at the center of this debate. The discussion of scales can trigger an important dissension in the conservative historical crossroads at which we find ourselves. It may better define the field of decision-making and the arenas in which liberating civic actions and the contestation of power can be promoted.

Finally, it is worth remembering that any attempt at elaborating on a theorization of decisions and political subjects at multiple scales requires:

Isolating and ordering the endogenous and exogenous factors which determine, condition, or accompany the social, economic, and political processes, as well as developing the pertinent theoretical, historical (and, one might also say, institutional, territorial, political, etc.) mediations.

Challenges of Reconstruction

Currently, a great challenge is identifying and qualifying the potentialities, but also the absences, omissions, and limitations, of critical historical-structural thinking in Latin America that are noteworthy for the formulation of highly complex collective research.

A central point would be to question if and how critical Latin American thought dealt with the spatial scales. There is also an urgent need to deal dynamically with the role of spatial scales (local, regional, national, world, etc.) in these structural processes. Another similar point of investigation would be to question what the peculiarities of the Latin American state and its specific forms of rescheduling would be.

The spatial scale, socially produced, must be seen as a snippet to apprehend the determinations and conditions of the social phenomena related to the territory. It is necessary to avoid the reification of a certain scale. And Latin American structuralism has reified the national scale.

What is the nature of the national scale in a peripheral "national" space, without decision-making and dependent-associated, and subordinate position in the concert of international/interstate relations and divisions?

In case of spatial scales, we can say that their analysis does not go down to the subnational level. At the regional level, the LAS do not have the interregional and the intercity connections, or a more advanced conception of scale of the urban network. They have no idea of interregionality or interurbanity (Brandão 2015b), do not contain the scale of daily life and the central elements to think about the scale of social reproduction of the "bottom" or the level of material life of Braudel. Even worse, as the greatest challenge for the rescue and dialectic overcoming of this scientific patrimony, not wasting their original and daring experiences of reflection, they do not have a substantive conception of the state and its scalar relations of state rescheduling.

It is not that LAS did not have a certain conception of spatial scales, but that it is not fully expressed. In fact, spatial scales were implicit in their creative analyses of the international division of labor, the exogenized decision centers of endogenous structural heterogeneities, and center-periphery relationships.

The emphasis was on movements (according to an interesting and promising awareness of hierarchical rigidity) of the hegemonic "main cyclical center" (first in England and then in the United States). Primacy was placed on the national scale, but this was taken as an abstract entity, without a differentiated and varied structural context.

At the same time, Latin American historical structuralism had, partly in its theoretical horizon, but especially in its propositions of development strategies, the construction of a supranational scale. That is, the political action advocated would undergo a kind of upscaling to continental space.

Subnational scales had little or no relevance. The exception was Furtado's concern with the "intra-country discontinuities" (1967) and a few "regional economists" who dealt with the intranational inequalities of some Latin American countries (Rofman 1974; De Mattos 1972; Coraggio 1979).

Latin American critical thinking treated the state and scales as static and abstract entities. A more dynamic and sophisticated approach to spatial scales has not been developed. These were taken as static and exact entities, endowed with a certain mechanism. The national level was privileged above all, but in an approach to sheltered structures and agents, as if they were only located and inserted in a framework of limited and statically restricted framing. In sum, although presenting an underlying reflection of spatial scales, they appeared basically as a fragment, circumscription, and above all fixed and confined. They were not conceived as conflicting, relational, contestable, procedural, and contingent social constructs, as the critical geographic literature reviewed here reworked them from the nineties.

Certainly, one of the limitations of Latin American historical structuralism to understand current capitalism will be to develop another notion of state, of conflicts and of multi-scalarity.

Concluding Remarks

Beyond its perception of the national scale as a receptacle, a shelter, a harmonious and passive homogeneous platform of a given geometric plane, one would have to take the various scales in which material processes and loci are inscribed, sculpted, and erected, materially and symbolically, in which social life is organized and reproduced dynamically.

In the ECLAC's interpretation was conceived a bi-scalarity (national versus worldwide), even if with some criticism. This school of thought analyzed only the nucleus versus the periphery, that is, the unidirectional forms of coupling of the latter in the central space. The dynamic and relational character of the endogenous-exogenous linkages has not been deepened.

In this way, a bold agenda of investigations needs to be structured, seeking to overcome the conception of a static scalarity, which interprets scales as closed and self-sufficient entities.

Despite the originality of its reflections on the peripheral condition, Latin American historical structuralism has not been able to adequately recover and analyze the richness of the diversity of its national trajectories (with its specific processes of accumulation, regulation, domination, alienation, and legitimation), without incurring some kind of methodological nationalism.

It could be said that they maintained a static national scalar conception, taking it as a container, receptacle of object agents (idealized), as a homogeneous platform equalized and passive, in a given geometric plane. They neglected or failed to capture the dynamics of variable geometry, the multiplicity of national and regional spaces, and their respective peculiar response capacities, given the constant penetration and reconfiguration carried out by multi-scale institutional and economic networks and agents (Fernández 2017).

In fact, its main authors have remained trapped in a certain methodological nationalism that exaggerates in horizontal relations, neglecting the potent relational vertical relations and contradictory co-evolution (center-periphery, global economic, and political networks).

Even the national spatial scale needs to be understood according to a dynamic and relational interpretation (not contained in a restrictive analytic and nationalistic basis). One must not neglect the exogenous and contextual determinations that emanate from the hegemonic imperial supranational states in a global context of insertion into the interstate systems in dispute. The theoretical tradition of merely positioning and situating Latin America within rigid center-periphery relations, "it's not enough anymore to understand the United States with its 'supranational economic territory', unlike what had happened to Great Britain" (Fiori 2014, 215).

A theoretical reconstruction that values Latin American intellectual heritage must question the role of the national scale in the context of the specifics of peripheral spaces.

Overcoming the reifying methodological nationalism to understand from its internal dynamics for globalized behaviors and the complexity of the center-periphery relations is a challenge today, especially to try to capture the scalar complexity of current capitalism from the periphery.

Certainly, Latin American structuralism did not have a concept of closed economies; however, it did not develop a scalar perspective with a more sophisticated relational approach, sometimes assuming a linear, static, and schematic view on the relations between the "main cyclical center" and its satellite economies.

The implicit character of the treatment of the scales in the LAS, where a certain methodological nationalism prevailed, should be better qualified and contextualized. It is strongly conditioned by the peculiarities of the very distinct historical moment in which a remarkable centrality of the national scale dominated (e.g., to control Polanyi's three fictional commodities) in the context of Fordist-Keynesian materialist and intellectual reproduction.

The worst time was when world capitalism underwent a deep crisis and transformation since the seventies, imposing its hierarchical and unequivocal logic, thus requiring redoubled boldness and creativity in Latin American critical thinking. The continent's response to more institutionalized spaces of reflection, such as ECLAC and most of the members of the epistemic community on development issues, was the consolidation of neo-structuralism.

The transformation of concrete reality required profound theoretical and analytical changes, that is, it demanded that Latin American structuralism assume a multi-scale perspective, especially incorporating new and old power relations.

The reality was to deepen the research on the mechanisms, instruments, devices, and logic of subalternity that were re-creating and perfecting the forms of domination in multiple dimensions and of long historical duration, which weakened its theoretical-methodological arsenal and suffered a ruinous collapse with the emergence of neo-structuralism.

Therefore, in a crucial moment after the crisis and the profound capitalist restructuring, launched since the seventies, when a new cumulative and regulatory form has taken shape and gained materiality and substance on a globalized scale, Latin American structuralism lost the vitality and the innovative talent it had over the previous two decades.

These had been decades of the heightened capacity for response undertaken at the national level, which had instruments with some sovereignty to argue development strategies and some autonomy by thinking their singularities of nature in the context of international relations.

During the four decades up to 1970, coinciding with the emergence of neo-structuralism, spatial metamorphoses took place that should have been worthy of scientific and political attention. Combined processes of decentralization and fragmentation and network connections were driven by aggressive strategies that were developed and disseminated by global policy networks, controlled by the supranational agencies monitored by the center.

This multi-scale logic of the great powers and interests had two objectives—on the one hand, to deactivate the devices and instruments of state intervention that retained and regulated the expansion and sophistication of the global economic networks, and on the other hand, to stimulate the penetration of the financial, productive, and mercantile fractions of global capital, favoring institutional mechanisms that ensure a pairing and selective and subordinate coupling to these networks (Fernández 2017).

The multi-scale redefinition strategies for powerful entities have therefore been a key element of the neoliberal restructuring that has expanded concomitantly to the progressive crises of the American hegemonic cycle.

The contrast between Latin American critical thinking needs to be built by incorporating the role of power and re-creating forms of domination through the spatial reordering of state capabilities, making the space-competition-regulation connection. There are often illicit devices that integrate the reuse of peripheral states for global capital strategies and their renewed regulatory forms that require accurate analysis.

In this context, marked by a new field of action in the contemporary scenario, the dissolution of power and its relations with space by neo-structuralism resulted in a key element in the aggravation of the weaknesses already presented by structuralism. Its limits to associate power and domination with scalar and spatial reordering devices were evident in the dissolution in this approach of the conflicting dimensions of power and domination, the role of space, state, and scales.

The theoretical and political effort must be to rethink a multi-scale cohesive and counter-strategic organization with a capacity for re-articulation sustained in the regional-local protagonism bottom up, national centrality, and macro-regional reach, resulting in a fundamental element.

The theoretical and political effort should be to rethink a cohesive and counter-strategic multi-scale organization based on a local regional dynamic built from the bottom up, but with a national centrality and a macro-regional scope.

It is necessary to seek new building of an analytical framework of the complex geopolitical and geo-economic tensions (see Chap. 5), a new strengthened statehood (as suggested in Chap. 6) and, from it, an alternative to the strategies of the global class fractions (financial, mercantile, and productive) that propagate and disseminate their power relations from the center of the system.

References

Arrighi, G. 1994. *The Long Twentieth Century: Money, Power and the Origins of Our Times*. London: Verso.

Bértola, L., and J. Ocampo. 2012. *Learning from Latin America: Debt Crises, Debt Rescues and When and Why They Work*. Institute for the Study of the Americas, School of Advances Study (University of London) y Development Bank of Latin America (CAF).

Bielschowsky, R. 1998. *Fifty Years of ECLAC Thought: A Review*. Reprint in: *ECLAC Thinking – Selected Texts (1948–1998)*. Chile Santiago: United Nations. Web Services Division, 2016, pp. 7–44.

Boyer, Robert. 1990. *The Regulation Theory: A Critical Introduction*. New York: Columbia University Press.

Boyer, Robert, and Yves Saillard. 2002. *Régulation Theory: The State of the Art*. London: Routledge.

Brandão, C. 2015a. *Capitalismo(s) y Región(es) en el singular y en el plural: desafíos para renovar el pensamiento crítico y original latino-americano e intervenir vía planificación regional*. CEPAL, Serie Seminarios y Conferencias. Santiago de Chile. Santiago, Cepal/Ilpes.

———. 2015b. Regional Dynamics of South Atlantic Brazilian Capitalism: Theoretical and Methodological Notes. Terceiro Milênio: Revista Crítica de Sociologia e Política. *Campos Goyatacazes* 4 (1, January/July): 13–30.

Braudel, F. 1979. *Civilisation matérielle: economie et capitalisme XVe–XVIIIe Siècle*. París: Armand Colin.

Brenner, N. 2001. The Limits to Scale?: Methodological Reflection on Scalar Structuration. *Progress in Human Geography* 25 (4): 591–614.

Cardoso, F.H. 1979. The Originality of the Copy: The Economic Commission for Latin America and the Idea of Development. In *Toward a New Strategy for Development: A Rothko Chapel Colloquium*, ed. D. Seers et al. New York: Pergamon Press.

Cardoso, F.H., and E. Faletto. 1979. *Dependency and Development in Latin America*. Berkeley: University of California Press.

CEPAL. 2012. *Cambio estructural para la igualdad: una visión integrada del desarrollo*. Santiago de Chile: CEPAL, agosto.

Coraggio, J.L. 1979. *Possibilities and Difficulties of Radical Spatial Analysis, Comparative Urbanization Studies*. School of Architecture and Urban Planning, University of California, Los Angeles.

Crouch, C. 2005. *Capitalist Diversity and Change: Recombinant Governance and Institutional Entrepreneurs*. Oxford: Oxford University Press.

De Mattos, C. 1972. Algunas consideraciones sobre la movilidad espacial de recursos en los paises latinoamericanos. EURE – Revista De Estudios Urbano Regionales. *Santiago Chile* 2 (6): 31–42.

ECLAC. 2016. *ECLAC Thinking – Selected Texts (1948–1998)*. Chile Santiago: United Nations. Web Services Division.

Fajnzylber, F. 1983. *La industrialización trunca de América Latina*. Buenos Aires: Centro Editor de América Latina.

Fernández, V.R. 2017. *La trilogía del erizo-zorro: redes globales, trayectorias nacionales y dinámicas regionales desde la periferia*. Buenos Aires and Santa Fe: Editorial Anthropos and Ediciones de la Universidad Nacional del Litoral.

Filgueiras, Luiz. 2013. A natureza do atual padrão de desenvolvimento brasileiro e o processo de desindustrialização. In *Novas interpretações desenvolvimentistas*, ed. Inez S.B. Castro. Rio de Janeiro: E-Papers/Centro Celso Furtado.

Fiori, José Luís. 2014. *História, estratégia e desenvolvimento: para uma geopolítica do capitalismo*. São Paulo: Boitempo.

Furtado, C. 1964. *Development and Underdevelopment*. Berkeley: University of California Press.

———. 1967. Intra-Country Discontinuities: Towards a Theory of Spatial Structures. *Social Science Information* 6: 7–14.

Gore, C. 1996. Methodological Nationalism and the Misunderstanding of East Asian Industrialization. *European Journal of Development Research* 8 (1): 77–122.

Hall, P.A., and D. Soskice. 2001. *Varieties of Capitalism: The Institutional Foundations of Comparative Advantage*. Oxford: Oxford University Press.

Harvey, D. 1982. *Limits to Capital*. Oxford: Basil Blackwell.

———. 2005. *A Brief History of Neoliberalism*. Oxford: Oxford University Press.

Lefebvre, H. 1974. *Le production d'espace*. Paris: Anthropos.

Leyva, F. 2008. *Latin American Neostructuralism. The Contradictions of Post-Neoliberal Development*. Minneapolis: University of Minnesota Press.

Marston, S.A. 2000. The Social Construction of Scale. *Progress in Human Geography* 24 (2): 219–242.

Marston, S.A., et al. 2005. Human Geography Without Scale. Transactions of the Institute of British Geographers. *New Series* 30 (3): 416–432.

Medeiros, C.A. 2010. Instituições e desenvolvimento econômico: uma nota crítica ao nacionalismo metodológico, *Economia e Sociedade, Campinas* 19, n. 3 (40): 637–645.

Palma, G. 1978. Dependency: A Formal Theory of Underdevelopment or a Methodology for Analysis of Concrete Situations of Underdevelopment? *World Development* 6: 881–924.

Peck, J. 2017. Neoliberalism. In *The Wiley-AAG International Encyclopedia of Geography*, ed. D. Richardson et al., 1–12. Oxford: Wiley-Blackwell.

Pendenza, Massimo. 2016. Intimations of Methodological Nationalism in Classical Sociology. *European Journal of Social Theory* 19 (4): 468–484.

Pinto, A. 1970a. Nature and Implications of the 'Structural Heterogeneity' of Latin America. Reprint in: *ECLAC Thinking – Selected Texts (1948–1998)*. Chile Santiago: United Nations. Web Services Division, 2016.

———. 1970b. Styles of Development in Latin America. Reprint in: *ECLAC Thinking – Selected Texts (1948–1998)*. Chile Santiago: United Nations. Web Services Division, 2016, pp. 315–340.

Prebisch, R. 1948. The Economic Development of Latin America Economic Survey of Latin America 1948 (E/CN.12/89). Reprint in: *ECLAC Thinking – Selected Texts (1948–1998)*. Chile Santiago: United Nations. Web Services Division, 2016, pp. 45–84.

———. 1963. Towards a Dynamic Development Policy for Latin America. Reprint in: *ECLAC Thinking – Selected Texts (1948–1998)*. Chile Santiago: United Nations. Web Services Division, 2016, pp. 255–276.

Rodríguez, Octávio. 2009. *O estruturalismo latino-americano*. Rio de Janeiro: Civilização Brasileira.

Rofman, A.B. 1974. *Dependencia, estructura de poder y formación regional en América Latina*. Buenos Aires: Siglo Veintiuno.

Sassen, S. 2014. *Expulsions: Brutality and Complexity in the Global Economy*. Cambridge: Harvard University Press.

Smith, N. 1984. *Uneven Development*. Oxford: Blackwell.

———. 1992. Geography, Difference and the Politics of Scale. In *Postmodernism and the Social Sciences*, ed. J. Doherty, E. Graham, and M. Malek, 57–79. New York: St. Martin's Press.

Swyngedouw, E. 1997. Neither Global nor Local. 'Glocalization' and the Politics of Scale. In *Spaces of Globalization: Reasserting the Power of the Local*, ed. K. Cox, 137–166. New York/London: Guilford Press/Longman.

———. 2004. Globalisation or 'Glocalisation'?: Networks, Territories and Re-Scaling. *Cambridge Review of International Affairs* 17 (1): 25–48.

Tavares, M.C. 1981. *Problemas de industrialización avanzada en capitalism tardíos y periféricos. Economia de América Latina, n. 6.* Mexico: CIDE.

Wallerstein, I. 1974a. *The Modern World-System: Capitalist Agriculture and the Origins of the European World-Economy in the Sixteenth Century.* Nueva York y Londres: Academic Press.

———. 1974b. *The Modern World-System.* New York: Academic Press.

———. 1979. *The Capitalist World-Economy.* Cambridge: Cambridge University Press.

CHAPTER 5

Geopolitics, Geoeconomics, and Development Strategies in the New Millennium

Carlos Aguiar de Medeiros and Numa Mazat

Introduction

During the Cold War, several peripheral countries under the United States' hegemony were encouraged to follow the path of developmentalism. In Latin America and Asia, development-oriented states promoted industrialization and improved infrastructure. The intent to establish a modern industry (heavy industry, automobiles, and chemicals) was more or less successful, according to internal as well as external factors. In this period, open access to the US market and international financing created external conditions for accelerated growth. Thus, we can characterize by "development by invitation"[1] the American strategy of not only allowing but also in several cases to deliberately promote the economic development of the allied countries in the regions of greater strategic importance for the conflict with the USSR. From the US point of view, the expansion of exports of its Allies and the reconstruction of the regional economy in Western Europe and Southeast Asia were important strategies for the growth of the world economy and for the construction of an international economic order that could isolate the Soviet bloc. Latin America was far from the

The author thanks CNPq for financial support.

C. A. de Medeiros (✉) • N. Mazat
Federal University of Rio de Janeiro, Rio de Janeiro, Brazil

V. R. Fernández, G. Brondino (eds.), *Development in Latin America*,
https://doi.org/10.1007/978-3-319-92183-9_5

warmer areas of the Cold War and received less favorable external conditions to the continuation of industrialization, since neither a Marshall plan nor a regional economy supported by aid and privileged access to US markets was made available for the region (Medeiros 2011).

Thus, according to their geopolitical importance, developing countries followed different patterns of growth. Diversification of exports was much higher in East Asia than in Latin America. Income and land distribution was much more unequal in some regions and countries (Latin America, India, Indonesia, and the Philippines) than others (East Asia). The structure of the ownership of industrial companies was also very heterogeneous in the periphery.[2] Prebisch (1949a [2000]) observed that structural change was a necessary step to reduce the external constraints and industrialization was the main lever to achieve high growth rates and low unemployment. Beyond the somewhat artificial distinction between import substitution[3] and export-oriented strategy, a common feature of all successful experiences was the central role played by developmental state (Medeiros 2013a). In this cold-war geopolitical context, the United States provided support to the countries according to their importance in this conflict but never allowed the emergence of regional autonomous powers.

The USSR's decline and collapse, which created the conditions for the Reagan-Thatcher offensive against social democracy in the "Centre", were also decisive for the end of US friendly attitude toward developmentalism in the eighties. The abandonment of developmental macroeconomics and industrial policy in the periphery was the mirror of the end of the subordination of monetary and fiscal policy to full employment in the "Centre". Nevertheless, the 1982 debt crisis affected the developing countries in much contrasted ways. Different from what happened in Latin America, East Asian countries faced no similar external crisis, preserving their developmental institutions. They also began to participate in global value chains (GVCs) in manufacture production particularly in information and communication (ICT) goods.

In Latin America, the agenda of liberalization reforms that spread all over within the region in the nineties dismantled their developmental institutions. The outcome was a higher integration to the world economy through foreign investment and international finance but with a disappointing rate of economic growth. While Mexico signed a free-trade and investment agreement with the United States and Canada (NAFTA), other countries particularly in South America followed through free trade schema and strong political alliances with the United States this same "integrationist" way even without a formal treaty (Amsden 2001).[4] Panitch and Gindin (2012) and Petras and Veltmeyer (2016) dubbed this strategy adopted by developing countries as "imperialism by invitation" stressing the association between domestic and international firms under the leadership of US State. Given its geographic location, Mexico joined the regional supply chains led by the United States and adopted a growth strategy based on industrial exports and low unit labor costs. The other Latin American countries received significant inflows of foreign direct investment (FDI) mainly in services and extractive industries pushed by mass privatization deals (Medeiros 2013a).

This reality changed in the first decade of the new century. In the two-thousands, the GDP growth was much faster in developing countries than in developed economies. Under this "decoupling" of growth tendency was the strong uprising in commodity prices and a rapid growth in domestic demand in large developing countries, which has led to a major intensification of South-South trade. The geography of world trade changed during this period, and China, boosted by its heavy industry boom, has taken a leading role in this process becoming the main trading partner for many developing countries, particularly in Africa and South America. Many natural resource-rich countries of the periphery adopted the so-called nationalism of natural resources (Medeiros 2013b), taking partial or total control over the raw material production and their ground rents. It has allowed these countries to increase their fiscal revenues and public spending and to achieve higher growth and significant poverty reduction, but without structural change.

These economic changes have given greater political prominence to developing countries, particularly China, whose economic impact on the world economy is far greater than any other nation. New Global South's geopolitical strategies and new economic regional blocks aimed for greater multilateralism (no longer centered in the United States) emerged. As Celso Furtado (1967 [2000], 331) stated, "integration policy [is] an advanced way of developmental policy".[5]

This change in the global scenario challenged the post-Cold War American strategy and its security concerns based on a pro-automatic alignment with the United States in several multilateral institutions: the International Monetary Fund (IMF), the World Bank, the World Trade

Organization (WTO), NATO and even the EU, and a considerable part of non-governmental organizations (NGOs). The regionalization advocated by the United States through agreements such as NAFTA and mega initiatives such as the Trans Pacific Partnership (TPP) or Transatlantic Trade Investment Partnership (TTIP) agreements (today they are discontinued or are in the process of restructuring; see last section) focused on free trade was part of this architecture. Their goal was the promotion of the leadership of the large corporations and the outstanding prominence of the United States. These multilateral trade agreements aimed to control China's influence on the world economic order and were fundamentally opposed to the construction of a new institutional framework led by the countries of the South.

This reality changed again. Under new external economic circumstances created by lower growth in developed countries and lower commodity prices in the last decade and under external and internal political conflict, the evolution in many countries is undoing in the last years both the characteristics of the higher growth rate of developing countries and the South geopolitical independent strategy. Brazil and Argentina, under economic and political pressures, abandoned their regional power ambition, and the South American regionalization projects have gone into crisis. South Africa seems to follow the same path. New leaderships committed to a passive, "integrationist", and strong political alliance with the United States reinforcing and regressing to the nineties' "imperialism by invitation". Although domestic political forces led this evolution, the United States strongly encouraged it. This change, nevertheless, was not homogeneous among countries. Russia, China, and India have intrinsic national interests (especially in security and defense) that enable them to preserve their national and autonomous strategy.

The liberal order promoted by US strategy along the last decades favored their big businesses particularly in innovative and financial sectors but generated high unemployment and great divide in US society. The new American nationalist strategy, promoted since the election of Donald Trump in 2016, points in the direction of a replacement, at least partial, of this US-centered multilateralism by a closed bilateral relationship in order to promote employment and old industrial sectors at the expense of the employment in the other countries. This strategy aims to contain China's exports into US market through bilateral negotiations and to increase foreign countries' concessions in exchange of access to American market.

This chapter is an attempt to examine the evolution of the economic, geo-economic and geopolitical paths followed by the countries of the South since the two-thousands and the geopolitical and geo-economic response of the United States to these more assertive strategies. The chapter also aims to articulate the study of the economic evolution with both internal and external power relations. The chapter is organized as follows. Section "The Functionalist Role of the State in Latin American Structuralism" focuses on the way structuralist analysis dealt with the question of the role of the State. Section "The Economic Rise of the South: The Decoupling of the Growth Trend Between Developed and Developing Countries in the Two-Thousands" takes a closer look at the decoupling and its economic consequences in the two-thousands. Section "The Geopolitical and Geo-Economic Rise of the South" deals with the geopolitical and geo-economic rise of the South during the same decade. Section "Continuity and Change in the Economic Performance and the Geopolitical and Geo-Economic Insertion of the Periphery in the Two-Thousand and Tens" discusses the continuity and change in the economic performance of the periphery and in its geopolitical and geo-economic insertion during the two-thousand and tens. The last section offers brief final remarks.

The Functionalist Role of the State in Latin American Structuralism

Latin American structuralism has developed powerful hypotheses on the differences between the center and the periphery, focusing essentially on productive structures and power relations. However, in the specific analysis on the dynamics of the peripheral process and of industrialization, a very functionalist view of the State has been adopted.[6]

Despite its wide perspective on economic development under a hierarchical world system, Latin American structuralism shares with Keynesian the same functionalist theory of State as a rational power filling the gaps and failures created by markets. While State intervention in macroeconomic policies in Keynesian paradigm is a necessary step to stimulate economy, and bring about a socially needed full employment, for Latin American structuralist the role of State intervention has a wider meaning consisting in an adaptation of Keynesianism to another social and economic context. In this different reality, in order to bring about full employment, the State, argued Prebisch (1949a) [2000], must engage on development policies aimed to achieve higher levels of industrialization and autonomy from international markets.

Since World War II, these progressive perspectives have disputed the market fundamentalism of liberal economists and modernization theorists but have not discussed why and in which political circumstances some states followed these rational agenda and why others, the majority, did not. These approaches do not have an analysis of State formation and of social and political constraints that explains differences in historical national trajectories. As Fiori (2011) argued,[7] these perspectives have developed a very "imprecise, homogenous and a-historical" concept of State as an actor intellectually created to solve economic problems.

Keynesian's economic policy, observed Hossein-Zadeh (2014, 33), "is largely a matter of technical expertise or economic know-how, that is, a matter of choice. Thus, the effectiveness of the Keynesian model is, therefore, based largely on hope, or illusion; since in reality the power relation between the state and the market/capitalism is usually the other way around". Full employment policies were not an option taken by progressive governments but were the outcome of class struggle and by the reality created by the 1930 crisis. After World War II, it was generalized by the growing dispute of American-led world against the USSR. The demise of Keynesianism since the eighties is an expression of the extraordinary geopolitical change that occurred in this decade.

Latin American structuralism was born in the United Nations Economic Commission for Latin America and the Caribbean (ECLAC), a branch of the United Nations, thanks to efforts led by intellectuals and Latin American governments' diplomacy. The United States agreed reluctantly to the new regional organization in an international context of institutional building led by the United States and aimed to isolate Western countries from the URSS. Probably because of this origin, and despite of its originality and clear defense of economic planning, two important consequences resulted from it: a prudent distance both from Marxist thinkers and from socialism. Thus, structuralism did not refer to Marxist analysis of imperialism and of social and international origins of Latin American countries, focusing essentially in what States should do to promote development. As Celso Furtado confirmed in an oral presentation (quoted in Bracarense 2012), "Prebisch was very careful with the terms he used … But he had succeeded in his prowess of saying what we wanted. For me underdevelopment was a matter of imperialism. But he would talk about the center and the periphery, a neutral description" (Furtado 2007, 4).

One consequence of this neutrality not only in center-periphery analysis, but at least some versions of dependency school that emerged from this perspective, was to consider the world system as a bipolar structure; the national strategies and the rivalry among States have been frequently inconsiderate. Sunkel (1970) [2000], Cardoso and Faletto (1979), and Furtado (1978) examined the huge impact created by transnational corporations and the predominance of the United States as the major headquarters of those companies on Latin American-dependent economies. Nevertheless, they did not explore the changing conditions created by State competition in the world economy center and its impacts and opportunities that were asymmetrically exploited by peripheral countries.

In most of this analysis, there is not a political economy of the economic and development policies followed by States. Underdevelopment (and underdevelopment countries) was conceptualized as a homogeneous reality in opposition to development (and developed countries), conceptualized, as well, as a homogeneous reality, underestimating the differentiated State formation, class struggle, and different geopolitical insertion (Fiori 2011). Why some States in backward economies led their economies to achieve a higher level of development and why some Developmental States in underdevelopment countries followed this same road is not explained. Modern "new developmentalism" (Bresser-Pereira 2010) shows the same shortcoming failing to explain why some countries sustained competitive real change rate of domestic currency, a policy that according to this perspective is the most important explanation factor of developmental performance observed in some countries. Nor different geopolitical insertion or social classes are present in this perspective.

The absence of geopolitics and State analysis in Latin American structuralism can be seen in Octavio Rodriguez's deep synthesis "*El Estructuralismo Latinoamericano*" (2006). In 15 chapters covering 50 years of ECLAC and Latin America structuralism authors, there are only two entries that carry State in the title and the analysis is exclusively concerned with the necessary role played by State. Although geopolitical factors are clearly assumed as a constraint factor for State autonomy, the only quotation in its support refers to Cardoso and Faletto (1979) where there is a fixed dimension of domination but not a geopolitical analysis.

We will show in this chapter how international changes influenced the relations of power and the national strategies of Latin American countries through their impacts on their balance of payments and consequently on the possibilities of growth, distribution, and the conflicts that these policies generate. In the next session, we will identify some factors that have allowed peripheral countries, particularly those in Latin America, to gain autonomy from central countries and to have a higher rate of growth, in sharp contrast with the experience observed in the nineties.

The Economic Rise of the South: The Decoupling of the Growth Trend Between Developed and Developing Countries in the Two-Thousands

As we can see in Table 5.1, in the two-thousands, the growth trend has been consistently higher in developing countries than in developed countries. The improvement of the balance of payments constraints and the adoption of expansionist economic policies in most of these economies in the two-thousands in relation to the nineties (Freitas et al. 2016) explain this "decoupling" of the economic growth of developing countries from the relatively low rates of growth of developed economies.

All the periphery has experienced high growth rates during the two-thousands, even after the global financial crisis of 2008. Large disparities appear between regions of the periphery, but all of them saw their growth rate increase during the two-thousands compared to the nineties (Table 5.2).

Both phenomena, the "decoupling" of developing countries growth trend and the increase in the relative prices of primary commodities during the two-thousands, occurred in a context characterized by elements of continuity in relation to the previous decade, such as the flexible dollar pattern (Serrano 2003) and the existence of large flows of external private capital. We would like to emphasize that it was a change not only in external economic circumstances but also in economic policies.

Table 5.1 Average growth rate of GDP (constant prices) of advanced economies and emerging markets and developing economies (1980–2016)

Region	*1980–1989*	*1990–1999*	*2000–2009*	*2009–2013*	*2013–2016*
Advanced economies (1)	3.1	2.8	2.4	0.8	1.9
Emerging markets and developing economies (2)	3.3	3.6	6.5	5.4	4.3
Difference (2) – (1)	0.2	0.8	4.1	4.6	2.4

Source: Author's elaboration based on IMF (2017)

Table 5.2 Average growth rate of GDP (constant prices) by regions of the periphery (1980–2016)

Region	*1980–1989*	*1990–1999*	*2000–2008*	*2009–2013*	*2014–2016*
Latin America and the Caribbean	2.1	2.9	3.7	3.0	0.1
Middle East and North Africa	0.6	4.2	5.7	3.7	3
Sub-Saharan Africa	NA	2.0	5.9	5.1	3.3
Emerging and developing Asia	6.8	7.2	8.2	7.8	6.6

Source: Author's elaboration based on IMF (2017)

In this context, important changes in the macroeconomic policies occurred in developing countries. To understand these changes, we need to look back at the balance of payments conditions that characterized the periphery in the nineties. In that decade there was low growth in the value of exports in dollars (both in price and *quantum*), still lower than the high interest rates related to these flows. In addition, short-term capital flows prevailed even in some of the more dynamic East Asian countries. The adoption of fixed exchange rates, trade liberalization, and other neoliberal reforms led to rapid import growth and worsened the competitiveness of peripheral exports. Following the crisis sequence in East Asia (1997), Russia (1998), and Argentina (2002), in the next decade there was a relatively rapid recovery of the US economy following the dot-com bubble crisis and in conjunction with this occurred a sharp increase in domestic demand in both China and other Asian countries.[8] This recovery explains the trend of commodity price increases observed during the two-thousands (at least until the global crisis of 2008), starting with oil and then followed by minerals and food.

In order to address the higher rates of growth of peripheral countries, we must consider some factors (Serrano 2013):

1. The low interest rates in the US and the international finance system provided large flows of private capital to developing countries;
2. High and sustained increase in commodity prices until 2012;
3. The higher growth of domestic demand in large developing countries (China and others) led to a major intensification of South-South trade;

4. Major improvement in balance of payments administration policies occurred in developing countries. This included: (a) generalization of flexible managed exchange regime replacing dollarization or fix exchange rate regimes; (b) taxation of some commodity exports; (c) early repayment of public external debt (or moratorium or default), creation of sovereign wealth funds; (d) substantial accumulation of foreign-exchange reserves, even in countries with current account deficits;
5. Many countries in the periphery (Russia, South America countries) adopted the so-called natural resource nationalism, and governments exerted partially or totally control over the exploitation of commodities. These countries could considerably increase their fiscal resources and public spending (Medeiros 2013b).
6. Many countries in the periphery (Russia, South America countries) adopted the so-called natural resource nationalism, and governments exerted partially or totally control over the exploitation of commodities. These countries could considerably increase their fiscal resources and public spending (Medeiros 2013b).

These combined factors led to more than ten years of high growth without any balance of payments crises in the periphery and a rapid economic recovery from the global crisis of 2008, at least until 2013.[9]

In these years, most of developing countries became more financially integrated (Akyüz 2012)[10] with developed countries,[11] which also occurred in the nineties, but there was a significant difference in outcomes between the two decades. Financial integration explained the temporary decoupling of growth in the first half of the nineties, but it also led to the balance of payments crises in the second half of the decade that disrupted this process. The external circumstances of the growth of the two-thousands were different in the sense that no balance of payments crisis occurred.

Many countries have incurred into current account deficits. However, these capital flows did not cause currency crises because, as we have seen, there was a radical improvement in the administration of the balance of payments in the two-thousands, especially the accumulation of high amounts of foreign-exchange reserves, compared to the previous decade. A considerable increase in South-South trade occurred.[12]

Along this period initiated in the early two-thousands, China occupies a central place, having greatly increased its share of world trade and South-South trade. South America became a major trading partner of China.

Table 5.3 Average growth rate of Chinese trade with other BRICS countries

	Brazil	*India*	*South Africa*	*Russian Federation*
China's exports to BRICS countries				
2000–2008	42.2	45.5	31.7	46.2
2009–2016	5.9	9.0	7.0	7.5
China's imports from BRICS countries				
2000–2008	48.0	44.9	33.0	21.7
2009–2016	6.9	−3.9	20.2	6

Source: Author's elaboration based on UN Comtrade (2017)

Observations: Data 1999 unavailable for South Africa

China, in particular, achieved a great trade expansion with other large developing countries, like Brazil, Russia, India, and South Africa[13] (Table 5.3). Besides, China, thanks to its position as the center of Asian value chain and to its strategy to follow a "second phase of catching-up" (Chang 2006) based on the construction of domestic technological capabilities, has an increasing number of state-owned transnational companies (TNCs). It allows China to be more and more integrated in the commanding of the GVCs and projecting its interests around the world.[14]

During the commodity cycle of the two-thousands, the composition of exports from primary export countries to China became less sophisticated and more concentrated in raw material than the composition of their exports to North countries (Klinger 2009). This specialization of developing countries in raw material exports showed a classic trade complementarity. But, despite this situation, many countries like Argentina, Brazil, and South Africa diversified their exports to other markets. When after 2010 the rate of growth of the world economy fell, Chinese exports dislocated these countries from these markets as well as their internal markets.

According to Medeiros and Cintra (2015), the Chinese rise had both a "demand effect" or macroeconomic effect, through its impact on exports, trade balance, and investment[15] and a "structural effect" or sectoral effect through its unequal impact on the sectors or activities according to the degree of complementarity and rivalry. Depending on the country's structure, natural resource endowment, size, technological stage, and domestic economic policies, the combination of both effects generates different results on economic growth. The growth of exports came both from a direct channel, through the increase of Chinese imports, and from an indirect one, when exports to other countries rose, due to the expansive effect on the capacity to import from these countries (Kaplinsky and Messmer 2008). The relative size of these channels depends on the intensity of the growth of the imports generated by the expansion of the exports and, therefore, the evolution of the balance of payments.[16]

As Medeiros and Cintra (2015) observed, the "structural effect" has several dimensions. On the one hand, there is a complementarity between Chinese demand for raw material and its industrial exports. But, on the other hand, there is also a rivalry between China and the other industrialized economies when it comes to industrial production. The growing Chinese industrial exports challenge both directly the domestics markets and indirectly the foreign markets for manufactured goods of the other countries. Following Lall et al. (2005), most of the studies on this subject assess the impact of Chinese expansion on a given economy through the effects it has on the market share of the industrial goods exported by this country. The greatest risk to other countries brought about by the rise of China could therefore be a loss of foreign and domestic markets for industrial goods and a tendency to the growth of raw material share in exports.

Following Medeiros and Cintra (2015), we notice that the situation can be more complex. Due to the "demand effect", the industrial exports of a country can grow but at a slower rate than Chinese ones, as it was the case in Latin America. Moreover, the complex implications of GVCs on the structure of the world trade require a more detailed analysis. The "structural effect" should not be measured only in terms of impact on the nature of the goods exported (categorized into technological classifications) and its market shares for world exports (Lall 2000, 6–7). The evolution of export pattern is better defined by the level of technological content used in the production process and therefore the domestic value added of exports. Thus, the increase of the share of industrial goods in exports does not necessarily reflect a technological upgrade of the productive structure. Some developing countries, like Mexico, essentially specialized in simple assembly of foreign parts (maquilas) and heavily depend on imported intermediate goods so that their industrial exports have low domestic value added.

The share of exports in GDP increased in all Latin American countries during the two-thousands, reaching different levels according to the economic features of the countries. In countries specializing in the export of raw materials, increased exports directly account for a significant part of

Table 5.4 Average growth rate of GDP (constant prices) of South American countries (1980–2016)

	1980–1989	*1990–2002*	*2002–2008*	*2009–2013*	*2013–2016*
South America	1.0	2.7	5.3	4.1	0.6
Argentina	−0.9	2.1	8.0	2.3	−0.7
Bolivia	−0.2	3.6	4.5	4.9	4.9
Brazil	3.0	2.0	4.2	3.3	−2.3
Chile	3.6	5.6	5.3	4.0	1.9
Colombia	3.4	2.8	5.2	4.2	3.1
Ecuador	2.4	2.6	4.9	4.5	0.9
Guyana	−3.1	3.8	2.2	4.6	3.4
Paraguay	3.9	2.1	4.5	5.3	3.9
Peru	0.6	3.1	6.8	5.5	3.2
Suriname	−1.8	1.4	5.6	3.9	−4.3
Uruguay	1.5	1.5	5.3	5.1	1.7
Venezuela	−0.4	1.8	7.5	1.3	−8.9

Source: Author's elaboration based on IMF (2017)

economic growth. In the case of countries with less trade openness and a larger domestic market, such as Colombia, Argentina, and Brazil, the positive impact of rising exports on the balance of payments has led to increases in domestic demand (consumption and investment) which raised the GDP growth rate (Table 5.4).

This economic situation was completely different from what happened during the nineties, when the neoliberal policies adopted in South America failed to bring about sustained growth and employment and culminated in the balance of payments crises in the region between 1998 and 2003. Taking advantage of favorable international economic circumstances, these new governments have adopted economic and social policies that break with those of the previous decade.[17] They increased social spending (education, health, pensions, social transfers). These active policies of social redistribution, including substantial increases in minimum wage, brought about important reduction in poverty, inequality and the labor share increased (Weisbrot 2015). They also abandoned most of the privatization programs and the macroeconomic austerity policies that had characterized the nineties. Thanks to the rapid improvement of their balance of payments, these countries repaid or restructured their international debts, thus moving away from oversight of multilateral financial institutions such as the IMF. Some South American governments have also practiced "nationalism of natural resources", that is, the national control of high priced natural resources (particularly oil and gas) and their rents, both to increase their tax revenues and to assert greater geopolitical and geo-economic independence (Medeiros 2013b). This was particularly the case in Venezuela, Bolivia, and Ecuador, for whom oil and gas revenues constitute the bulk of tax revenues.[18]

They also improved income distribution and reduced poverty and the weight of the informal sector. It was the "Latin American Spring" of the two-thousands (Weisbrot 2015, 167), allowing most South American countries to launch several foreign initiatives supporting a developmental regionalization, as we will discuss in Subsection "New Arrangements and Consolidation of Blocks and Initiatives in the Periphery".

The Geopolitical and Geo-Economic Rise of the South

US Geopolitical Strategy in the Post-Cold War Era

As pointed out by Mazat and Serrano (2012), the United States combined a military and civil power far above any country (Medeiros 2004; Ruttan 2006) after the end of the Cold War. The American geopolitical strategy has followed two main objectives after the end of the Cold War and the collapse of the USSR. The first one is to weaken the countries aspiring to be regional powers, especially—but not only—those with nuclear weapons (Fiori 2004). The other priority is the attempt to maintain control over the access to the world's major reserves of energy resources. The central point is not primarily the guarantee of the routes of the United States' energy supply, but rather the maintenance of the capacity to veto, if and when necessary, the supply of other important countries, whether these are allies or rivals.[19] Moreover, the United States has increased considerably its oil and gas domestic production in the recent years thanks to the "shale revolution". The United States practically does not import natural gas from Russia and/or Eurasia, which would make it difficult to understand the American interest in the region if the objective was only the energy security of the American economy. This geopolitical strategy aims to maintain the US leading position in the world system and, at the same time, goes hand in hand with the general economic interests of the industrial-military complex (Hossein-Zadeh 2007) and the financial sectors. These sectors have major influence in the decisions of the American state and explain largely the militarism and aggressiveness of its diplomacy. However, neither the state nor American capitalism is monolithic (Panitch and Gindin 2012). One can observe this in US relations with China. Economic complementarity in manufacture production tasks counterbalances the growing political rivalry aroused by the dispute for resources. Although complementarity does not eliminate this general orientation, it tends to moderate it substantially.

This general geopolitical strategy operates in both military and diplomatic terms and is tacitly present as a bias for automatic alignment with the United States in several multilateral agencies (the IMF, the WTO, the World Bank, NATO, and the EU). The ideological orientation of global media and many NGOs tends to accept the US diplomatic leadership and the defense of free trade of goods and capital, widening the American soft power. As Petras and Veltmeyer (2016) observed, this "economic imperialism" and multilateralism has evolved lately to a "raw imperialism" at least in some areas (in Asia and the Middle East) where the United States is engaged in unilateral projection of military force.[20]

In this context, as we argued below, the attempts of some countries (Russia, China and, in a smaller extent, peripheral countries like India, South Africa, Brazil and Venezuela) along the 2000s to exert a regional leadership are perceived as threats by the United States. However, the degree of reaction of the United States varied greatly from one country to another, depending on the degree of threat it poses.

US Geo-Economic Strategy in the Post-Cold War Era

Geo-economics is defined by Blackwill and Harris (2016, 19) as:

> the use of economic instruments to promote and defend national interests, and to produce beneficial geopolitical results; and the effects of other nations' economic actions on a country's geopolitical goals.

In order to promote its "economic imperialism" toward emerging countries, the American strategy since the eighties worked to create an enabling environment for the expansion of its TNCs, reducing or eliminating protectionist policies and embargoes or restrictions on investment and creating free trade agreements. Given the frustration of Doha Rounds in including services and intellectual property rights under a multilateral agreement, this strategy focused on the construction of mega regional agreements (NAFTA, TTIP, and TPP), along with several bilateral free trade and investment agreements (De Ville and Siles-Brügge 2015; Nayyar 2008).[21]

Besides the general goal toward free capital mobility, these initiatives, like the TPP agreement, aimed to contain the growing influence of China on international economy.

The regionalization advocated by the United States, through agreements such as NAFTA, TPP, or TTIP, focuses on free trade, guarantee of property rights, strengthening the large corporations of the Core (Ryner and Cafuny 2017), and US investment regimes. It is fundamentally opposed to the construction of alternative international institutional frameworks led by the countries of the South and particularly addressed against the Chinese international presence (Tellis 2014, 49). The alleged neutrality of US advocacy for these new trade frameworks hardly hides the advantage the United States could take from its implementation.[22]

Since the early nineties, the United States (and up to a certain extent, the other developed countries) not only wants to move forward free trade of goods, but also the free circulation of capital. Thanks to the growth of global (and regional) value chains organized and controlled by TNCs, activities like research and development, production, support services, distribution, marketing, finance, and after-sales services are more and more geographically separated (Millberg and Winkler 2013). In these chains, FDI and trade in intermediary goods deeply interconnect. This trade and the growing expansion of trade in services create a need to establish a regulatory framework to protect the US investment regime and US property rights (Panitch and Gindin 2012). Even under US leadership, the WTO did not fully build this regulatory architecture creating economic and political space for those treaties where the targets are the liberalization of services, investment, and the control of intellectual property rights.

In this context of growing expansion of transnational investment and trade in services, major global companies and investors created a huge demand for the generalization of the "rules of law" as the solid guarantor, to quote Panitch and Gindin (2012), of the "laws of value". Given the predominance of American corporations in global investment and the American internal market on world investment, the US government acquired a predominant influence on regulatory provisions and juridical decisions related to investment in the world economy. As argued by these authors, the US efforts have been to subordinate the "national law making" of foreign countries to the "global norm making", wherever the extraterritorial application of US law is not possible.[23] This includes not only an international standard pattern for government procurement, regulatory regimes, price controls, and subsidies, but also an international jurisprudence on arbitration in investor-government disputes and guarantees against expropriation.

This juridification of economy goes hand in hand with the juridification of politics. An internationalization of American law, through the creation of an "arbitration community" controlled by American law firms, gave the United States a new form of power. These firms assist and provide consulting services to enterprises from developing countries that want to follow the global (American) rules (Panitch and Gindin 2012). This deep involvement in business and law generated a kind of what they termed as "imperialism by invitation". In Latin America, Mexico under the NAFTA is the most notorious example. The acceptance of the foreign institutional rules by elites and government as it were of their own interests was of course very common during the nineties in countries that followed the Washington Consensus. In South America, given its natural resource richness and its geography, the acceptance of American leadership—the "peripheral realism" explicitly assumed in Argentina in the nineties or the "autonomy for integration" advocated by Brazil in the same decade (Bastos and Hiratuka 2017)—has another additional meaning. It endorsed the Monroe Doctrine, an American old geopolitical strategy based on America for the Americans (North America) (Boron 2013). As we observe in the next section, the growing presence of China in the region and the natural resource nationalism that spread in the beginning of the new century challenged this geopolitical setting.

Although the new US government elected in 2016 discontinued these mega trade agreements and political initiatives in order to achieve a higher employment at the expense of other countries, the economic interests behind them have not vanished. They correspond to the solid demand of American transnational corporations particularly in sectors where intellectual property rights are of the utmost importance.[24] Before we discuss this change, it is important to consider another use of the "rule of the law". When countries do not follow the international rules or economically and politically collide with the principle of "regional power policy" or with the "energy control policy", the use of the law can assume a more political function, as an instrument to promote a regime change.[25]

New Arrangements and Consolidation of Blocks and Initiatives in the Periphery

The economic transformations of the last decade previously considered have given greater prominence to developing countries, particularly China, whose economic international impact is far bigger than any other nation. Global South's geopolitical strategies in the new millennium seeking greater multilateralism (no longer centered on the United States) are then an extension of the process of economic expansion taken in many peripheral countries in Africa and Latin America. This process was not only built by political decisions but also depended on the very logic of the material expansive process, which makes China, for example, to set up deep alliances with strategic suppliers of its raw materials. The G20 initiative (designed over the G7) seems to materialize this growing importance of the emerging countries. Particularly the BRICS bloc was conceptualized as a new geopolitical platform that could reduce their dependence on US diplomacy and on the rule played by Washington organizations (Panitch 2015, 65).

The association of Brazil, Russia, India, and China into a political outfit known as the BRIC, which became BRICS in 2010, with the introduction of South Africa, is the result of this economic success of the periphery in the two-thousands. In the case of Russia, the initiative was a way out of its geopolitical isolation, particularly after the Georgian war in 2008 (Sakwa 2015). Russia and Brazil (that launched explicit diplomatic and economic initiatives toward South countries) seemed to have been the leaders in the creation of BRICS (De Conning et al. 2015). The BRICS summits have happened annually since 2009 and are the sign of a new South-South geo-economic force less dependent on the North-South relationship. This idea became materially strong with the decision, taken by the BRICS countries in 2014, to form a New Development Bank (NDB), making loans available to promote infrastructure and development projects and a Contingent Reserve Arrangement (CRA), providing balance of payments financial support. The NDB and the CRA are alternatives to the Bretton Woods institutions like the IMF and the World Bank.

Other South-South regional agreements were born during this period: Bolivarian Alliance for the Peoples of Our America (ALBA), UNASUR (USAN—Union of South American Nations), and the Shanghai Cooperation Organization (SCO). In a world economy historically led by Washington institutions, these initiatives and projects of developing countries are contrary to the main lines of the post-Cold War geopolitical American strategy.

Since the nineties, political and economic relations between China and Russia have become closer (Leão et al. 2011, 214). However, it was only in the two-thousands that Russia and China developed a strategic partnership.[26] Both countries want to counterweight US geopolitical ambitions in either Eastern Europe, the Caucasus, Central Asia, or the Pacific. The creation of the SCO in 2001 established an alliance between Russia and China in military terms against terrorism terms, religious fundamentalism, and separatism in the Asian region.[27] The two countries have come to support convergent positions at the UN and other international forums, such as the G20. The partnership between China and Russia also exists in the arms sector. Russia has been China's largest supplier of modern weapons in the two-thousands (Lo 2008).[28]

In South America, the ascent to power of "progressive" governments meant also a change in the geopolitical and geo-economic integration of these countries. The choice of a developmental regionalization led to the creation of institutions such as UNASUR and ALBA. The integration model chosen was an alternative to US-led free trade proposals, either through the failed Free Trade Area of the Americas or through bilateral agreements.[29] Latin American countries have launched other projects of financial and monetary cooperation like the *Banco del Sur* (Bank of the South)[30] or the Unified System for Regional Compensation (SUCRE).[31] This regionalism aimed to build institutions to support the development of each country as well as to foster regional cooperation. The need for macroeconomic coordination between South American countries was also very clear to these new political leaderships, especially after the balance of payments crisis of 1998–2003.[32]

Developmental regionalization aimed at reproducing at the regional level the national development strategies followed by Argentina and Brazil based on the expansion of their internal markets and by Bolivia, Ecuador, and Venezuela with the focus on the control of royalties and their distribution directed to the poorest and to social projects. One of the results of this regionalization was the great expansion of intra-Southern Common Market (MERCOSUR) trade, the reduction of the importance of the United States as a trading partner, and the growing importance of China. The "primarization" of South American exports during the two-thousands is an undeniable phenomenon. But external transformations and agreements in the MERCOSUR have enabled intra-regional trade in which manufactures have grown much more than in total exports. So, despite the Chinese rise, Brazil was benefited and had a growingly positive trade balance with the other MERCOSUR partners. Brazil also became the main market for Argentina's industry.

Most of South American countries will abandon part of these strategies in the two-thousands and tens. We will discuss this change in the next session.

Continuity and Change in the Economic Performance and the Geopolitical and Geo-Economic Insertion of the Periphery in the Two-Thousand and Tens

The global financial crisis of 2008 hit differently developed and peripheral countries. In this last group of countries, it apparently had a more limited extent. Nevertheless, we can observe a tendency to the recoupling of the economic growth of developing countries to the rates of growth of developed economies, particularly after 2013, when international commodities prices fell. Although developed countries have experienced an economic recovery from 2014, this is mainly due to the significant decline in the average growth rate of developing countries as a whole. However, this observation covers heterogeneous realities inside the periphery since growth performances in the aftermath of the crisis have followed very different tendencies according to the country (Table 5.2).

The average growth rate of manufacturing-producing countries in Asia fell slightly. However, other regions such as the Middle East and North Africa and Sub-Saharan Africa experienced a sharper contraction in their economic growth rates (Table 5.3). Latin America and the Caribbean, after a slight slowdown in growth during the period 2009–2013, entered a stagnation phase in 2014–2016.

The BRICS countries have showed very heterogeneous performances: India and China sustained high although lower rate of growth, whereas Brazil and Russia entered a deep economic crisis and South Africa has got closer to stagnation (Table 5.5).

This different evolution can be partially associated with the composition of exports and their impact on government budget. The fall in energy and commodity prices hit badly natural resource exporter's countries and consequently their capacity to import and to finance public investment

Table 5.5 Average growth rate of GDP (constant prices) of BRICS countries (1980–2016)

	1980–1989	*1990–1999*	*2000–2008*	*2009–2013*	*2014–2016*
Brazil	3.0	1.7	3.8	3.3	−2.3
China	9.8	10.0	10.4	9.0	7.0
India	5.5	5.7	6.8	7.5	7.3
Russia	NA	−4.9	7.0	1.1	−0.8
South Africa	2.2	1.4	4.2	1.9	1.1

Source: Author's elaboration based on IMF (2017)

and social transferences. The mineral extractive countries like Chile, Ecuador, Peru, and Venezuela faced deterioration in their balance of payments and economic shortfalls and declining political support. However, this decline in commodity prices did not undermine all the features that allowed the "decoupling" tendency explained earlier. Particularly remarkable, as previously observed, was the absence of currency crisis in developing countries in contrast to what occurred in the nineties.

With large reserves and wide access to financial markets, developing countries followed different routes. One route was to keep the strategy previously taken in a context of lower growth. Some countries in South America like Chile and Bolivia followed this route. In fact, different from Chile and Colombia that are aligned with the United States,[33] Bolivia[34] is one of the few South American countries still run by a leftist government, which preserved the social and economic model adopted after 2005. Bolivia has been the fastest growing Latin American economy during the period 2014–2016, with an average rate of 4.9%. In other South American countries, like Uruguay and Ecuador, governments of the left or center-left are still in power and continue to adopt policies like those practiced in the two-thousands, but with less favorable economic results (see Table 5.4). Venezuela also maintained the same strategy since a "Bolivarian" government is still ruling the country. However, in a context of deep political crisis, the current economic collapse in Venezuela has internal political dimensions that cannot be generalized to the rest of South America.

All the "progressive" governments that have ruled South American countries in the two-thousands faced a growing internal opposition. Even before being ruled out, most of these governments have weakened and began to change their strategy, some of them even adopting conservative fiscal policies.[35] Regime changes occurred in Paraguay (2012) with the impeachment of Fernando Lugo; in Argentina (2015), with the election of Mauricio Macri, and in Brazil (2016), with the impeachment of Dilma Roussef, and signaled a radically new direction. The main economies of South America shifted their political development strategy (internal and external economic policy) toward the right, interrupting the previous center-left political cycle and retaking the agenda of the Washington Consensus reforms (deregulation, privatization) amplified by institutional reforms as flexibilization of labor relations. Part of this change has been the opening of the energy sector in Argentina (agreements with Chevron), Brazil (allowing the participation of private and foreign companies in the pre-salt layer blocks), Ecuador (agreements with the China National Petroleum Corporation), and Venezuela (Orinoco Basin).

This change in political and growth regime had some similarities to the process of liberalization of the eighties, when the main private economic groups that benefited from the developmental state led the political opposition to this State (Medeiros 2013a).[36] Industrial and financial groups that benefited from the previous pattern of growth managed to form political coalitions to interrupt this growth regime.[37] Together with the abandonment of the development model chosen in the two-thousands, South American countries like Brazil and Argentina began to give up their regional power ambition. South American regional integration projects are nowadays in crisis.[38] "Integrationist" governments and "imperialism by invitation" replaced progressive and nationalist governments following a strategy based on free trade schemes and strong political alliances with the United States. South Africa seems to follow the same path. With the economic and political problems of some member countries, the very sustainability of the original BRICS project is threatened.

However, other countries did not follow this change. Russia, despite its economic difficulties, has an increasingly assertive geopolitical strategy, as proved by the annexation of Crimea in 2014 and the Russian participation in Syrian civil war (with the discreet backing of China). In other emerging countries such as India, the business sector, although discontent with nationalism and the growing presence of China, have not been so successful or have found vested interests in attacking developmental institutions but continue to advocate greater integration with the United States to the detriment of the countries of the South. China continues to develop new multilateral institutional arrangements where it holds the lead, such as the Asian Infrastructure Investment Bank (AIIB),[39] set up in 2016, with the goal of supporting the Chinese Belt and Road initiative (BRI).[40]

These disparities in the trajectories of developing countries show a great heterogeneity in their ability to follow persistently an independent geo-economic and geopolitical strategy, depending on the relation between the State and the big business. Countries such as Russia, China, and India have intrinsic national projects, especially on security, that resist changes in the ideological, political, and economic position of the leaders in power. However, countries like Brazil, Argentina, or South Africa do not have this characteristic. In these countries, the adherence to regional or multilateral South-South (BRICS) construction projects depends on the choices of political leadership. This diversity in the South economic strategies is explained by domestic political and economic decisions but US action took the opportunities to promote their interests.

The new American nationalist strategy, promoted since the election of Donald Trump, seems to point in the direction of a replacement of this US-centered multilateralism for a closed bilateral relationship. Trump has politically used the rejection (including in a part of the Democratic Party) of multilateral agreements,[41] and appropriates this rhetoric in favor of a higher employment. The idea is to reformulate multilateral agreements or replace those agreements with bilateral agreements so that the terms become favorable to US companies but probably in favor of American employment at expenses of employment in developing countries.[42]

In South America, with the fall or weakening of "progressive governments" in the mid-two-thousand and tens, most of the countries abandoned their assertive geopolitical and geo-economic strategies. Regional institutions like the MERCOSUR and the UNASUR have declined since the new right-wing governments of Argentina, Brazil, and Paraguay do not back these initiatives. These governments now favor free trade agreements on the model advocated by the United States, be they bilateral or with blocks already constituted (the European Union, NAFTA,…). The independent foreign policy of the two-thousands is substituted in many countries like Brazil or Argentina by an alignment with the US State Department. It is the comeback of the "peripheral realism" and the "autonomy for integration" of the nineties (Bastos and Hiratuka 2017).

It is interesting to observe that the conservative wave has submerged much of South American countries almost simultaneously. Three hypotheses can be advanced to explain this regionalization of the political cycle. The first hypothesis rests on political aspects. After the relative "attention deficit" in Latin America observed in the two-thousands, the United

States would have demonstrated growing concerns toward the region.[43] The growing influence of China in the region[44] and "progressive extractive nationalism" in ALBA countries backed by Brazil and Argentina[45] would have motivated a growing US engagement and support to opposition movements, including in some cases typically lawfare strategies.[46] Besides, the regime change that occurred in Argentina and Brazil in 2016 and the profound crisis in Venezuela have enlarged America's influence in its traditional backyard.[47] Moniz Bandeira (2016) and Weisbrot (2016) have endorsed this interpretation. They claim that this process has been relatively like what occurred in North Africa during the "Arab Spring" started in 2010. It would have been politically subtler and more efficient than the failed attempts against the Chavist and other progressive Latin American governments during the two-thousands.[48] However, this first hypothesis lacks an analysis of the internal mechanisms that led to political and electoral discontent that would have politically propitiated the right-wing victory.

A second hypothesis mixing external and internal economic aspects would be that the expansion of public and social expenditures in South America during the two-thousands depended heavily on the growth of exports of natural resources. So, when there was a fall in the price of commodities and a decrease in external demand, a phenomenon that manifests itself already in 2012, but was still stronger in 2015–2016, the previous economic cycle would have been disrupted and the economic growth declined sharply in the region. The economic crisis would then have undermined popular support for leftist governments and precipitated their end. However, this purely economic hypothesis has weak points. Not all the mineral economies, which were the most affected by the reversal of terms of trade, suffered the same economic and political impacts. Moreover, there has not been a currency and financial crisis like those that historically marked the disruption of economic and political cycles in Latin America in the eighties and nineties, because of the adoption of a better administration of the balance of payments (see Section "The Economic Rise of the South: The Decoupling of the Growth Trend Between Developed and Developing Countries in the Two-Thousands").

A third hypothesis is based on the notion of distribution conflict. In Argentina and Brazil, at least until 2014, the decline in the economic growth did not lead to a substantial fall in employment and real wages. As it has been shown by Kalecki (1943 [1990]), a situation of full employment in a capitalist economy would create the conditions of a wage explosion. Even if Argentina and Brazil were not in an actual situation of full employment in 2015, strong inflationary pressure was still present in these countries. As a result of those tensions, and even in the absence of a currency crisis, there would have been an opportunity for a new political cycle commanded by the right-wing parties and backed by the big business, opposite to the anterior one controlled by the center-left. Indeed, this new political cycle has led to the reversal of the social and economic policies adopted during the two-thousands in these countries.

Final Remarks

We explored in this chapter how it is necessary to integrate geopolitical and geo-economic dimensions to analyze the development strategies followed by the states. Our discussion began with the transformations brought about by the commodity cycle of the two-thousands and the associated economic, social, and political transformations.

The high economic growth of developing countries during the decade of the two-thousands led to a geopolitical and geo-economic rise of the South. This evolution occurred under the leadership of the United States as the main economic and military power and in a liberal international environment led by transnational corporations. In this evolution, China played a central role in this movement. If the United States (and Europe) remains the "cyclical center" (Prebisch 1949b [1993], 422) for Chinese exports, China has become a new "cyclical center" for raw material exports, especially from Latin America and Africa, with a strong increase in South-South trade. Many initiatives to promote multilateralism centered on developing countries emerged in the two-thousands, either through the establishment of cooperation institutions or South-South trade agreements. In South America, the developmental regionalization took in this decade aimed to support the national development strategies followed by Argentina and Brazil (based on the expansion of their internal markets) and by Bolivia, Ecuador, and Venezuela (with a focus on the control of raw materials royalties and their distribution targeting the poorest populations and funding social projects). This regionalization colluded in many aspects with the one promoted by the US centered economically on free trade and capital mobility and geopolitically on the prevention of new regional power. In this context, the growing presence and influence of China in natural resource (energy) rich regions like South America, the BRICS initiatives, and nationalism in the South challenged the previous status quo followed in many countries, particularly in Latin America during the nineties.

This geopolitical and geo-economic autonomy movement in the periphery seems to have entered a critical phase in the two-thousand and tens. The decline in commodity prices and the world rate of growth and the adoption of contractionary economic policies in many countries led to a sharp slowdown in economic growth. In the case of the biggest countries in South America, as Argentina and Brazil, changes in political leadership have led to abandon (at least partially) of their regional integration and South-South cooperation projects.

Notes

1. The expression "development by invitation" was invented by Wallerstein (1979) to refer specifically to the invitation to the development made by large companies to small countries. It is used here in a different sense (see Medeiros and Serrano 1999).
2. In Latin America, public companies were common, with also a strong presence of transnational firms, whereas in Asia national conglomerates were dominant.
3. The import substitution strategy followed by developing countries, mainly in Latin America, was successful, at least partially. For a study of some of the main weaknesses of the import substitution strategy, see Tavares (1964).
4. Or a passive strategy according with Lall (2000).
5. Author's translation.
6. For a discussion of different dimensions of state relations both in the structuralist tradition and in the more recent neo-structuralist perspective, see Chaps. 2 and 6.
7. For a discussion of this problem see Fiori (2011).
8. Historically no country that entered in modern industrialization had a population size similar to China and India (Kuznets 1973).
9. For the new developmentalists (Bresser-Pereira 2010; Frenkel and Rapetti 2011), these changes generated a chronic overvaluation of the currency of each country. In our view, they prevented the periodic tendency to currency crisis and devaluation that historically took place in peripheral currencies (Serrano 2013).
10. For a discussion of this topic, see Chap. 8.
11. In Latin America, the main exceptions to this phenomenon were Argentina and Venezuela.

12. The share of developing countries' merchandise exports to other economies of the "rest" rose from 42% in 1995 to 46% in 2005 and 58.5% in 2013 and the share of South-South imports increased from 37.9% in 1995 to 52.4% in 2005 and 59.6% in 2013 (UN Comtrade 2017).
13. The so called BRICS are formed by Brazil, Russia, India, China, and South Africa.
14. China alone accounts for over 30% of the developing world's share in GVCs' trade (Medeiros and Trebat 2017).
15. The "demand effect" induced by the rising exports increases if the macroeconomic policy is more expansive and if income distribution improves.
16. For a discussion of this aspect, see Chap. 7.
17. These governments range from the "Bolivarian" left (Venezuela with Hugo Chavez (1999), Bolivia with Evo Morales (2006), Ecuador with Rafael Correa (2007)) to the less radical and more liberal center-left of the other countries (Lula in Brazil (2003), Néstor Kirchner in Argentina (2003), Tabaré Vazquez in Uruguay (2005), Michelle Bachelet in Chile (2006), Fernando Lugo in Paraguay (2008), Ollanta Humala in Peru (2011)). See analysis of the "pink tide" in Chap. 1 (Introduction).
18. For a discussion of this aspect, see Petras and Veltmeyer (2016, 96).
19. If the objective of the strategy was merely to secure US supplies, it would be difficult, for example, to understand its strong military presence in the Middle East, since the United States could in principle be able to source itself fully from the Americas (Canada, Mexico, Venezuela…).
20. These transformations are currently in a process of change with Trump's administration. There is a shift from multilateral agreements to bilateral arrangements and growing nationalist pressures (see Section "Continuity and Change in the Economic Performance and the Geopolitical and Geo-Economic Insertion of the Periphery in the Two-Thousand and Tens").
21. See also Chap. 7.
22. "It is precisely because the system works to America's advantage that U.S. policy makers have all the more incentive to hold up as neutral the disciplines of trade, investment, and finance that together comprise rules-based order, vesting them with the authority of Rawlsian impartiality, blind to the national interests of any one country over any other" (Blackwill and Harris 2016, 189).
23. One remarkable example discussed by Panitch and Gindin (2012) was the extension to the NAFTA agreement of the US "regulatory takings", a US jurisprudence that protects American investors from expropriation.
24. As we argue in the next sections, the new government will reinforce theses interests in bilateral investment treaties.
25. The use of the law as power politics appears in the concept of "lawfare", a term originally developed in the context of war by Charles Dunlap, a for-

mer American general who is now the Executive Director of Duke Law School's Center on Law, Ethics and National Security. In his words, lawfare means "the strategy of using—or misusing—law as a substitute for traditional military means to achieve an operational objective".

26. Putin settled the last territorial disputes with China in 2004, on the Eastern border.
27. SCO permanent members are China, Russia, Kazakhstan, Kyrgyzstan, Tajikistan, and Uzbekistan since 2001, being joined by India and Pakistan in 2017.
28. The autonomous economic strategy followed by many peripheral countries included a more assertive geopolitical positioning. Investment in new weapons has grown and many countries in the South have modernized their armed forces. Initiatives to develop industrial-military complexes have emerged (in particular in the case of China—see Medeiros and Trebat (2014)). In the case of the BRICS countries, there were increasing growth rates of military expenditures, mainly in China, but also in India and Russia. The average growth rate of real military expenditures between 2000 and 2016 was 9.5% in the Russian Federation, 10.8% in China, and 4.6% in India (author's calculation based on SIPRI (2017)).
29. The US established bilateral free trade agreements with Chile (2004), Peru (2007), and Colombia (2011). Colombia, Peru, and Chile built a regionalism centered on free trade and the Pacific Alliance, but, unlike Mexico, they did not really change their productive and institutions after the integration. They remain close to the economic cycle of the other South American countries.
30. The Bank of South was established in 2009 by Argentina, Bolivia, Brazil, Ecuador, Paraguay, and Venezuela as an investment bank and a monetary fund, to finance development and social projects. As of 2017, it has not been funded.
31. The SUCRE is the regional currency of the ALBA, first used in 2010.
32. For example, the devaluation that occurred in the Brazilian exchange rate crisis of 1998 had a strongly negative impact on Argentina, which maintained a fixed and appreciated exchange rate up to 2002.
33. Colombia, Peru together and Chile built free trade agreements with the US and a regionalism centered on free trade, the Pacific Alliance, but unlike Mexico, they have little changed their productive structures and institutions and are close to the economic cycle of other countries of **South America** as well as relations with MERCOSUR.
34. US-Bolivia relations have been actually very tense since the election of Evo Morales in 2005 (Weisbrot 2015, 198–199).
35. In the case of Brazil, the adoption by Dilma Roussef of more conservative fiscal policies led to lower economic growth (Serrano and Summa 2015)

and created political opportunities for big business and other internal and external group of interests, discontent with the previous social and distributive evolution led by the centre-left coalition, to destabilize the PT (Worker's Party) government.

36. In Brazil, for example, the sectors that were most strongly opposed to the nationalization during the presidency of Geisel (1974–1979) are precisely the industrial groups that were promoted by heavy industrialization.
37. As Petras and Veltmeyer (2016) put, the commodity exporters perceived an opportunity to rid from their connections with nationalist states and participate in more lucrative arrangements in a low tax and low wage economy.
38. See also Chaps. 6 and 7.
39. The AIIB aims at funding the construction of infrastructure in the Asia-Pacific region.
40. Formerly known as "New Silk Road" or "One Belt, One Road" (Li 2017), the BRI has two pillars: the Silk Road Economic Belt (SREB) and the "Maritime Silk Road" (MSR).
41. "The Obama administration has pushed ahead with doubling-down and further entrenching the neoliberal policy box. This is most visible in its approach to globalization. In 2010, free trade agreements modelled after NAFTA were signed with South Korea, Colombia and Panama. The Trans-Pacific Partnership (TPP) and the Trans-Atlantic Trade and Investment Partnership (TTIP), two mega-agreements negotiated in secrecy and apparently bearing similar hallmarks to prior trade agreements, are also being pushed by the Obama administration" (Palley 2015, 24–25).
42. For example, Trump's administration wants to impose on Mexico restrictions on exports to the United States to reduce the bilateral trade deficit between the two countries. Other target is to force Mexico to replace imported components from China by others made in America, especially for Mexican exports to American market (Office of the United States Trade Representative 2017). In this way, US strategy is more than ever committed to the use of "economic tools" to achieve its goals (President of the United States 2017, 34).
43. The US supported a military coup in Honduras, institutional change in Paraguay and destabilization in Bolivia and Venezuela (Petras and Veltmeyer 2016; Moniz Bandeira 2016).
44. China has signed agreements on the purchase of ore and oil and Chinese companies have bought strategic assets in the infrastructure and energy sectors of many Latin American countries (Cui 2016).
45. "In this context of US-Latin American relations, countries in the region can be placed into three categories: (1) Chile, Peru, Colombia-Mexico—aligned with the US; (2) Venezuela—to some extent Bolivia, Ecuador,

Argentina, Brazil, even Honduras and Nicaragua—in the US's backyard as it were—pursuing a path of relative autonomy and alternative integration; (3) other countries lie somewhere in between—relatively autonomy but commercially competitive—not an ally to be counted on, yet still very much 'client states' " (Petras and Veltmeyer 2016, 97).

46. Through resources from USAID, National Endowment for Democracy, Freedom House, and other conservative organizations, the United States gave support to opposition groups in economies led by nationalist governments in Venezuela, Paraguay, Argentina, and Brazil, the leader of UNASUL, all of them great trade partners of China that became great investor as well (Moniz Bandeira 2016).
47. "The economic downturn in some of the post-neoliberal economies, namely Brazil, Argentina and Venezuela, and the rightward moving political spectrum, has opened a window of opportunity for US economic imperialism to work in tandem with the rising neoliberal political opposition" (Petras and Veltmeyer 2016, 110).
48. "In the sphere of military influence and political intervention, collaborators of the US suffered major setbacks in their attempted coups in Venezuela (2002, 2003) and Bolivia (2008), and in Ecuador with the closing of the military base in Manta; but they were successful in Honduras (2009). The US secured a military base agreement with Colombia, a major potential military ally against Venezuela, in 2009" (Petras and Veltmeyer 2016, 33).

References

Akyüz, Yylmaz. 2012. The Boom in Capital Flows to Developing Countries: Will It Go Bust Again? Ekonomi-tek, 1: 63-96.

Amsden, Alice. 2001. *The Rise of "the Rest": Challenges to the West from Late-Industrializing Economies.* Oxford: Oxford University Press.

Bastos, Pedro Paulo Zaluth, and Célio Hiratuka. 2017. A política econômica externa do governo Dilma Rousseff: comércio, cooperação e dependência. *Textos para Discussão*, Instituto de Economia, UNICAMP, n° 306.

Blackwill, Robert D., and Jennifer M. Harris. 2016. *War by Other Means? Geoeconomics and Statecraft.* Cambridge, MA: The Belknap Press of Harvard University Press.

Boron, Atilio. 2013. *América Latina en la geopolítica del imperialismo.* Buenos Aires: Ediciones Luxemburg.

Bracarense, Natália M. 2012. Development Theory and the Cold War: The influence of Politics in Latin American Structuralism. *Review of Political Economy* 24 (3): 375–398.

Bresser-Pereira, Luiz Carlos. 2010. *Globalização e Competição*. Rio de Janeiro: Campus.

Cardoso, Fernando Henrique, and Enzo Faletto. 1979. *Dependency and Development in Latin America*. Berkeley: University of California Press.

Chang, Ha-Joon. 2006. *The East Asian Development Experience, the Miracle, the Crisis and the Future*. London: Zed Books.

Cui, Shoujoun. 2016. China's New Commitments to LAC and Its Geopolitical Implications. In *China and Latin America in Transition. Policy Dynamics, Economic Commitments, and Social Impacts*, ed. Shoujoun Cui and Manuel Pérez García, 15–34. New York: Palgrave Macmillan.

De Coning, Cedric, Thomas Mandrup, and Liselotte Odgaard. 2015. *The BRICS and Coexistence: An Alternative Vision of World Order*. London: Routledge.

De Ville, Ferdi, and Gabriel Siles-Brügge. 2015. *TTIP: The Truth About the Transatlantic Trade and Investment Partnership*. Cambridge, UK: Polity.

Fiori, José Luis. 2004. O poder dos Estados Unidos: formação, expansão e limites. In *O poder americano*, Fiori (Org.). Petrópolis: Editora Vozes.

———. 2011. Estado e desenvolvimento, na América Latina. Notas para um novo 'programa de pesquisa'. (mimeo).

Freitas, Fábio, Carlos Aguiar de Medeiros, and Franklin Serrano. 2016. Regimes de política econômica e o descolamento da tendência de crescimento dos países em desenvolvimento nos anos 2000. In *Dimensões estratégicas do desenvolvimento brasileiro. Continuidade e mudança no cenário global: desafios à inserção do Brasil*, ed. CGEE, 17–46. Brasília, DF: Centro de Gestão e Estudos Estratégicos (CGEE).

Frenkel, Roberto, and Martín Rapetti. 2011. Fragilidad externa o desindustrialización: ¿Cuál es la principal amenaza para América Latina en la próxima década? Serie macroeconomía del desarrollo, CEPAL, no. 116, November.

Furtado, Celso. 1978. Criatividade e dependência na civilização industrial. Rio de Janeiro: Paz e Terra.

———. 2000. *Teoria e política do desenvolvimento econômico*. Rio de Janeiro: Paz e Terra.

———. 2007. The Oral History Interview, January 7th 2000. In *The Complete Oral History Transcripts from UN Voices, CD-ROM*. New York: United Nations Intellectual History Project.

Hossein-Zadeh, Ismael. 2007. *The Political Economy of U.S. Militarism*. New York: Palgrave Macmillan.

———. 2014. *Beyond Mainstream Explanations of the Financial Crisis*. New York: Routledge.

Kalecki, Michal. 1943 [1990]. Political Aspects of Full Employment. In *Collected Works of Michal Kalecki*, ed. Jerzy Osiatynski, vol. I, 347–356. Oxford: Clarendon Press.

Kaplinsky, Raphael, and Dirk Messmer. 2008. Introduction: The Impact of Asian Drivers on the Developing World. *World Development* 36 (2): 197–209.

Klinger, Bailey. 2009. Is South-South Trade a Testing Ground for Structural Transformation? *Policy Issues in International Trade and Commodities Study Series*, no. 40, United Nations.

Kuznets, Simon. 1973. Modern Economic Growth: Findings and Reflections. *The American Economic Review* 63 (3): 247–258.

Lall, Sanjaya. 2000. The Technological Structure and Performance of Developing Country Manufactured Exports, 1985–98. *Oxford Development Studies* 28 (3): 337–369.

Lall, Sanjaya, John Weiss, and Hiroshi Oikawa. 2005. China's Competitive Threat to Latin America: An Analysis for 1990–2002. *Oxford Development Studies* 33 (2): 163–194.

Leão, Rodrigo Pimentel Ferreira, Aline Regina Alves Martins, and William Vella Nozaki. 2011. A ascenção chinesa e a nova geopolítica e geoeconomia das relações sino-russas. In *China na nova configuração global: impactos políticos e econômicos*, ed. Luciana Acioly, Rodrigo Pimentel Ferreira Leão, and Eduardo Costa Pinto, 195–234. Brasília: Ipea.

Li, Yuan. 2017. Belt and Road: A Logic Behind the Myth. In *China's Belt and Road: A Game Changer?* ed. Alessia Amighini, 13–34. Milan: ISPI.

Lo, Bobo. 2008. *Axis of Convenience. Moscow, Beijing and the New Geopolitics*. London: Chatham House and Washington: Brookings Institution Press.

Mazat, Numa, and Franklin Serrano. 2012. A Geopolítica da Federação Russa em Relação aos Estados Unidos e à Europa. In *O Renascimento de uma potência? A Rússia no século XXI*, ed. André Gustavo de Miranda Pineli Alves, 9–50. Brasília: IPEA.

Medeiros, Carlos Aguiar de. 2004. O desenvolvimento tecnológico americano no pós-guerra como um empreendimento militar. In *O poder americano*, ed. José Luis Fiori, 225–252. Petrópolis: Editora Vozes.

———. 2011. The Political Economy of Institutional Change and Economic Development in Latin American Economies. *Journal of Economic Issues* 45 (2): 289–300.

———. 2013a. The Political Economy of the Rise and Decline of Developmental States. In *Sraffa and the Reconstruction of Economic Theory. Volume Two: Aggregate Demand, Policy Analysis and Growth*, ed. Sergio Levrero, Antonella Palumbo, and Antonella Stirati. London: Palgrave Macmillan.

———. 2013b. Recursos Naturais, Nacionalismo e Estratégias de Desenvolvimento. *Oikos* 12 (2): 146–167.

Medeiros, Carlos Aguiar de, and Maria Rita Vital Paganini Cintra. 2015. Impacto da Ascenção Chinesa sobre os Paises Latino-Americanos. *Revista de Economia Política* 35 (1): 28–42.

Medeiros, Carlos Aguiar de, and Franklin Serrano. 1999. Padrões monetários internacionais e crescimento. In *Estados e moedas no desenvolvimento das nações*, ed. José Luis Fiori, 119–151. Petrópolis: Vozes.

Medeiros, Carlos Aguiar de, and Nicholas Trebat. 2014. Military Modernization in Chinese Technical Progress and Industrial Innovation. *Review of Political Economy* 26 (2): 303–324.

———. 2017. *Finance, Trade, and Income Distribution in Global Value Chains: Implications for Developing Economies and Latin America*. Instituto de Economia, UFRJ, Discussion Paper, 002/2017: Rio de Janeiro.

Milberg, William, and Deborah Winkler. 2013. *Outsourcing Economics: Global Value Chains in Capitalist Development*. Cambridge: Cambridge University Press.

Moniz Bandeira, Luiz Alberto. 2016. *A Desordem Mundial*. Rio de Janeiro: Civilização Brasileira.

Nayyar, Deepak. 2008. *Trade and Globalization*. New Delhi: Oxford University Press.

Office of the United States Trade Representative (Executive Office of the President). 2017. *Summary of Objectives for the NAFTA Renegotiation*. Monday, July 17, 2017. Accessed https://ustr.gov/sites/default/files/files/Press/Releases/NAFTAObjectives.pdf.

Palley, Thomas. 2015. The US Economy: Explaining Stagnation and Why It Will Persist. Accessed http://www.thomaspalley.com/docs/research/Interpretations%20of%20the%20Crisis%20-%20WEBSITE.pdf.

Panitch, Leo. 2015. BRICS, the G20 and the American Empire. In *BRICS. An Anti-Capitalist Critique*, ed. Patrick Bond and Ana Garcia. London: Pluto Press.

Panitch, Leo, and Sam Gindin. 2012. *The Making of Global Capitalism. The Political Economy of American Empire*. London: Verso.

Petras, James, and Henry Veltmeyer. 2016. *Power and Resistance, US Imperialism in Latin America*. Boston, Leiden: Brill.

Prebisch, Raúl. 1949a [2000]. O Desenvolvimento Econômico da América Latina e alguns de seus principais problemas. In *Cinquenta Anos de Pensamento da Cepal*, ed. Ricardo Bielschowsky, 69–136. Rio de Janeiro: Record/CEPAL.

———. 1949b [1993]. Teoría Dinámica de la Economía (con Especial Aplicación a las Economías Latinoamericanas). In *Raúl Prebisch. Obras 1919–1948, Vol. IV*. Buenos Aires: Fundación Raúl Prebisch.

President of the United States. 2017. *National Security Strategy of the United States of America*. Accessed https://www.whitehouse.gov/wpcontent/uploads/2017/12/NSS-Final-12-18-2017-0905.pdf.

Rodriguez, Octavio. 2006. *El Estructuralismo Latinoamericano*. México, D.F: Siglo XXI/CEPAL.

Ruttan, Vernon W. 2006. *Is War Necessary for Economic Growth? Military Procurement and Technology Development*. New York: Oxford University Press.

Ryner, Magnus, and Alan Cafuny. 2017. *The European Union and Global Capitalism: Origins, Development and Crisis*. London: Palgrave.

Sakwa, Richard. 2015. *Frontline Ukraine: Crisis in the Borderlands*. London: I.B. Tauris.

Serrano, Franklin. 2003. From 'Static' Gold to the Floating Dollar. *Contributions to Political Economy* 22 (1): 87–102.

———. 2013. Continuity and Change in the International Economic Order: Towards a Sraffian Interpretation of the Change in the Trend of 'Commodity' Prices in the 2000s. In *Sraffa and the Reconstruction of Economic Theory. Volume Two: Aggregate Demand, Policy Analysis and Growth*, ed. Sergio Levrero, Antonella Palumbo, and Antonella Stirati. London: Palgrave Macmillan.

Serrano, Franklin, and Ricardo Summa. 2015. *Aggregate Demand and the Slowdown of Brazilian Economic Growth from 2011–2014*. Washington: CEPR.

Sunkel, Osvaldo. 1970 [2000]. Desenvolvimento, Subdesenvolvimento, Dependência, Marginalização e Desigualdades Espaciais: Por um enfoque totalizante. In *Cinquenta Anos de Pensamento da Cepal*, ed. Ricardo Bielschowsky, 521–566. Rio de Janeiro: Record/CEPAL.

Tavares, Maria da Conceição. 1964. *Da Substituição de Importações ao Capitalismo Financeiro. Ensaios sobre Economia Brasileira*. Zahar: Rio de Janeiro.

Tellis, Ashley J. 2014. *Balancing Without Containment: An American Strategy for Managing China*. Washington: Carnegie Endowment for International Peace.

Wallerstein, Immanuel. 1979. *The Capitalist World-Economy*. Cambridge: Cambridge University Press.

Weisbrot, Mark. 2015. *Failed. What the 'Experts' Got Wrong About the Global Economy*. Oxford: Oxford University Press.

———. 2016. *The Brazilian Coup and Washington "Rollback" in Latin America*. Washington: CEPR.

Data Bases

IMF (International Monetary Fund). 2017. *International Financial Statistics*. Available at: http://data.imf.org/?sk=5DABAFF2-C5AD-4D27-A175-12534-19C02D1&ss=1409151240976.

SIPRI. 2017. *Military Expenditure Database*. Available at: http://www.sipri.org/research/armaments/milex/milex_database.

UNCTAD. 2017. *UNCTADstat*. Available at: http://unctadstat.unctad.org/EN/.

CHAPTER 6

The State in the Capitalist Periphery: From the Structuralist Vacuum to the Neo-Structuralist Deviations and Beyond

Víctor Ramiro Fernández and Emilia Ormaechea

Introduction

One of the most important limitations of the theoretical approaches that address the state in the context of capitalist development, in both the institutional (Mann 1986) and Marxist (Poulantzas 1978) perspectives, even in those who have endeavored to address the "third world" scenario (Migdal 2001; Kholi 2004), is that, in general, they have neglected the peripheral conditions under which the state was constituted and its interventions were developed. In a center-periphery relational context, such conditions are relevant to understand the variable performance that capitalism had in recent decades, as well as the different trajectories that took place within the periphery.

Although perspectives such as the World-Systems Theory (WST) have carried out an explicit recognition of such existence and established the

V. R. Fernández (✉) • E. Ormaechea
Institute of the Humanities and Social Sciences of Litoral, National Scientific and Technical Research Council (CONICET) and National University of Litoral (UNL), Santa Fe, Argentina
e-mail: rfernand@fcjs.unl.edu.ar

V. R. Fernández, G. Brondino (eds.), *Development in Latin America*,
https://doi.org/10.1007/978-3-319-92183-9_6

bonds between central and peripheral states within its analytical framework (Chase-Dunn and Inoue 2011; Chase-Dunn and Anderson 2005), they have not specified which are the aspects that represent and differentiate them, beyond pointing out that the central spaces give place to "*strong state machinery*" different to the "*weak state machinery*" that dominate the periphery (Wallerstein 1974). Thereby, the limits derived from this tautological positioning that represents a significant part of the WST (Fernández 2017) are understood as that weak capability of identification of the complex camp of action/processes, national and transnational (Sanderson 2005), that operates in the configuration of accumulation processes and the formation of peripheral states.

For its part, Latin American structuralism developed a perspective that, as we saw in Chaps. 1 and 2, was presented as a variant in the identification of the center-periphery relationship, in relation with the WST and dependentism. Unlike those approaches, the analytical core was not the unfeasibility of development within capitalism, but the restrictions derived from the absence of an industrialization strategy capable of reversing the asymmetries in the diffusion of technical progress, whose main manifestation was the deterioration of the periphery's terms of trade. Within this framework, without demeaning the consideration of the global dynamic of capitalism, its "unit of analysis" did not retract centrality to the national spaces and its trajectories, but placed them as a platform for the analysis and a strategic space of action, from which to bolster the Import Substitution Industrialization (ISI) guided by the state.

Nevertheless, the central role that structuralism designated to the state did not count initially with a treatment on the constitutive conditions of its peripheral character (Gurrieri 1987). Beyond the progressive recognition of the power and conflict particularities that later emerged inside the "cepaline" circle, the structuralist approach did not deploy a conceptual device that acknowledged how the peripheral condition(s) of the state affect(s) its organizational configuration and forms of involvement, and, therefore, its capability to influence the structural changes expected in the accumulation level. It did not either manage to deploy tools capable of accounting the differentiated trajectories that affected the state constitution and the way these influenced the accumulation dynamics of the periphery, as well as the possibilities for the different peripheral spaces of confronting the transformation of capitalism after its structural crisis and the process of globalization.

As a way of contributing to the structuralist proposal, in this chapter we will offer an argument that endeavors to analyze those constitutive specificities of the peripheral states, particularly of those that configure the Latin American scenario in the expansive postwar process, under the consolidation cycle of the US hegemony and then throughout the new cycle of global capitalism. To this end, we will analyze the different state capabilities that result from (a) the variable geopolitical and geo-economic empowerments/obstructions promoted from the center; and (b) the interaction between those states and their civil societies, within the framework of the differentiated weight and conflictivity assumed by the actors that make up these last ones.

Operating in a comparative perspective, the argument contrasts the weakness of the structural and implicative configuration of Latin American states with other experiences situated on the inside of the enormous peripheral space, particularly with the one of East Asia (EA)[1]; evaluating how the different capabilities to construct cohesive state structures and coherent forms of implication affected the state projects in one case and another, conditioning and enabling different accumulative strategies.

As a step forward, first, we go back to the differentiation between strong and weak states, from a series of conceptual clarifications referred to how the elements of conflict are constructed in the relation of civil society-state, and the geo-economic/geopolitical links deployed from the hegemonic center and its capital agents. Second, we evaluate how under the "indispensability" of the states during the period of relative autarky of the periphery, the social conflict within peripheral civil societies together with the differentiated geopolitical and geo-economic behavior of the hegemonic center (enabling or obstructive) with such peripheral states, configured different capabilities to pursue projects that impacted, also differentially, on the way of responding to the processes of capitalist transformation in its new phase of globalization.

Third, we will analyze, in relation to these processes, how the Economic Commission for Latin America and the Caribbean (ECLAC) treated the state, first under structuralism and later under neo-structuralism; to then, finally, point certain limitations contained under those approaches in relation to the analytical device proposed here. Such limitations relate to both the weakness or disability of structuralism to identify the requirement that would have been necessary, regarding the weak peripheral states, to accomplish the process of industrialization proposed; and subsequently, to offer an alternative that allows facing, over the reconstruction of those states, the offensive dismantlement and reconfiguration of the state projects that were promoted, first, by the extended authoritarian exercises, and then fully by the Washington Consensus (WC).

Strong and Weak States in Spatial Variations Under Peripheral Capitalism: Its Effects on Development

The rigid character that comes along with the hierarchical configuration of capitalism, with little alterations in the center-periphery positions of the world-system (Arrighi and Drangel 1986), must not be understood as an unmovable system. On the contrary, capitalism has been set through diverse dynamic cycles, in which the center changes its hegemonic leading through "specific complexes of governmental and business agencies" (Arrighi and Silver 1999, 22). Through these cyclical processes, over-accumulation crises are overcome, transferring the over-accumulated capital from its financial forms to new forms of accumulation and realization, which in turn inaugurate new cycles under new spatial fixes (Harvey 1982). These spatial fixes imply the extension of these renewed forms of accumulation toward new territorial scenarios or new ways of linking to these territories, preserving the predominant hierarchical links (Fiori 2015).

Through the cyclical development of capitalism and the complex interstate system, the central and peripheral states interrelate through geopolitical—strategies of territorial control—and geo-economic—territorial strategies of accumulation, or the geostrategic use of economic power to expand the forms of accumulation[2] (Wigell 2016)—processes, working interrelatedly and varyingly (Lee et al. 2017; Arrighi 1999), with different levels of subordination among them according to the circumstances. This interaction between geopolitics and geo-economy acts equally in the periphery as a configuration factor of the characteristics that the civil society and its main actors assume. For their part, these actors act internally in their peripheral societies, playing a key role in the configuration of its own states (peripheral as well) and, through them, in the processes of accumulation that set the exit or reinforcement in the peripheral positioning.

Precisely, within the framework of temporal changes that manifest from one cyclic configuration to another, spatial variations within the periphery are produced, which form "different peripheries" (Fiori 2015) from the different constitutive forms of the peripheral states and the development of different national and macro-regional trajectories of accumulation (Fernández 2017).

In consequence, the characteristics adopted by states in terms of "strong" or "weak" state (Migdal 2011) within the periphery show their different possibilities to shape strategies that aim to enhance or hinder the development; the latter understood as the deployment of accumulative forms substantiated in the configuration (late regarding the center) of an endogenous and dynamic industrial core.

On the one hand, strong states emerged in the periphery during the twentieth century, within the framework of a relationship where they combined and replenished particularly the prevalence of the geopolitics over the center geo-economy, allowing the creation of "relative autarky"[3] under which endogenous and dynamic processes of industrialization were generated, directed by the states. These states interacted with weak civil societies that, under such global context and geopolitical shoring, did not have a conditioning capability over the state, but they were actually tied to its disciplinary and consensual action.

On the other hand, weak states emerged within the framework of global processes in which the geopolitics of the center, in connection with the periphery, stayed subordinated to the geo-economic interests of the hegemon. Even though that generated determined spaces of relative autarky, in these cases, the process did not allow the configuration of strong and managerial states, but the strengthening of civil societies based on the repositioning of actors that demonstrated, on the one hand, the *status quo* of capital and land control (oligarchies and local bourgeoisie) and, on the other hand, the organized workforce. Without geopolitical protection to any addressing from the states, these states were finally captured by such actors and became main protagonists in their conflicts. Consequently, they were limited to address the accumulative process through industrialization.

The presence of strong or weak states, being the result of that special interaction between geopolitics and geo-economy, and these with the creation of strong or weak societies, was translated throughout the twentieth century in the differentiated capability to shape cohesive state structures and articulated/coherent forms of state implication for conducting an endogenous and dynamic industrialization process. That is, the formation of strong or weak states has been a critical element to explain the differentiated path followed within the periphery.

Explanation About the Cycles, Crisis, and Temporal and Spatial Variations in the Periphery

The process of strong and weak state formation in the periphery needs to be analyzed within the framework of the British hegemony crisis and the emergence of the US hegemony, established after post-World War II (Arrighi and Silver 2003). Both hegemonic cycles were characterized by developing and preserving hierarchal center-periphery relationships, although under differentiated characteristics.

In the case of the British hegemony, such relation took place under a subordinate integration of the periphery to global markets, structured by the hegemon state, as a natural resource supplier to feed the latter's process of industrialization, under the growing and sophisticated support of the "haute finance" (Arrighi 1999). For its part, the US hegemony "was instead the 'container' of a self-centered, largely self-sufficient, continent-sized economy" (Arrighi and Silver 2003, 339) that demanded a limited construction of institutions and financial networks to control its vast territory.

The US hegemony, under this logic, arose progressively during the "revolutionary thirties" within the context of the end of the pound-gold standard, the emergence of fascism, and the consolidation of the Russian Revolution, imposing complex protectionist policies that trickled down to the rest of the economies, and the periphery in particular, causing national economies to triumph over the international monetary order (Gilpin 1987, 128).

This scenario, and the more self-centered pattern of US hegemony, coexisted with the global expansion of its capital—supported by financial assets and technological infrastructure developed from the hegemonic state (Arrighi and Silver 2003; Gilpin 1975)—and gave place to the aforementioned relative autarky of the periphery. That is, it allowed the possibility of undertaking autonomous processes of accumulation addressed by the state and structured through industrialization, without implying an alteration, on a global level, of the hierarchical structure center-periphery. Nevertheless, within the periphery, important different bases were formed, with clear divergent trajectories followed in EA and Latin America.

In different contexts, the dialectics of external (geopolitical and geoeconomic) and internal (formation of weak or strong civil societies) processes formed strong states in one case and weak ones in the other. From there, different capabilities to structure the processes of industrialization, which guided the accumulation of the periphery during the postwar period (i.e., the relative autarky period), were consolidated.

That differentiation, apart from producing exceptional displacements from the periphery to the center of the world system (Japan, Korea, and Taiwan), created a framework of divergent immunologic capabilities to face the later crisis and restructuring of capitalism by the end of the sixties. On the one hand, these capabilities allowed the consolidation of EA as the most dynamic region of the world system and configured, through China, the most challenging national unity to the unilateral hegemony of the United States. On the other hand, it maintained Latin America (and others peripheral regions) in a framework of external subordination, becoming the most unequal region of the world.

Therefore, we must analyze the construction of strong and weak states in the framework of the US hegemonic relay and the processes of relative autarky under which they were configured; to consider then how, from its results, the crisis of that hegemonic cycle and the emergence of a new restructuring scenario, dominated by globalization, reconfiguration of productive processes, and financing were faced.

Capitalist Crisis, Relay of Hegemony, and Relative Autarky in the Periphery: The Emergence of Weak and Strong States

The countries that mobilized the development of EA under the relative autarky period did it from strong states—and weak civil societies—that directed strongly the process of accumulation, configuring an endogenous and dynamic industrialization. This resulted, internally, in higher levels of inclusion and equality, and externally, in a competitive insertion. Instead, in Latin America, there were weak states—and strong civil societies, captured by the actors/conflicts of civil society, which lacked that capability to lead the accumulative dynamic. Therefore, the result was a truncated industrialization, unable to alter the structural heterogeneity and overcome the limits of an insertion based extremely on the primary sector.

Strong States in EA Under Relative Autarky

The origin of strong states, in EA, took place in a context where the US geopolitical interest predominated over its immediate geo-economic interests (i.e., interest in controlling territory over the immediate interest of accumulation), in order to create “defensive bastions” to face the communist threat.

It implied, besides the assistance of capital and raw material price subsidies, the granting of the US markets for manufactured products elaborated in EA (Stubbs 2009). The need of EA countries to reach those markets required certain quality standards. It demanded the capitalist actors to avoid any market speculation, and the workforce to reach a high level of education, sustained by the state, preserving its low costs as a condition of their competitiveness (Fernández 2017).

At the same time, this geopolitically protective task for the formation of those “defensive bastions” implied the hegemon’s support for the formation of strong states (Cumings 1984). These were “vassal” states (Castells 1992), subordinated to a transnational geopolitical dynamic (Glassman 1999), but with inner capabilities to direct the behavior of capitalist actors and labor toward ways that prioritize the productive re-investment of the surplus (Stubbs 2009).

That was possible to the extent that the actors of those civil societies were fragmented and highly conditioned, product of: A postwar scenario that had decimated the economic system and the institutional and political networks (Stubbs 2009); the limited material resources; the presence of external threats that attempt against its own existence (Doner et al. 2005); the realization of several agrarian reforms, supported by the hegemonic center itself (Kay 2002); and the workforce control (Deyo 1989; Castells 1992).

Fragmented capitalist actors and workforces authoritatively controlled constituted, therefore, a comparatively weak society, that reduced pressure and demands, allowing those states elites to configure “autonomous” and achievable objectives. Thus, and by being geopolitically endorsed, these states did not find structural resistance or ways of capture from civil society to particular interests (Stubbs 2009).

To accomplish those objectives, strong states counted with organizationally cohesive state structures (Kholi 2004; Chibber 2002), from centralized instances that acted as “pilot agencies” (Johnson 1982; Chibber 2002; Weiss 2000) related to the financial system control (Amsden 1989; Papanek 1988; Zysman 1983) and qualified bureaucracies (Evans 1995). This allowed the deployment of strategically coherent and long-term mechanisms of involvement, through which capital—including external capital—and labor could be disciplined (Kim 1999; Amsden 1989).

In consequence, it was possible to shape the accumulative strategy founded in industrialization with an endogenous and dynamic base, combining an inclusive (Gough 2001) and equalizing (Jomo 2003) pattern of production, with a dynamic/competitive insertion in international markets, through a progressive control in the strategic functions of global chains.

Weak States in Latin America Under Relative Autarky

On its part, the process of relative autarky that took place in Latin America, during the same period, implied the development/strengthening of weak states that combined a larger presence, intervention, and size, with a progressive weakness in their capability to lead the accumulation strategies.

Unlike EA, in Latin America, concomitant with the unaltered claim of regional geopolitical control—that did not tolerate questioning or economical political autonomy (Fiori 2015) and that promoted the intranational Balkanization of the region (Spykman 1942)—the US hegemony did not contemplate the propping up of strong states from an industrializing geo-economy based on an endogenous productive structure with a dynamic external insertion.

This is to say that, in Latin America, the United States did not enable the formation of strong centers that acted as platforms of geopolitical balances, as it did in Europe and Asia during the postwar period (López 2012). That would have demanded a "geo-economic granting" that would have implied opening its markets to an industrial production that neither the center demanded nor Latin American ruling classes were willing to develop.

A transformative industrialization would require to give an effective geopolitical support to the fragmentation of the Latin American dominant classes' power (oligarchies and bourgeoisie) and to modify its rentier forms of accumulation. On the contrary, the hegemon's actions did not address the weakening of local oligarchies, but maintained a reasonable harmony with them, operating increasingly over the peripheral states. First, by tolerating this process of state fragmentation configured to address from a "top-down" dynamic the contradictory claims of the "activated" actors (O'Donnell 2010) and of the oligarchies—and its mutated forms of pseudo-industrialized bourgeoisie (Peña 2014). And, second, by allowing the settling of such tensions in favor of the latter, encouraging authoritarian intervention and the deactivation of the formers (O'Donnell 1982).

In this respect, the hegemon's implication, keeper of the *status quo* from a geopolitical perspective, contributed to develop a process of social transformation within Latin American periphery. The ISI (together with the protectionist measures after the crisis of 1930) and the bigger processes of urbanization (Almandoz 2008) activated new sectors and actors (O'Donnell 2010), carriers of multiple social and political demands, that challenged the absence of wealth distribution and lack of institutional participation. All of this led to a complex civil society, multiplied in organizations, whose actors did not find the restrains such as those visualized in the Asian experience.

Far from armed conflicts and in the absence of external threats that could legitimize the reconstruction of an actor from the statewide-authoritarian control (as happened in EA), the complexity of the Latin America civil society was accompanied by a major social and political organization of the workforce, and by a growing development of the middle strata (Graciarena 1972). The multiplied requests of these actors coexisted in tension with the local oligarchies' efforts to preserve power, which were favored by the absence of agrarian reforms that restricted its conditioning power (Kay 2002), and the "new bourgeoisie" that, despite having emerged under ISI, were related to traditional oligarchies.

While, on the one hand, active actors claimed inclusion and distribution policies, on the other hand, those "survivors" demanded the non-alteration/consolidation of the *status quo*, hindering the accumulation processes and limiting the transforming tools of the industrialization process.

With all variants and specificities, the Latin American state ended up being captured and subordinated to diverse opposed actions. While preserving the dominant classes' interests—local oligarchies and foreign capitals—and attending, at the same time, the demands of subaltern actors, the states deployed diverse forms of redistribution that enlarged its structures, its regulatory-organizational forms, and its interventional actions in a disconnected manner (Cardoso and Faletto 1977). Therefore, they became weak states, captured, colonized, and conditioned in its structures by those actors and interests.

In clear contrast with EA, this forged in Latin American the inability to address the behavior of the economic actors toward a deepened industrialization able to make stronger its endogeneity and dynamism, and to overcome two of the main "structuralist restrictions to development": The primary peripheral insertion and the socio-productive heterogeneity.

In this context (as it was discussed in this book—see Chap. 2), the more active presence of external capital, represented by transnational corporations (Kerner 2003), gained legitimacy. Far from operating in a transforming way to qualify the process of industrialization, that presence, geopolitically endorsed, ended up progressively favoring an extrovert way of accumulation that intensified the external imbalances at the same time that exacerbated the inner heterogeneity of the productive system (Mariño 1981). This, finally, weakened the endogenous production capabilities (Sunkel 1970) and strengthened the power of rentier-concentrated capital benefited by/molded to market protectionism.

The fragmentary and captured configuration of the Latin American states, increasingly conditioned internally and geopolitically, resulted in not only a differential to understand the interrelated restrictions experienced under industrialization, but also to capture the divergent answer capability that those states found when the capitalist crisis and its restructuration took place toward the end of the sixties and the beginning of the seventies.

Crisis, the Weakening of US Hegemony, and the Emergence of Global Capitalism: Divergent Peripheral Integration from the Differentiation in State Projects

The crisis at the end of the sixties meant a huge challenge in the reconstruction of the dominant accumulation and regulation logics developed during the postwar. Particularly, it implied recomposing the rate of profit (Duménil and Lévy 2001) by redefining the productive forms and decompressing the conditions of capitalist reproduction configured in the center given the offensive of the workforce (Bowles and Gintis 1982) and the increasingly expensive building of the Welfare States (Offe 1984).

In that context, the technological revolution offered the capitalists the capability to prosecute a "jumping scale" (Smith 1993), with the purpose of avoiding the strict domestic regulation, deploying renewed production processes based in a multi-localized decomposition and centralized control of production and realization (Sassen 2010; Dicken et al. 2001). From the point of view of the center-periphery relation, the latter became an important space for the search of productivity at lower costs, through partial integration of relocated activities—developed in the periphery—and global networks; the centers not losing, but rather strengthening the control of the same (Dunning 1981) (see also Chaps. 2 and 3).

Such logic of decomposition—leached increasingly for the mechanism of financialization (Milberg 2008; Serfati 2008)—was accompanied with the global capital shoring in strategic sectors, resources and services, obtained from a monopolistic positioning through dispossessive mechanisms (Harvey 2003), dressed up of private sanitation logics, and the restoring of market self-regulatory mechanisms.

All this demanded a renewed regulatory device of transnational nature capable of assembling the multiple arrangements—and new locations—that global capital fractions performed in the periphery (Simmons et al. 2008). This device, formed by Global Political Networks (GPN) (Fernández and Cardozo 2012; Fernández 2017), commanded by central states—particularly, by the United States (Wade 2013)—and with international organizations operating as "hubs", was in charge of configuring programs and actions that, far from relativize the role of the peripheral states, ensure their rearrangement and subalternation inside a reproductive dynamic that turned asynchronous the idea of exclusively domestic decision processes (Simmons et al. 2008).

The modes of accumulation and regulation that under relative autarky had contributed considerably to forming the protagonism of the peripheral states—strengthening in EA and weakening in Latin America—and industrialization processes—dynamic in EA, truncated in Latin America—were challenged by the new global accumulative and regulative logics that demanded the relocation of a huge over-accumulated financial capital stock (Arrighi 1999) and the redefinition in the capital operative space-time (Harvey 1982). That, at the same time, demanded new forms and foundations of state implication in the periphery, centered on dismantling protectionist barriers, and granting liberties to the global capital to penetrate selectively the economic and institutional actors that took part in the national and regional trajectories (Arrighi and Silver 2003).

As a result of this process, a new conflictive map centered on the power of the global capital was established. The interest of global capital, sponsors of the "market self-regulatory power", collided with the compound of activated actors developed under the ISI, who required a state orientated to favoring its positions in a scenario of subordinating penetration.

Faced with this scenario, the national and macro-regional trajectories and the different characteristics of the peripheral states shaped under relative autarky were important to explain the different paths followed by EA and Latin America.

For its part, EA had the possibility to answer the penetrating logic of the global capital through the fortress of its cohesive and qualified state structures, from which it could lead a historical process of endogenous and highly dynamic accumulation, and upon which, from an associated logic—not necessarily horizontal—to the "flying geese" (Akamatsu 1962), the most dynamic macro-regional space of global capitalist accumulation was created. That is, it forged an immune macro-regional capability in front of the subordinating action of the center.

That did not impede, although, since the eighties, and then more actively since the nineties, a clear offensive of the financial global capital to be conducted, articulated by large conglomerates of leading countries of the "flying geese", that pushed for dismantling the set of regulations and the economic actors that had characterized the developmental states in EA (Kim 2007; Crotty and Lee 2005). To that process contributed, from the geopolitical point of view, the dilution of many Cold War factors that had played a permissive role of the United States to the building of those strong states (Bello 1999) and the active paper of the international funding agencies, such as the International Monetary Fund, always under the command of the US hegemony.

Nevertheless, that immunologic capability derived from the strong states and the endogenous industrial accumulation had already given the multiples effects of ejecting the leaders of the "flying geese" from the periphery, and formed an increasingly consolidated macro-regional space, whose leading role was assumed by China. After working in the construction of a strong state with growing capabilities to direct its industrial policy, and inspired by the Japanese experience (Heilmann and Shih 2013), the Asian giant has recaptured the idea of the "flying geese" as a tool of geopolitical reconstruction (Escobar 2017)—subordinated to its geo-economy—to lead a large-scale project, in a context that makes it the unique space born in the South that has real autonomy from the US imperial domain.

Latin America, instead, represented a space for the reconfiguration of the peripheral state projects in key tools to the penetration of accumulative strategies that favored new exogenous and financial accumulation forms impulsed by the global capital. Such permeability implied as well, and not secondarily, the subordination of Latin American states to the global renewed regulatory complex that the hegemon proposed.

Indeed, the new institutional complex that accompanied the process of reconstruction from the growing role of supranational organizations in the supervision and reformulation of the peripheral states, found in the weakness of the Latin American states a favorable scenario to their reconfiguration; first, since the end of the sixties and throughout the seventies, from the trail of authoritarian experiments, and then, from the end of the eighties and throughout the nineties, through the imperial power assumed by the speech and practices of the self-regulating market of the WC (Fernández 2017).

This reconfiguration meant an adaptation of their structures and actions, internally and with the social actors, to the discipline imposed by the new regulatory transnational forms, congruent with the global capital expansion (Gill 1995). These forms did no longer start from the own state to act in the domestic order over capital and labor, as happened in EA during the postwar, but from the transnational instances—controlled by central states—capitalizing the Latin American states weakness and delegitimization to adapt their organization and intervention to the expansion of the surplus of productive and financial capital.

The transnational instances counted with the legitimacy to discredit and recapture geopolitically those states, in order to subordinate them geo-economically to the new accumulation strategies that accompanied the global capital expansion. The weakness of Latin American states associated with a disarticulated implication and fragmented organization inherited from the relative autarky period, fed back, on the one hand, with the accumulative matrix that combined concentration, progressive transnationalization, and rent-seeking behavior; and, on the other hand, with a traumatic macroeconomic disruption, expressed in deficit and external imbalances (Katz 2000).

All this, together, made the Latin American states unable to adapt themselves to the new accumulative conditions demanded to the capitalist statehood. Such conditions were no longer based on the closing of internal markets, but on a "strategic activism" (Weiss 2003) associated with a Schumpeterian endowment (Jessop 2008) of tangible/hard and intangible/soft infrastructures, to strengthen the complexity and innovation of the productive structure, and to dispute the positioning in the global value chains.

The inability to confront such a challenge took place in a complex setting marked by strong conditionings of global capital—both productive and financial—that, together with central states and supranational organizations, demanded the dismantling of the institutional architecture of ISI as a condition to promote investments and finance debt in peripheral spaces.

This resulted in the conformation of dependent state projects (Kholi 2009), that subordinated their organization/implication mechanisms to the regulatory discipline and hierarchy of the GPN, and promoted accumulative strategies that ensured the attachment of domestic conditions to the dispossessing, subordinating, and impoverishing expansion of global capital reproduction logics.

Under that new role, the state was not diluted in the world of horizontal networks that displaced the hierarchies, but repositioned for their control. Therefore, there was a need of the center (in its state and capital form) to reuse/rework the hierarchies to impose discipline—accompanied by a speech linked to the micro and macro consensus—under the growing hegemony of the global-institutional architecture, where the peripheral states played a relevant role in its different devices of expansion and implementation.

The imposed discipline, showing the persistent relation of power and capitalism dominance, had a double form that contributed in transforming the peripheral states into protagonists of their own dismantlement, and in "officious promoters and implementers" of the fragmentary forms of socio-productive legitimation; that had not been orientated to be questioned, but to functionalize the subaltern forms of integration, in a way that some have called "inclusive neoliberalism" (Ruckert 2006).

The first of those disciplining forms is associated with the supranational bodies—central agents of the GPN—over the national bodies of the state. The second, complementary to the first, is based on the conformation of a strong concentration of intra-state decisions in areas of macroeconomic and financial decision-making, and the subordination of politic power to the technical knowledge associated with the international funding agencies.

Both disciplinary mechanisms, combined with micro and macro consensual forms, were intended to ensure the alignment of the different organizational and territorial instances of the state, under a process that some scholars call "rollback neoliberalism" (Peck and Tickell 2002). That meant the dismantling of the structures and implicative forms of the states (i.e., of the state projects) built under the ISI period that restricted the income of financial and productive fractions of the global capital and pointed to strengthen the local productive segments and income distribution of domestic actors that conformed the national subalternity.

Since the increasing capital inflow involved a process of inequality, exclusion, and new forms of precarious subalternity, peripheral states were forced to act bipolarly. On the one hand, as strategic actors in the compensation of these effects through the formulation of a panoply of instruments to serve sectors and actors that were excluded from the process of marketization. On the other hand, as facilitators of this subaltern integration to economic networks controlled by the global capital.

This was the scenario of the *rollout neoliberalism* (Peck and Tickell 2002), which strengthened an organizational device of intervention that reused the state, maintaining a paradoxical logic of strategic presence under a parallel reinforcement of its weaknesses. This process meant the introduction of several programs in the form of "fast policy" (Peck and Theodore 2015), that gained space fragmentarily and disjointedly within several state structures related to attend, also in a fragmentary form, the social and productive effects generated by the triumph of the idea of market self-regulation.

The reconditioning of the states meant, therefore, the continuity in other forms of their capture and reuse, now by the directing, institutional, and economically exogenous matrix—in connivance with local dominant classes—where the geopolitics and the geo-economy of the center re-articulated to grant the re-composition of its productive and increasingly financial accumulation forms.

That renewed capture meant, once more, the inability of Latin America to consolidate a state project based on an endogenous cohesion and a strategy of coherent implication, from where to direct the actors responsible of accumulation and define their forms of external insertion, like that deployed since the postwar in EA and currently finds continuity in China.

Approaches (and Analytical Omissions) of the State in Latin American Structuralism and Neo-Structuralism

Latin American structuralism has a paradoxical weakness, sustained in the fact that, although it appeals actively to the state as a promoter of development, the original treatment given to it has important analytical limitations. The analysis omitted that the (re)production of the peripheral condition does not stop in the unequal productive structure that generates an asymmetric relation with the center, but rather links, closely, with the peripheral conditions where the states are constructed and to which huge tasks are demanded.

As analyzed previously, such "peripheral" character of the Latin American state is conditioned by the presence, as we saw above, of a set of external and internal elements that help to explain the different trajectories followed by national spaces within the periphery. The absence of part of those aspects for the identification of the analyzed process limited the understanding of the historical dynamics that influenced the peripheral state formation, and of those that led to the weakness of the Latin American states to conduct an industrialization process.

Certainly, the structuralist analysis of the state was not static, and its evolution acquired new theoretical inputs, including a perspective over power and domination that approach to the systematic consideration of those aspects. Nevertheless, the path undertaken since the neo-structuralist restructuring vanished that possibility and ended up hiding new fundamental issues to qualify the structuralist thought in general, and to orientate ECLAC, in particular, both in the diagnosis and in the strategies to take under the capitalist reconstruction process.

The State Under Structuralism: Undisputed Centrality for Directing the Development Process

Initially, the structuralist proposal conceived the centrality of the state direction during the period of relative autarky, appealing to a positive and promising conception of its interventionist and ordering capabilities. The states were supposed to be configured based on neutrality, efficiency, and rationality principles (CEPAL 1953, 1955), and capable of analyzing objectively the development needs (CEPAL 1954), designing and coordinating/leading the required actions to those objectives (Prebisch 1952; Furtado 1958).

They were positioned as actors who developed vertical—but not necessarily arbitrary—actions (CEPAL 1953). The assumption of programming, regulation, and direct intervention functions were based on certain expertise and neutrality conception which allows the states to direct the behavior of private actors (Furtado 1962), without being permeated by the politic and social dynamics that, in any other way, could block the state planning (Prebisch 1952).

Nevertheless, that neutral and efficient conception of state planning soon manifested certain changes[4]; that, although they did not dismiss the deposited expectation in the state intervention (Prebisch 1960, 1963), they did recognize that the interventions deployed under ISI were not the expected ones. In this way, the socioeconomic transformations experienced during the industrialization processes gave rise to divergent interests at the political realm (Furtado 1964), conditioning and limiting the mechanism of the state action/intervention (Furtado 1965).

As a result of the insufficient dynamic of the industrial activity, the state enlarged its structures, employees, and functions, increasing the public expenditure to cover major economic and employ one part of the workforce that the industry could not absorb (Prebisch 1956, 1963). In Prebisch's perspective, those "morbid and spurious" mechanisms of state actions (Prebisch 1963, XVIII) were functional to the recreation and legitimation of the limitations manifested in the accumulation level, in a context of growing tension as a result of the impossibility of making it compatible the transformation of the productive structure with claims of income redistribution.

The Contributions of "Late" Structuralism: State, Class Conflict, and Domination

The progressive recognition that ISI could not overcome the condition of underdevelopment led to the elaboration of new contributions—within ECLAC and other surrounding academic circles—that pointed out the need of complementing the predominantly economic-technocratic analytical matrix, and incorporated sociological and political perspective on power, domination, and social conflict.

Thus, the analysis/understanding of the peripheral condition incorporated in its explanation the historical process of link/rupture of the former colonies with the metropolis, and the way in which local dominant classes established their domain in the region, preserving the links with the central economies and recreating, later, the relations of dependency to the internal national territory (Cardoso and Faletto 1969; Quijano 1968).

At the same time, this analysis reevaluated, in a larger extent, the recognition of the Latin American sociopolitical tensions because of the coexistence of traditionally dominant actors and those who emerged from the industrializing process, whose demands positioned strongly in the political scene. Thus, when reassessing the historical dimension that refers to the formation of local dominant actors, the establishment of different political alliances and the emergence/consolidation of new political actors, the state, and its modes of action were positioned as an important structural element to explain both the subordination and the developing possibilities of countries (Sunkel 1967; Cardoso and Faletto 1969; Furtado 1964).

On his part, as mentioned in Chap. 1, the "last" Prebisch was very receptive of the sociological contributions that were elaborated inside and outside ECLAC, and the referential analysis to classes (or stratum) and conflict. The synthesis of his works in the seventies (Prebisch 1971, 1976, 1978, 1980) recovers the contributions elaborated previously based on the "dynamic insufficiency" concept (Prebisch 1963) to explain the difficulties that the

Latin American economies still got through the impossibility of altering the productive structure, and under a growing conflictive scenario because of the surplus redistribution. The accumulation-redistribution disputes and the impossibility of solving them through the industrializing process made the state develop diverse mechanisms of intervention that, ultimately, also generated a drain over the surplus. That is, when acting relieving the consequences of the dynamic insufficiency and when increasing constantly its functions and structures, the state could not solve the tensions of the accumulation process but, instead, legitimated and aggravated them. Finally, when the surplus pressure was unbearable, the state intervened deactivating the organized working class, mainly through repression.

In any case, although these contributions could not offer a theory regarding the Latin American state, they can be seen as a progressive recognition of the conflictive logics operating in the peripheral capitalism, that act permeating and conditioning those states, and that should be taken into account to explain the specificities of regional underdevelopment.

At the same time, those analysis recognized the growing presence of the transnational capital in the region—especially, through transnational companies from the United States—and how through the emergent process of the capitalism reconfiguration in a global scale, new dependence and subordination relationships for Latin America regarding the central/hegemonic states were outlined (Sunkel 1971; Cardoso and Faletto 1969).

Evolution and Persistence of Limitations in the Structuralist Treatment of the State

The structuralist approach experienced a clear evolution, from conceiving a supposed state full of capabilities to lead the industrialization process, to a position that recognizes its limitations to develop such a task. In this change, the contributions of the "late" structuralism regarding a progressive and explicit recognition of power, interests and conflicts, and the evaluation of the state within that framework, played a central role.

However, the structural limitations persisted. The recognition of the state situated in a dominance relation and in a conflictive scenery did not have a parallel attention over the way how, under a peripheral dynamic, the state's devices and its activities were developed (Gurrieri 1987). That is, although a progressive recognition of internal conflicts between traditional and activated actors in the region was made, the consideration on how such processes coagulated in certain state structures/devices and the bond with the different forms of implication assumed by the state was deficient. Specifically, the contributions, still in evolution, found limitations to answer what limits did the resultant state find to work in the accumulation process through the industrialization.

It is within these problematic boundaries that the argument and categories employed in this chapter take place. As analyzed, within the framework of that geopolitical subordination to geo-economy, and in a clearly differential context regarding EA, the Latin American industrialization process developed together with the constitution of a "weak state", product of its capture by the main actors of a densified and conflictive civil society. More precisely, the increasingly organized interests of actors activated by the ISI and their redistributive demands over a surplus with enlargement difficulties collided with the rentier nature of oligarchies and the new bourgeoisie that attempted to preserve their power.

The tensions and demands of that set of actors moved progressively to the state and made it a receptive agent of constant demands, potentiating the malformation of its structures from a multiplied and uncoordinated enlargement of its regulatory/interventive action (Guimarães 1997). As a result, organizational and operational states that lacked cohesion and articulation capabilities emerged, incapable of imposing on central actors a behavior linked to deepening the industrialization process with the purpose of overcoming critical phases and exploring the insertion of external markets (Hirschman 1968).

The trajectory of the Latin American state under ISI can be expressed, then, as an essential actor, but structural and implicatively weak from its organizational and operational configuration. This forged, as aforementioned, its inability to: (1) Alter the industrialization processes' obstacles, for not having the ability to discipline and conditionate strategically the internal and external capital; (2) solving the intranational tensions between the capital that hegemonized the power block, and the distributive activation of subaltern sectors; (3) lead in a conditioned way the growing income of foreign capital—under transnational corporations—that arrived as ISI approached an exhaustion phase; and (4) face the new scenario of global restructuring that will follow the capitalist crisis.

Neo-Structuralism: Displace of State-Centrality and Dilution of Power/Conflict

As we have mentioned, the transformations that followed the crisis of the end of the sixties were accompanied by a new conflictive dynamic, controlled jointly by the capital global fractions, the central states, and supranational organizations; with the purpose of expanding the operational base of the accumulation process through the penetration of the economic networks and global policies (Fernández 2017; Sassen 2010). This included the subordination of economic and institutional peripheral actors to such networks, installing a hegemonic perspective (Cox 1996) that presents itself as beneficial to everyone but in reality hides the recreation of the peripheral condition.

In this scenario, the financial capital will take the lead in the Latin American periphery through loans and financing mechanisms that resulted in a huge process of indebtedness (Thorp 1998), increasing the state vulnerability. Precisely, such vulnerability made the state a fundamental tool of destructuration of subaltern actors grown under ISI, from the wave of the authoritarian processes, geopolitically supported by the hegemon.

The return to democracy, encouraged by the economic and socially regressive results of the authoritarian project, was contextual to the new reality of Latin American states dominated by indebtedness and the incapability of managing macroeconomic imbalances. This facilitated the insertion of a new global regulatory project, expressed in the WC, through which the global capital—productive and financial—assured its positions from an unprecedented machine of "accumulation by dispossession" (Harvey 2003), combining several mechanisms of deregulation and privatization.

It was within this framework, under the deployment of the neoliberal project at the end of the eighties, that the neo-structuralist proposition was developed, presenting itself as a renovation/update of structuralism and, at the same time, as an alternative to the dominant neoclassical vision of the WC. Among other things, this revision implied a new form of understanding the role of the state in development, related to the "new challenges" associated with a sophisticated extern insertion, based on the industrialization oriented to knowledge and innovation (Bielschowsky 2009).

The state was integrated to a perspective for attaining systemic competitiveness (Esser et al. 1996; CEPAL 1996) that, while it observes critically the possibility of solving the processes through the markets, it relativizes/redefines the part of the hierarchies that dominated the postwar "frivolous protectionism" (Fajnzylber 1990). The speech claimed the centrally of networks for competitiveness through the collective development of learning and innovation (see Chap. 2). Thus, the state was incorporated as a stimulator/promoter of public-private cooperation, over which such networks should be constructed and the learning processes developed (Fajnzylber 1990; Sunkel and Zuleta 1990).

This "systemic-cooperative" spirit, with states that stimulate organizational assemblies and where the market and the state complement, will be frequent in the central documents of ECLAC. In the proposals of "productive transformation with equity" (CEPAL 1996) and "structural change" (CEPAL 2012), the state intervention is presented in terms of "concerted strategy" (CEPAL 1996) and/or "pacts" generating (CEPAL 2014); in which the state, through a minimum platform of agreements, will achieve the integration of sectors, agents and practice/actions.

Increasingly influenced by the proposals of evolutionism and institutionalism, the state under the neo-structuralist perspective was circumscribed to operate as an active collaborator in the gestation of this public-private cooperation, as well as a promoter of the development of learning aimed at overcoming the technological gap. In such context, the role of recreated forms of power and domination, that renew the peripheral condition in the new cycle of global capitalism, and the consideration of the role of the state in its formation or reversion, were completely eradicated.

By downplaying the role of power and domination—as well as excluding these categories in their historical analysis-, the neo-structuralist approach ends up deepening structuralist's limitations to evaluate the peripheral state configuration and the exogenous and endogenous factors that made the Latin American states weak. That configuration and those factors are key to observe that the limits of the ISI (with all its market-intern pathologies and protection over-intervention) are not attributable to the state's hierarchical dominance, but to the shape that such hierarchy took within the state, which was dependent on domestic social conflict and the dialectics between geopolitics and geo-economics.

The recognition of those aspects was of vital importance to understand the—differential—positioning that resulted from the constitution and implication of the states, not only during the relative autarky period but also after the crisis of the end of the sixties. In this scenario, the trajectory of the strong states (as the ones in EA) was essential to analyze the persistence of state hierarchical actions able to offer new forms of center-periphery articulation facing those transformations. That is, alternatives to the subordinate and peripheral role imposed by the global economic and political networks, based on new contradictory logics, by deepening the development and the controlling position of its own economic and political networks in an increasingly multipolar scenario.

In this sense, still recognizing the successful trajectory of the Asian experiences (Fajnzylber 1990; CEPAL 2012), the promoters of neo-structuralism relativize the disciplinary and hierarchical role of the strong states. The continuity of the accumulation process by "the high ways of global chains" that showed EA after the crisis, was marked for the lasting capability not just of breeding and qualifying the public-private coordination, but the durability of those capabilities and directing practice over productive and financial actors, producing networks and positioning dominantly over them.

That hierarchical and disciplinary role of the state (deployed first in Japan and Korea under the relative autarky period and currently growing strength in China) (Fernández 2017), led to the formation of regionally integrated accumulation and state implication nucleus, which combine an increase in the substitution of domestic products (Koopman et al. 2012) with a successful performance in the integrated control of global value chains (Abe 2016). This acted as a brake to the neoliberal offensive led by the productive and financial capital of the hegemonic center, and deployed once the geo-economic protection and geopolitical interest was no longer required at the end of the Cold War (see Chap. 5).

Neo-structuralism's restriction to assimilate this aspect was extended to its limitations to understand the contrasting path of EA and Latin American. Unlike EA, in Latin America the practice of the hierarchies was persecuted within the framework of a balkanized capture of the states (Fiori 1992) by a part of a strengthen and conflictive civil society, where associated oligarchies and bourgeoisie survived, and where the geopolitics was hostile to the construction of autonomous instances (Fiori 2001) (see Chap. 5).

As it was pointed out, the accumulative weakness inherited from the relative autarky period, sustained in the fragility to deepen industrialization—and the growing macroeconomic decoupling—emerged as the result of weak states incapable to alter/direct the behavior of the actors that ended up leading such process—represented by transnational capital, oligarchies, and new local bourgeois-. That shaped a new conditional base to the successful development of any public-private corporation logic orientated to give "net-answers" in order to qualify the productive system and enter competitively in a new global scenario from more equitable and inclusive forms.

The neo-structuralist limitations to read adequately that link between the inheritance of the state and accumulative weakness, and the capability of penetration of actors that dominate the new conflicting scenario, placed over the economic net and global policy, prevented (and prevent) an adequate diagnosis of the form under which the state—however the speech associated with its reduction spread by international funding agencies and its GPN—was strategically reused inside the regulatory restructure of WC.

The desire of alternate a neoclassic perspective, introducing "actors, interests and learning articulated intervention", impeded neo-structuralism to consider the actual involvement of peripheral states in networks that are not horizontal. Instead, these networks incorporated them as disciplinary agents under a power structure and new—and not that new—domination relationships; and, at the same time, coupled them as disciplinary and consensual instruments of international and multi-scale order. That is to say, the state dilution, inside a cooperative subject to win-win games, impedes the analysis of the translation of its structures and implication forms into a fundamental piece of a new regulatory global map, deployed from the center, to adequate the peripheral state to the creation of conditions that the insertion of global capital demands (Fernández and Cardozo 2012). Furthermore, that "cooperative logic" ended up being captured and functionalized by the financial networks and policies that, within the recreated forms of commodification, formed the "inclusive neoliberalism" (Ruckert 2006) and the neoliberal *roll-out*, and, finally, reaffirmed the subaltern inclusion to those devices.

Concluding Remarks

A central purpose of this chapter was to contribute to the deficit of the academic production, both in the center and in the periphery, concerning the conditions and specificities over which the peripheral states are built. That is, those conditions that intervene in their variable constitution and forms of implication. In this regard, we tried to enrich the Latin American structuralism, marking at the same time the limits and derivations that accompany the treatment given to the state by neo-structuralism.

To do this, we analyzed, from a comparative perspective, the temporal variations that capitalism experienced from the crisis and redefinition of its systemic cycles throughout the twentieth century; the spatial variations that took place in the inner periphery; and the differential conformation of weak and strong states that influenced considerably in the divergent capability to act over the accumulation process by the deployment of industrialization. From these processes, we also analyzed the divergent capabilities of strong and weak states to face the new subordination forms that the global and neoliberal restructuring of emergent capitalism imposed.

The argument aims to recognize the need to observe the historical dynamics, with their continuities and differentiation, under which the peripheral states are constructed and developed; and, from it, the role of power and domination forms that emerge, interrelated, from a combination of extern (geopolitical and geo-economic) and internal (different strength/conflict and weakness/malleability) processes.

We highlighted that such processes form different state structures and implicative forms that not only give specificity to the state configuration but also form different capabilities, enabling or disabling the conduction of an accumulation process based on an industrial development, internally inclusive and distributive, and externally inserted in activities that would close the technological gap. The creation of that development pattern in determined national trajectories, as happened in EA, has been nuclear to visualize the creation of macro-regional spaces with growing integration that strengthen the accumulative capabilities sustained in the industrialization.

When focusing in the Latin American experience, in contrast with the Asian one, we highlighted the way in which internal and external factors have worked interactively in the fragmentation and capture of the states, whose growing protagonism was accompanied by the weakening of its leadership capability over the main actors that structured the accumulation process, disabling the creation of a macro-regional space as mentioned before.[5]

That fragmentation and the state's capture was a result of a double and interrelated process. First, under the relative autarky, the distributive demands of an increasingly densified and a conflictive civil society collided with the "industrializing opacity" of the local ruling classes and transnational actors, who preserved the control of concentrated capital. Such collision of actors, classes, and interests was transferred to the state, promoting its corporative and fragmentary capture, and, hence, dissolving its capability for strategic and coherent intervention.

Second, under the hegemonic center exhaustion and the restructuring of global capitalism, the disciplinary and fragmentary capture of peripheral statehood was functional to the GPN action that gained power under the

WC. In this way, they sought to functionalize the peripheral statehood to the global economic networks requirements, addressed by productive and financial fractions of the global capital.

Both macro-processes reinforced the historical lack of cohesion and the disarticulation of the Latin American state structures and their implicative forms, consolidating their operational weakness and, thus, preventing the states to face the recreation of the subaltern forms that the center imposed on the periphery.

As we have seen, the analytical limitations of structuralism were aggravated in neo-structuralism. By considering the state as a promoter of public-private cooperative networks, neo-structuralism dissolved from its analysis the rôle of power and domination, and the importance of considering the organizational structure of the state.

These restrictions have a significant impact on both the analytical and the propositional fields. One the one hand, regarding the first aspect, the neo-structuralist approach does not have elements to analyze how these weaknesses reappeared under the new neoliberal forms of state involvement that characterized most of the recent Latin American neo-developmentalist experiences. On the other hand, regarding the propositional field, it is not a matter of ignoring the relevance of recognizing the new reproductive scenario under which center-periphery relations take place and the role of the state in stimulating cooperative logics, and the development of systemic processes of learning that help to introduce innovation and complexity to the productive system. However, the argument developed throughout this chapter reaffirms the priority of building a strong and directive statehood, capable of operating in external inhospitable environments (inexistence of geopolitical support and promotion of docile statehood to the global regulatory logics) and internal resistances (corporative power historically built, who fragmentarily captures the state).

To achieve this, it is necessary to assume the great challenge of building a socially and economically sustainable project for the wide range of subaltern actors of the periphery. Such a project demands the construction of a cohesive and well-articulated statehood,[6] endowed with financial and conceptual autonomy to confront, in an inhospitable environment, the logic imposed by the matrix of actors that represent the powerful interests of transnational and concentrated local capital. These actors will always be willing to face the attempts of breaking the *status quo* that reinforces the peripheral condition and reuses the peripheral state for that purpose.

Notes

1. Naturally, the civil societies and the states of the periphery, both within Latin American and EA, have their own specificities. Notwithstanding the recognition of the existence of particular trajectories and characteristics that are specific to each country, the argument developed through this chapter operates on a plane of generality that admits the consideration of certain characteristics common to Latin America and to EA to study the economic and political processes that took place within each of the regions, first during the postwar period, and subsequently under the advent of global capitalism.
2. To see more about the concept of "geo-economics", see Chap. 5.
3. "Relative autarky" is understood as the achieved space of self-determination/autonomy that emerges in the periphery, in spatial forms and temporary variably, that allows the development of strategies of endogenous accumulation, driven by/from the state, within the conditioning framework of the hierarchic and uneven structure that the center/semi-periphery/periphery system place under the latter.
4. In relation to the "disenchantment" of Furtado and Prebisch regarding the state planning it can be consulted, respectively, the works of Almeida and Elesbão (2011) and Ormaechea and Fernández (2017).
5. About the current limitations that face the Latin American state to direct an industrialization policy, as well as the current restrictions to promote an autonomous industrialization, see Chap. 7.
6. The direction of a development strategy is a complex process that also includes the analysis of the multi-scale dimension of the state. In this regard, see Chap. 4.

References

Abe, Shigeyuki. 2016. *Global Value Chains in East Asia*. MCTI Conference, East-West Center.

Akamatsu, Kaname. 1962. A Historical Pattern of Economic Growth in Developing Countries. *Journal of Developing Economies* 1 (1): 3–25.

Almandoz, Arturo. 2008. Despegues Sin Madurez. Urbanización, Industrialización Y Desarrollo En La Latinoamérica Del Siglo XX. *EURE* XXXIV (102): 61–76.

Almeida, de, and José Elesbão. 2011. Encantos E Desencantos de Celso Furtado Com a Racionalidade Do Planejamento Estatal. *Cadernos Do Desenvolvimento* 6 (8): 717–737.

Amsden, Alice. 1989. *Asia's Next Giant: South Korea and Late Industrialization*. New York; Oxford: Oxford University Press.

Arrighi, Giovanni. 1999. *El Largo Siglo XX*. Madrid: AKAL.

Arrighi, Giovanni, and Jessica Drangel. 1986. The Stratification of the World Economy: An Exploration of the Semiperipheral Zone. *Review* 10 (1): 9–74.

Arrighi, Giovanni, and Beverly Silver. 1999. *Chaos and Governance in the Modern World System*. Minneapolis: University of Minnesota Press.

———. 2003. Polanyi's 'Double Movement': The Belle Époques of British and U.S. Hegemony Compared. *Politics & Society* 31 (2): 325–355.

Bello, Walden. 1999. *Dark Victory: The United States and Global Poverty*. London: Pluto Press.

Bielschowsky, Ricardo. 2009. Sesenta Años de La CEPAL: Estructuralismo Y Neoestructuralismo. *Revista de La CEPAL* (97): 173–194.

Bowles, Samuel, and Herbert Gintis. 1982. The Crisis of Liberal Democratic Capitalism. *Politics and Society* 11 (1): 51–93.

Cardoso, Fernando Henrique, and Enzo Faletto. 1969. *Dependencia Y Desarrollo En América Latina. Ensayo de Interpretación Sociológica*. Buenos Aires: Siglo XXI.

———. 1977. Post Scriptum a 'Dependencia Y Desarrollo En América Latina'. *Desarrollo Económico* 17 (66): 273–299.

Castells, Manuel. 1992. Four Asian Tigers with a Dragon Head: A Comparative Analysis of the State, Economy, and Society in the Asian Pacific Rim. In *States and Development in the Asian Pacific Rim*, ed. Richard P. Appelbaum and J.W. Henderson. Newbury Park, CA: Sage Publications.

CEPAL. 1953. *Estudio Preliminar Sobre La Técnica de Programación Del Desarrollo Económico*. Río de Janeiro: Naciones Unidas.

———. 1954. *La Cooperación Internacional En La Política de Desarrollo Latinoamericano*. Nueva York: Naciones Unidas.

———. 1955. *Análisis Y Proyecciones Del Desarrollo Económico*. México: Naciones Unidas.

———. 1996. *Transformacion Productiva Con Equidad. La Tarea Prioritaria Del Desarrollo de América Latina Y El Caribe En Los Años Noventa*. Santiago de Chile: Naciones Unidas.

———. 2012. *Cambio Estructural Para La Igualdad. Una Visión Integrada Del Desarrollo*. San Salvador: Naciones Unidas.

———. 2014. *Pactos Para La Igualdad. Hacia Un Futuro Sostenible. Trigésimo*. Lima: Naciones Unidas.

Chase-Dunn, Chris, and E. Anderson. 2005. *The Historical Evolution of World-Systems*. London: Palgrave.

Chase-Dunn, Chris, and Hiroko Inoue. 2011. Immanuel Wallerstein. In *The WileyBlackwell Companion to Major Social Theorists: Volume II, Contemporary Social Theorists*, ed. G. Ritzer and J. Stepnisky. Cambridge: Wiley-Blackwell.

Chibber, Vivek. 2002. Bureaucratic Rationality and the Developmental State. *American Journal of Sociology* 107 (4): 951–989.

Cox, Robert. 1996. Social Forces, States and World Orders: Beyond International Relations Theory. In *Approaches to World Order*, ed. Robert Cox and Timothy Sinclair, 85–123. Cambridge: Cambridge University Press.

Crotty, James, and Kang-Kook Lee. 2005. From East Asian 'Miracle' to Neo-Liberal 'Mediocrity': The Effects of Liberalization and Financial Opening on the Post-Crisis Korean Economy. *Global Economic Review* 34 (4): 415–434.

Cumings, Bruce. 1984. The Origins and Development of the Northeast Asian Political Economy: Industrial Sectors, Product Cycles and Political Consequences. *International Organization* 38 (1): 1–40.

Deyo, Frederic. 1989. Labor and Development Policy in East Asia. *The Annals of the American Academy of Political and Social Science* 505 (1): 152–161.

Dicken, Peter, Philip Kelly, Kris Olds, and Henry Wai-Chung Yeung. 2001. Chains and Networks, Territories and Scales: Towards an Analytical Framework for the Global Economy. *Global Networks* 1 (2): 89–112.

Doner, Richard, Bryan Ritchie, and Dan Slater. 2005. Systemic Vulnerability and the Origins of Developmental States: Northeast and Southeast Asia in Comparative Perspective. *International Organization* 59 (2): 327–361.

Duménil, Gerard, and Dominique Lévy. 2001. Periodizing Capitalism: Technology, Institutions and Relations of Production. In *Phases of Capitalist Development*, ed. R. Albritton, M. Itoh, R. Westra, and A. Zuege. London: Palgrave Macmillan.

Dunning, J.H. 1981. *International Production and Multinational Enterprise*. London: Allen & Unwin.

Escobar, Pepe. 2017. Xi's Wild Geese Chase the Silk Road Gold. *Asia Times*, May 15. http://www.atimes.com/article/xis-wild-geese-chase-silk-road-gold/.

Esser, Klaus, Hillebrand Wolfgang, Dirk Messner, and Meyer-Stamer Jörg. 1996. Competitividad Sistémica: Nuevo Desafío Para Las Empresas Y La Política. *Revista de La CEPAL* (59).

Evans, Peter. 1995. *Embedded Autonomy: States and Industrial Transformation*. Princeton, NJ: Princeton University Press.

Fajnzylber, Fernando. 1990. *Industrialización En América Latina: De La "caja Negra" al Casillero Vacío. Comparación de Patrones Contemporáneos de Industrialización*, ed. CEPAL. Santiago de Chile: Naciones Unidas.

Fernández, Víctor Ramiro. 2017. *La Trilogía Del Erizo-Zorro. Redes Globales, Trayectorias Nacionales Y Dinámicas Regionales Desde La Periferia*. Barcelona: Anthropos – Siglo XXI Editores – Ediciones UNL.

Fernández, Víctor Ramiro, and Lucas Cardozo. 2012. Nueva Estatidad Bajo La Re-Emergencia Regional. La Reelaboración Del Proyecto Neoliberal Y Sus Alternativas En La Periferia. *Estudios Urbanos E Regionais* 14 (2): 11.

Fiori, José Luis. 1992. Economía Política Del Estado Desarrollista En Brasil. *Revista de La CEPAL* (47): 187–201.

———. 2001. Para Um Diagnóstico Da Modernização Brasileira. In *Polarização Mundial E Crescimento*, ed. José Luis Fiori and Carlos Medeiros. Petrópolis: Vozes.
———. 2015. *História, Estratégia E Desenvolvimento Para Uma Geopolítica Do Capitalismo.* San Pablo: Editorial Boitempo.
Furtado, Celso. 1958. Fundamentos Da Programação Econômica. *Econômica Brasileira* 4 (1 e 2).
———. 1962. *A Pré-Revolução Brasileira.* Río de Janeiro: Fondo de Cultura.
———. 1964. *Dialética Do Desenvolvimento.* Río de Janeiro: Fondo de Cultura.
———. 1965. Obstáculos Políticos Para El Desarrollo Económico Del Brasil. *Desarrollo Económico* 4 (16): 373.
Gill, Stephen. 1995. Globalisation, Market Civilisation and Disciplinary Neoliberalism. *Millennium – Journal of International Studies* 24 (3): 399–423.
Gilpin, Robert. 1975. *U.S. Power and the Multinational Corporation.* New York: Basic Books.
———. 1987. *The Political Economy of International Relations.* Princeton, NJ: Princeton University Press.
Glassman, Jim. 1999. State Power Beyond The 'territorial Trap': The Internationalization of the State. *Political Geography* 18: 669–696.
Gough, Ian. 2001. Globalization and Regional Welfare Regimes: The East Asia Case. *Global Social Policy* 1 (2): 163–189.
Graciarena, Jorge. 1972. *Poder Y Clases Sociales En El Desarrollo de América Latina.* Buenos Aires: Paidós.
Guimarães, Roberto. 1997. *El Leviatán Acorralado: Continuidad Y Cambio En El Papel Del Estado En América Latina.* Documento 97/40. Serie Ensayos. Santiago de Chile: ILPES.
Gurrieri, Adolfo. 1987. Vigencia Del Estado Planificador En La Crisis Actual. *Revista de La CEPAL* (31): 201–217.
Harvey, David. 1982. *The Limits to Capital.* Oxford: Basil Blackwell.
———. 2003. *The New Imperialism.* Oxford: Oxford University Press.
Heilmann, Sebastian, and Lea Shih. 2013. The Rise of Industrial Policy in China, 1978–2012. *Harvard-Yenching Institute Working Paper Series* (31).
Hirschman, Albert. 1968. The Political Economy of Import-Substituting Industrialization in Latin America. *The Quarterly Journal of Economics* 82 (1): 1–32.
Jessop, Bob. 2008. *El Futuro Del Estado Capitalista.* Madrid: Los libros de la catarata.
Johnson, Chalmers. 1982. *MITI and the Japanese Miracle: The Growth of Industry Policy 1925–1975.* Stanford: Stanford University Press.
Jomo, Kwame Sundaram. 2003. *Globalization, Liberalization and Equitable Development: Lessons from East Asia.* Geneve: UNRISD.

Katz, Jorge. 2000. The Dynamics of Technological Learning During the Import-Substitution Period and Recent Structural Changes in the Industrial Sector of Argentina, Brazil, and Mexico. In *Technology, Learning and Innovation: Experiences of Newly Industrializing Economies*, ed. L. Kim and R. Nelson, 307–334. New York: Cambridge University Press.

Kay, Cristóbal. 2002. Reforma Agraria, Industrialización Y Desarrollo ¿Por Qué Asia Oriental Superó a América Latina? *Debate Agrario* (34): 45-94.

Kerner, Daniel. 2003. La CEPAL, Las Empresas Transnacionales Y La Búsqueda de Una Estrategia de Desarrollo Latinoamericana. *Revista de La CEPAL* (79).

Kholi, Atul. 2004. *State Directed-Development: Political Power and Industrialization in the Global Periphery*. Cambridge: Cambridge University Press.

———. 2009. States and Economic Development. *Brazilian Journal of Political Economy* 29 (2): 212–227.

Kim, Yu Tae. 1999. Neoliberalism and the Decline of the Developmental State. *Journal of Contemporary Asia* 29 (4): 441–461.

———. 2007. Regional Innovation Policy of South Korea, Compared with, and Learning from, the European Union. In *European Union Center of Excellence and Center for East Asian Studies*. Madison: University of Wisconsin.

Koopman, Robert, Zhi Wang, and Shang-Jin Wei. 2012. Estimating Domestic Content in Exports When Processing Trade Is Pervasive. *Journal of Development Economics* 99 (1): 178–189.

Lee, Seung-Ook, Joel Wainwright, and Jim Glassman. 2017. Geopolitical Economy and the Production of Territory: The Case of US–China Geopolitical-Economic Competition in Asia. *Environment and Planning A: Economy and Space* 50: 416–436.

López, José Ignacio. 2012. La Geopolítica de Nicolas Spykman. *Universidad EAFIT* 31 (97): 79–86.

Mann, Michael. 1986. *The Sources of Social Power*. Cambridge: Cambridge University Press.

Mariño, Luis. 1981. Las Empresas Transnacionales Y La Actual Modalidad de Crecimiento Económico. *Revista de La CEPAL* (14).

Migdal, Joel. 2001. *State in Society. Studying How States and Societies Transform and Constitute One Another*. Cambridge: Cambridge University Press.

———. 2011. *Estados Débiles, Estados Fuertes*. México: FCE.

Milberg, William. 2008. Shifting Sources and Uses of Profits: Sustaining US Financialization with Global Value Chains. *Economy and Society* 37 (3): 420–451.

O'Donnell, Guillermo. 1982. *El Estado Burocrático Autoritario. Triunfos, Derrotas Y Crisis*. Buenos Aires: Editorial Belgrano.

———. 2010. *Modernización Y Autoritarismo*. Prometeo.

Offe, Claus. 1984. In *Contradictions of the Welfare State*, ed. J. Keane. London: Hutchinson.

Ormaechea, Emilia, and Víctor Ramiro Fernández. 2017. Consideraciones Sobre El Cambio de Percepción de Raúl Prebisch En El Entendimiento Del Rol Del Estado Para El Desarrollo Latinoamericano (1949–1963). *Papeles Del Centro de Investigación* (18).

Papanek, G. 1988. The New Asian Capitalism: An Economic Portrait. In *Search of an East Asian Development Model*, ed. P. Berger and H.-H. Hsiao. New Brunswick: Transaction Books.

Peck, Jamie, and Nik Theodore. 2015. *Fast Policy. Experimental Statecraft at the Thresholds of Neoliberalism.* Minneapolis: University of Minnesota Press.

Peck, Jamie, and Adam Tickell. 2002. Neoliberalizing Space. *Antipode* 34 (3): 380–404.

Peña, Milcíades. 2014. (Pseudónimo: Testa, Víctor) 1. La Evolución Industrial Argentina. In Fichas de Investigación Económica Y Social Tomo I (Abril 1964). Vol. I, ed. Milcíades Peña. Argentina: Ediciones Biblioteca.

Poulantzas, Nicos. 1978. *Estado, Poder Y Socialismo.* México: Siglo XXI Editores.

Prebisch, Raúl. 1952. *Problemas Teóricos Y Prácticos Del Crecimiento Económico.* Santiago de Chile: Naciones Unidas.

———. 1956. El Papel de La Industria En El Crecimiento Argentino. In *Conferencia Del Doctor Raúl Prebisch, Pronunciada En La Sede Social de La Unión Industrial Argentina El 11 de Octubre de 1956.* Buenos Aires: Unión Industrial Argentina.

———. 1960. Exposición Del Dr. Raúl Prebisch, Representante Del Secretario General de Las Naciones Unidas Y Director Principal de La CEPAL. In *Tercera Conferencia Económica Interamericana*, ed. CEPAL. Santiago de Chile: Naciones Unidas.

———. 1963. *Hacia Una Dinámica Del Desarrollo Latinoamericano.* CEPAL – Décimo Período de Sesiones.

———. 1971. Transformación Y Desarrollo. La Gran Tarea de América Latina. In *CEPAL. Decimocuarto Período de Sesiones. Santiago de Chile, 27 de Abril Al 8 de Mayo de 1971*, ed. CEPAL. Santiago de Chile: Naciones Unidas.

———. 1976. Crítica Al Capitalismo Periférico. *Revista de La CEPAL Primer sem.*

———. 1978. Socio-Economic Structure and Crisis of Peripheral Capitalism. *Revista de La CEPAL* (Second Half).

———. 1980. Hacia Una Teoría de La Transformación. *Revista de La CEPAL* (96).

Quijano, Aníbal. 1968. Dependencia, Cambio Social Y Urbanización En Latinoamérica. *Revista Mexicana de Sociología* XXX (3): 525.

Ruckert, Arne. 2006. Towards an Inclusive-Neoliberal Regime of Development: From the Washington to the Post-Washington Consensus. *Labour, Capital, and Society* 39: 34–67.

Sanderson, Stephen K. 2005. World-Systems Analysis After Thirty Years: Should It Rest in Peace? *International Journal of Comparative Sociology* 46 (3): 179–213.

Sassen, Saskia. 2010. Global Inter-City Networks and Commodity Chains: Any Intersections? *Global Networks* 10 (1): 150–163.

Serfati, Claude. 2008. Financial Dimension of Transnational Corporations, Global Value Chain and Technological Innovation. *Journal of Innovation Economics* 2 (2): 35–61.

Simmons, Beth, Frank Dobbin, and Geoffrey Garret. 2008. *The Global Diffusion of Markets and Democracy*. New York: Cambridge University Press.

Smith, Neil. 1993. Homeless/Global: Scaling Places. In *Mapping the Futures. Local Cultures, Global Change*, ed. J. Bird, B. Curtis, T. Putnam, G. Robertson, and T. Tiickner, 87–119. Nueva York: Routledge.

Spykman, Nicolas. 1942. *Estados Unidos Frente Al Mundo*. Mexico: Fondo de Cultura Económica.

Stubbs, Richard. 2009. What Ever Happened to the East Asian Developmental State? The Unfolding Debate. *The Pacific Review* 22 (1): 1–22.

Sunkel, Osvaldo. 1967. Política Nacional de Desarrollo Y Dependencia Externa. *Estudios Internacionales* 1 (1): 43–75.

———. 1970. Desarrollo, Subdesarrollo, Dependencia, Marginación Y Desigualdades Espaciales; Hacia Un Enfoque Totalizante. *EURE* 1 (1): 13–49.

———. 1971. Capitalismo Transnacional Y Desintegración Nacional En América Latina. *Estudios Internacionales* 4 (16): 3–61.

Sunkel, Osvaldo, and Gustavo Zuleta. 1990. Neoestructuralismo Versus Neoliberalismo En Los Años Noventa. *Revista de La CEPAL* (42).

Thorp, Rosemary. 1998. *Progreso, Pobreza Y Exclusión. Una Historia Económica de América Latina*. Washington, DC: Banco Interamericano de Desarrollo.

Wade, Robert. 2013. Protecting Power: Western States in Global Organizations. In *Global Governance in Crisis: New Powers and the Restructuring of World Order*, ed. David Held and Charles Roger. Cambridge: Polity Press.

Wallerstein, Immanuel. 1974. *The Modern World-System: Capitalist Agriculture and the Origins of the European World-Economy in the Sixteenth Century*. New York; London: Academic Press.

Weiss, Linda. 2000. Developmental States in Transition: Adapting, Dismantling, Innovating, Not 'normalizing. *The Pacific Review* 13 (1): 21–55.

———. 2003. Gobernanza Global, Estrategias Nacionales: Cómo Los Estados Hacen Espacio Para Desenvolverse Bajo La OMC. *Documentos Y Aportes En Administración Pública Y Gestión Estatal* 4 (3): 7–40.

Wigell, Mikael. 2016. Conceptualizing Regional Powers' Geo-Economic Strategies: Neo-Imperialism, Neo-Mercantilism, Hegemony, and Liberal Institutionalism. *Asia Europe Journal* 14: 135–151.

Zysman, J. 1983. *Governments, Markets and Growth: Financial Systems and the Politics of Industrial Change*. Ithaca: Cornell University Press.

CHAPTER 7

The Possibilities of Industrialization and Structural Change for the Periphery in the Context of Globalization

Margarita Olivera

Introduction: Industrial Policy or Free Trade? That Is the Eternal Debate

Before analyzing the actual possibilities for industrial policy, given the constraints on the economic policy space imposed by the system of international rules and regulations, it is important to understand some salient features of the structuralist theory and the context in which these ideas were abruptly replaced with free trade theories.

After World War II, prominent works in economic development were published. A common characteristic emerging from these works is to stress the importance of the transformation of the productive structure of the economy in order to achieve economic development. Even more, most of them agree that the key determinants of the accumulation processes in the

The author thanks Andrés Lazzarini and the participants of the Seminar "Desarrollo en América Latina: Discusiones críticas desde la periferia" organized by the editors in July 2017 for their comments and suggestions.

M. Olivera (✉)
Federal University of Rio de Janeiro, Rio de Janeiro, Brazil

V. R. Fernández, G. Brondino (eds.), *Development in Latin America*,
https://doi.org/10.1007/978-3-319-92183-9_7

backward economies will greatly depend on the structural features of such economies.[1] Among the main specific characteristics, we have the duality of the economies, which is the presence of a very productive sector together with another sectors with very low productivity, the segmentation of the job market and the presence of disguised unemployment. Certainly, these ideas were encouraged by both the incipient processes of industrialization in the backward areas of the world and the experience of the planned economy in the former USSR.

Among the main theoretical contributions, it is possible to identify several types of analyses, with different emphases on the various aspects of the accumulation mechanisms; however, all of them acknowledge the existence of labor unemployment, as well as the asymmetrical determination of income distribution. Post-war development theories consider that capital is both inefficient and scarce relative to an abundant supply of labor, and that free trade is not a successful strategy to transform the productive structure and boost development (Olivera 2011). It is worth pointing out that these development theories have not been the only approaches within the heterodox tradition. It will also be seen that some of the post-Keynesian, neo-Ricardian, and post-Marxian theories have all contributed to growth theory of a more general character (i.e., they are not only meant for the study of less-developed countries). The structuralist approach within the development theories has been mainly focused on the paths to transform the productive structure of the economy as the only way to achieve economic development.

Changes in international markets originating during the interwar period triggered off incipient, though significant, development processes, particularly in Latin America. The two World Wars, together with the economic slump of the thirties, reshaped the economy, society, and politics on a global scale. As far as the economic sphere was concerned, both unequal exchange and market closure strongly inspired backward economies to rethink their own economic position in the world economy as well as their economic structures. Deep changes in international trade patterns arose out of these new circumstances, as well as changes in the international division of labor. The industrialization strategies adopted in many countries of the periphery are broadly known in the discipline as the *Import Substitution Industrialization* (ISI). In this context, following World War II, some Latin American economists started to focus on the study of the specific structural features that impinge on the economic development in the region.

This approach is based on the seminal works by Raul Prebisch, the first executive secretary of the Economic Commission for Latin America and the Caribbean between 1950 and 1963 (ECLAC). In "The Economic Development of Latin America and Its Principal Problems", Prebisch shows how the principle of comparative advantages (based on relative factor scarcities), and therefore free trade policy, is not valid for the periphery, especially in Latin America.

As is well known, this principle establishes that, if each economy specializes in the production of goods that use more intensively the factor of which it is relatively abundantly endowed with, then international trade would be more advantageous for all the participants in the exchange than it would in case of autarchy. As a result, the less-developed economies, whose productive structure is principally specialized in primary goods, would be able to reach similar levels of wealth as in the developed economies. As Prebisch remarks, this has not been verified for most peripheral countries:

> The enormous benefits resulting from increased productivity have not reached the periphery in proportion to those obtained by the population of these great countries [of the centre]. This explains the outstanding differences found in the standard of living of the masses of these two groups and the manifest discrepancies in their capacity to capitalize ... There is therefore an evident disequilibrium, a fact which, whatever its origin or justification, destroys the basic assumptions of the schema of the international division of labour. (Prebisch 1950, 2)

According to Prebisch, the slow and irregular spread of technical progress in the world has caused the emergence of two groups of countries: the rich and most developed countries[2]—the *center*—and the poor and less-developed countries—the *periphery*. The *center* is characterized by a high and continuous flow of technical progress, which has allowed these countries to develop a highly-diversified economic structure (since it covers a broad range of activities), which is also roughly homogenous because the several economic sectors show similar levels in labor productivity. On the contrary, the countries of the *periphery* have found a place in international trade as primary goods producers (i.e., primary products and natural resource-based manufactures). Their economic structures are characterized by being highly specialized, particularly in primary goods, but also heterogeneous, since they have high labor productivity levels in the sectors they are specialized due to an inflow of technical progress, but in all the remaining sectors productivity levels are very low. Furthermore, this heterogeneity in sectoral labor productivities produces persistent wage gaps and segmented labor markets across the different sectors, as exemplified by the industrialization experience after War World II.

Likewise, in the *periphery*, heterogeneity is strongly associated with structural disguised unemployment, underemployment, and informal employment. In fact, while activities with normal labor productivity can create employment, those industries with low productivity levels, which comprise the largest number of sectors and employ large numbers of workers, are associated with low wages and underemployment. In addition, economic specialization drives the whole economy to significant external disequilibria, since the elasticity of demand for imported capital goods on the part of the *periphery* is persistently higher than the elasticity of demand for primary goods on the part of the *center*.[3] Therefore, due to the international division of labor, less-developed countries end up focusing their economic resources on developing productive sectors with scarce elasticity of demand, poor job creation, very few linkages within the economy (normally considered as enclave sectors), and slow spillover effects both on growth and technology.

This is the main concern raised by Prebisch as well as by other Latin American economists. One significant way to overcome this divergent situation worldwide, according to this approach, is by industrializing the periphery. To achieve this goal, ECLAC proposed[4]: (1) to strengthen the industrialization process by ISI; (2) to implement a land (or agrarian) reform, since concentration of landed property checks the industrialization process; (3) to maintain, stimulate and improve state interventionism, with policies focused on fostering industrialization and development; and (4) to promote Latin American integration in order to overcome market restrictions and thus to enlarge the scales of production.[5]

According to this approach, the state must play an active role in the development process and one of its main duties should be to strengthen and diversify the industrial sectors through direct subsidies and protection of infant industry, in order to reduce the specialization in agricultural production and the heterogeneity that characterizes these economies (in Latin America, industrialization during the fifties was mainly centered on the machinery-producing sector).

Nevertheless, this boom of development ideas based on state intervention and high wages has found its end together with the end of the

Keynesian Golden Age in the United States and the beginning of the collapse of the USSR. In the seventies, major changes came together with the so-called Thatcher—Reagan era in the international sphere. Together with this shift in the geopolitical scenario, the ISI strategy followed by most Latin American countries starts to show some severe issues due to the increasing need of financial flows (see Diamand 1972) in order to overcome the external constraint (i.e., the increasing need of foreign currency to meet the increasing import requirements for industrialization). However, since domestic industries were not capable of being competitive on the international market, the outcome was a huge indebtedness process that ended up in the Latin American debt crisis in the eighties.

Supporters of the rebirth in neoliberal ideas underlined that the main reason for the flaws of the ISI strategy in Latin America, vis-a-vis the Asian experience, was precisely the excessive state intervention and the lack of an outward-looking strategy (see, e.g., Bhagwati and Krueger 1973; Balassa 1988; Bhagwati 2002). However, as Chang (2007) has shown, the development process in South Korea was far from a neoliberal free market strategy, being characterized by strong state intervention. Also, these supporters more often than not overlooked to mention that, unlike the East Asian countries and Japan, Latin American countries did not benefit from the international inflow of finance by the huge flows of trade and capital with the United States, in the context of the Cold War conflict (Medeiros and Serrano 1999); (more on this below).

Since the beginning of the neoliberal era in the late seventies, the policy space has been drastically reduced in peripheral countries. Industrial policies as part of the political agenda in backward economies have been shrinking as globalization progressed (Olivera 2011; Herrera 2011). The main target has been the state-driven ISI processes, as well as commercial policies involving tariff protection and direct subsidies to production. Even Latin American institutions, such as ECLAC, which had been characterized since their foundations by their concern with structural factors as determinants of the development process, were affected in the seventies and eighties by the so-called neoclassical counter-revolution (Toye 1993).

Unlike development theorists, orthodox economists supportive of the theory of comparative advantages have argued that free trade policies are the only way to achieve both sustained economic growth and growth convergence between dissimilar economies. Even if this idea could appear to be an old concept, we can also find it behind the current set of statements being used to hold the same policy suggestions. Nowadays this debate was rekindled under new clothes, although sharing the same old essence. In the beginning of the past century, free trade supporters underlined the inefficiency of tariff protection as a development strategy. Today, they argue that the best way to achieve development is by participating in the global value chains. To be "included" into these new international vertical integration processes, less-developed countries should have to pursue traditional free trade policies, based on the comparative advantage principle, good governance and investment agreements (see Gereffi 2014; Gereffi and Sturgeon 2013).

Is Free Trade the Best Strategy to Achieve Development?

If we analyze the historical evolution of the core economics during capitalism, we can observe that except for short periods economic convergence did not prevail among the regions of the world. The main exception could be certainly the golden age (1950–1970) in which the Cold War, with the Keynesian policies in the western developed countries and the USSR policies in socialist countries directly or indirectly influenced the industrialization processes in countries of the periphery. As Nayyar shows:

> By 1870, the share of 'The West' in world population had already increased to one-third while that of 'The Rest' had already decreased to two-thirds. And, by 1870, the share of 'The West' in world income had risen to 57 per cent while that of 'The Rest' had fallen to 43 per cent. For the world economy, the significance of 1870 is clear. The international division of labour had changed. The beginning of a divide between what are now described as industrialized countries and developing countries in the world economy was visible. (Nayyar 2013, 16)

> Between 1950 and 1980, the share of developing countries in world population rose from 67 per cent to 74 per cent, while their share in world GDP stopped its decline and rose from 27 per cent to 32 per cent ... This was a clear reversal of the trends in growth during the period from 1820 to 1950 when 'The West' fared so much better than 'The Rest'. (Nayyar 2013, 51)

With the beginning of the globalization, the results have drastically changed. If we analyze the evolution of gross domestic product (GDP) per capita in recent years (see Fig. 7.1), we can observe the rise of the gap between developed economies and backward economies (except for the

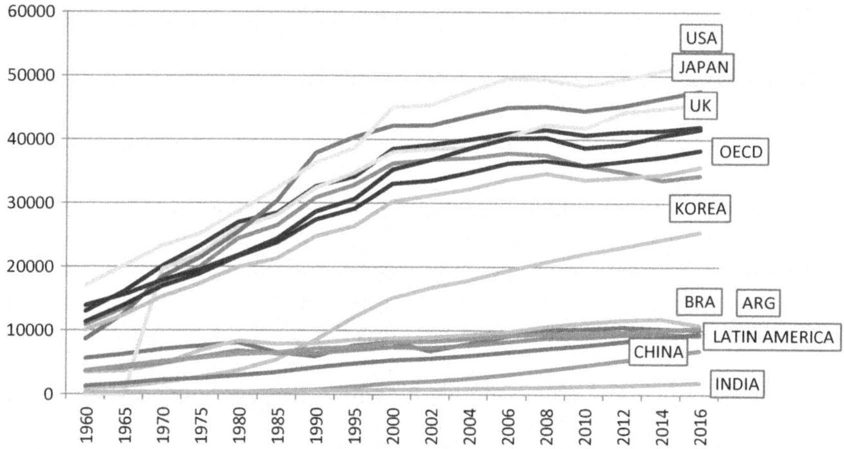

Fig. 7.1 GDP per capita (2010 US dollars). 1960–2016. Selected countries. Source: Author's own elaboration based on World Bank data

case of South Korea). Since the rebirth of free trade policies, the results were far from positive for peripheral countries, especially in Latin America and Africa. Several empirical studies have shown that for this period there has not been a correlation between economic growth and trade openness (Rodriguez and Rodrik 1999; Rodrik 1997; Moguillansky and Bielschowsky 2001; Di Maio 2008).

However, the effects were very different among backward economies, and in most cases, it had to do with the kind of liberalization processes that each economy has followed. As Shafaeddin has shown in his study of the processes of liberalization between 1980 and 2000:

> In several countries, mostly East Asian newly industrializing economies, rapid export growth was also accompanied by fast expansion of industrial supply capacity and upgrading. In these countries, after they had reached a certain level of industrial maturity, trade liberalization took place gradually and selectively. By contrast, the performance of the remaining countries, mostly in Africa and Latin America (majority cases), was not satisfactory. These countries embarked, in the main, on a process of structural reform in 1980s, including uniform, across-the-board and often premature trade liberalization. They further intensified their liberalization efforts in the 1990s. Consequently, half of the sample countries, mostly low-incomes ones, have faced de-industrialization. (Shafaeddin 2011, 19)

It is important to notice that the South Korean miracle was not only the result of the implementation of market friendly policies and good entrepreneurial skills but also of forceful state-driven policies designed to pick up the winner companies and of the aid provided by the United States. As mentioned above, Medeiros and Serrano (1999, 134–135) studied how, in the context of the cold war with the USSR, the United States followed a "development by invitation" strategy with countries located in disputed geographical areas, such as Korea, Japan, China in Asia, and Germany in Europe. The strategy consisted in ensuring both massive capital inflows and external markets for the country's exports. Hence, the transformation of the productive structure in East Asia was the result of strong state intervention coupled with US aid to overcome the external constraints.

Quite differently, as Fernandez and Ormaechea pointed out on Chap. 6, Latin America did not benefit from this collateral effect during the Cold War period, a relative autarky process of development took place in the region during this period and the results were not so great in terms of economic growth. However, if we consider the historical experience of these countries, it is evident that in order to achieve economic development it is necessary to transform the productive structure, as the structuralists have long held. Unfortunately, the industrialization strategies implemented during the golden age and in East Asia were based on economic policies that are no longer available, given the limitations that the regulatory frameworks of international relations impose.

In the next sections, we will analyze how the international trade and productive development policies have been built under the new regulatory framework created during globalization.

Globalization, Free Trade, and the WTO

In the last few decades, we have witnessed a profound transformation in the methods of production and technologies. After the end of the golden age and the abandonment of Fordism together with the collapse of the USSR, the accumulation model has drastically changed. From a strategy based on domestic demand and high wages, developed countries move to a strategy focused on external markets and the internationalization of the productive processes by offshoring parts of the production to lower-wages economies. Goods are produced essentially by Global Value Chains (henceforth, GVCs) spread all over the world and led by Transnational Corporations (henceforth, TNCs). These GVCs, promoted by the TNCs, have represented one of the greatest transformations in the world economy after the industrial revolution. The multiplication and success of this new mode of production have been possible thanks to the reduction in international transport costs, the advances in information and communications technologies, and trade liberalization. As Nayyar (2013) pointed out, a result of this transformation is an almost permanent increase in the share of international trade in economic activities. In particular, developing countries' share of world trade has been rising mainly since the late eighties, achieving in the last years the 45 per cent of total world trade (Nayyar 2013, Chap. 5). The rate of increase in international markets was even higher than economic growth. One result of the new international division of labor is the increase in the share of intermediate goods in international trade flows. As Medeiros and Trebat (2017, 14) have argued: "GVCs expanded rapidly after 2000, and this coincided with an increase in the technological sophistication of developing country exports and higher rates of GDP growth". However, this technological improvement has not being equally distributed within the economies. Bianchi and Szpak (2013) have studied that the productive segmentation that emerges from the internationalization of production generates the conformation of an international division of labor between the center and the periphery that evidences the technological asymmetry that prevails among them. As a result, central countries have deepened specialization in those segments of production, commercialization, and marketing with higher technological sophistication, while the countries of the periphery focused on the production of intermediate goods with little value added (as in the case of Mexican "maquiladoras", see Sargent and Matthews 2008). In this connection, the phenomenon envisaged by the structuralist theorists has not been reversed itself, but rather evolved. Developed countries have focused on the service sectors (marketing, financial services, R&D) and the production of high technological components while the less-developed countries, once again, have had to use their competitive advantages, specializing in the assembly of products and the production of parts with low value added. In this way, less-developed countries are under a constant pressure to keep their wage levels low and their economies open to foreign competition, both for trading imports and exports and for the establishment of branches of the TCNs in their territories.

Since the beginning of the so-called globalization in the early 1990s, two intertwined facts have turned apparent. On the one hand, as Villani and Zeolla point out in Chap. 8, capital flows have been largely raised from stock markets and from foreign direct investment (FDI). On the other hand, policy recommendations have insisted to move toward a free trade world, which is perfectly suitable with the needs of TNCs. As Chang (2003) remarks: "In 1995 the Uruguay Round of talks by the GATT (General Agreement on Trade and Tariffs) resulted in worldwide tariff cuts, tougher restrictions on trade-related subsidies, strengthening of trade-related intellectual property rights, and, most importantly, the transformation of the GATT into the more powerful World Trade Organization (WTO)" (Chang 2003, 267). Therefore, according to the WTO tenets, since this set of rules is necessary "to level the playing field", all countries should drastically cut their tariffs on an average level and, coupled with other agreements, guarantee free trade of goods, services, and capital. On this regulatory framework, three agreements meet with TNCs' needs which eventually reduce the industrial policy space: investment (TRIMS), property rights (TRIPS), and subsidies (WTO 2015).

Through the TRIMS agreement, governments cannot discriminate among local and foreign firms either by enforcing national origins of inputs or by limiting the volume/value of imported products on the grounds of export capacity of the firm, or by limiting the access of the foreign firms to foreign currency to purchase imported inputs. The TRIMS agreements do not limit the possibility for the state to demand some R&D levels, a minimum percentage of state participation, the creation of joint ventures and skilled workers trained by domestic institutions. However, given the structural constraints for economies of the periphery, it would likely be hard and expensive for them to use these measures to promote industry development.

The TRIPS are perhaps the most controversial agreements from a long-run perspective, since they allow for the monopoly of technological use. The agreement guarantees the protection for intellectual property rights to enhance technological innovation, transfers and dissemination, authors' copyrights, trademarks, geographical indications, designs and industrial models, patents (preventing the production, use, selling and import by outsourcing firms for 20 years), framework for designed integrated circuits, protection for undisclosed information. This treaty is clearly disadvantageous for countries of the periphery, since their production of inventions and patents is much lower than in central economies. Therefore, the agreement limits the access to technology and medicines for less-developed countries. It is notorious that trade liberalization does not matter for TRIPS.

The agreement on subsidies and countervailing measures forbids every type of direct subsidy like those used during the ISI period. Governments cannot subsidize any enterprise, industry, or sectoral production as a prize for its exporting performance or for the uses of domestic inputs for its production (which is the commonly known as import substitution subsidy). The only subsidies allowed for are those of non-specific kind, like subsidies aimed at promoting R&D, environmental, and regional subsidies (i.e., the agrarian common policy in the European Union is allowed within the WTO regulations).

As Chang pointed out, poor countries were the great losers of the negotiations of Uruguay Round,

> … in the name of 'levelling the playing field', the Bad Samaritan rich nations have created a new international trading system that is rigged in their favour. They are preventing the poorer countries from using the tools of trade and industrial policies that they had themselves so effectively used in the past in order to promote their own economic development—not just tariffs and subsidies, but also regulation of foreign investment and 'violation' of foreign intellectual property rights. (Chang 2007, 62)

In fact, among the main results, the reduction in tariff was mainly of primary and agricultural goods, while the protection for manufactured products is maintained (in 2001, during the Doha round the discussion around the reduction in tariffs for non-agricultural products started but no agreement was reached). Then, peripheral countries end up paying more in tariffs than developed economies due to the kind of product they trade. In addition, the drop in tariffs in proportional terms implied further drops for the periphery in absolute terms (they started in high tariff levels) and the burden of reducing the public budget for a backward economy is greater than for developed ones, preventing government from improving public policies. Most of the policies allowed by TRIPS, TRIMS, and Subsidies are indeed accessible only by rich economies. To finance R&D, environmental improvement, innovations, and/or to create joint ventures, public budgets should be higher than those that backward economies commonly can afford to. Finally, the treaties signed up and the norms and regulations behind WTO tend to consolidate the international division of labor, deepening the specialization patterns according to static comparative advantages.

One of the greatest achievements of the creation of the WTO and of the TCNs has been certainly to combine the agreements that significantly limited the industrial policy space along with a dispute settlement system for which countries should be accountable. In this sense, the creation of the WTO can be thought as an instrument to reduce policy space and sovereignty.

Doha: NAMA, IPR, and Services

After the creation of the WTO, the peripheral countries had to accept a greatest average tariff reduction, the de-regulation of FDI, which forbids any possible protection for local producers and benefits TNCs (Akyüz 2005), and the banning of direct subsidies for local producers. However, several issues remain outside the negotiations (as E-commerce, software, technological services, non-agricultural markets access, public procurement, among others) and "the existing (and prospective) rules of the WTO regime allow few exceptions and provide little flexibility to countries that are latecomers to industrialization" (Nayyar 2003, 78). This policy space was used in East Asia and especially by China to promote their industrial development in a sort of "hidden protectionism" in what Alice Amsden (2001) called "new mechanisms of resistance".[6] With the beginning of the new millennium, the process of internationalization of production has been extended and, with them, the needs of the TCNs. In 2001, a new round of discussions started in Doha, with the participation of 149 countries (including China) and in a few years discussions reached 157 countries after several ministerial meetings (Cancun 2003, Hong Kong 2005 and Geneva 2011, Bali 2013, Nairobi 2015 and Buenos Aires 2017). The main concern raised in the negotiations by less-developed countries has been the way in which the agreements signed in the Uruguay Round should be implemented, and the exceptions and differential treatments from which less-developed countries should benefit. According to Khor (2007), peripheral countries have argued that:

> many of the existing WTO agreements are biased against their interests, and that this situation must be rectified in order to attain a more balanced multilateral trading system. Among their arguments was that the Agreement on TRIPS puts onerous burdens on the developing countries (raising the cost of consumer products such as medicines, and hindering innovation and technology upgrading); the Agreement on TRIMs prohibits investment measures such as

local-content policy that are useful development tools; and the Agreement on Agriculture (AoA) has allowed the developed countries to maintain their high protection in this sector (through high domestic support and tariffs) while requiring the developing countries to liberalise their food imports, at the expense of food security and farmers' livelihoods. (Khor 2007, 3)

On the other hand, developed countries claim that the main issues should not concern development topics, but market access, in particular, to consolidate TRIPS by accessing non-agricultural markets (henceforth, NAMA) and liberalizing services.

While in the Uruguay Round there was an agreement regarding the reduction in tariffs, the discussion was always around average levels, leaving some space to governments to discriminate among sectors and products. As for NAMA, the countries must bind all their industrial tariffs by massively cutting their industrial tariffs on a line-by-line basis. The argument is that this harmonization process is the only way to guarantee uniformity between tariff structures among countries in order to leveling the play field. To do that, developed countries have been discussing (although they have not got an agreement) about possible strategic formulas differentiated by the stages of tariff reduction, the sunset clauses, the final coefficient, and/or the extent of the reduction in the dispersion. There is not a unified vision even among central economies.

The main implication of the adoption of a low and homogenous tariff structure is that it removes any possible strategy of differentiation between imports of inputs, intermediate goods, capital goods, and consumer goods (including luxury goods). Also, any strategy based on differential treatments to imports of manufactures according to the technological content to boost specific economic sectors has been removed. Therefore, by applying the NAMA framework, not only the space for industrial policy is reduced but also the external constraint could be worsened further.

In the short run, the main effects could involve higher trade flows (due to the impact on the costs of imports and exports), lower levels of production and employment of the sectors that highly reduce tariffs, and a reduction in tax collection. However, the main problems involve their long-term effects. Within NAMA, the specialization pattern for the periphery will be deepened. The possibilities of development and the transformation of the productive structure will be further reduced. As Chang holds, "there are strong theoretical and empirical arguments that show that the kind of tariff cuts proposed in the current NAMA negotiations are likely to damage the future of the peripheral countries. It may not be too much of an exaggeration to say that the peripheral country trade negotiators have to fight the developed countries' NAMA proposals as if the future of their countries depended on it" (Chang 2005, 102).

Following Akyüz (2005), in order to industrialize, less-developed countries do not need very high tariffs on average, since the protection scheme needed for the industrialization process could be designed by combining high tariffs in some sectors and low tariffs in others. This structure should be dynamic, according to the stage of the process of industrialization in which the economy happens to be. Therefore, average tariffs should not be higher than 25 per cent in the early stages of industrialization.[7] Akyüz finally concludes that developing countries should not leave their ability to discriminate among sectoral tariff levels. If peripheral economies have to accept the cut in industrial tariffs, they should only accept to target average level and not the entire tariff structure on a line-by-line basis (as in the Uruguay Round).

Going Beyond WTO: Investment Treaties and ISDS

As mentioned above, in 2001 a new round of negotiations started; however, after several years of discussions, no agreement has been achieved. Along with these failed attempts to advance in the liberalization of the economies, other phenomena have been perceived. First, a new player appeared on the international scene in a disruptive way. The rise of China and, to a lesser extent, other Asian countries, has brought into discussion the development and growth strategies of the periphery, and has rearranged the South-South relations. According to World Bank statistics, in 2016 China overtook the United States in terms of GDP (PPP)[8] and Chinese exports have indeed become a major economic engine. Second, some economies of the periphery have experienced important crises after a decade following the neoliberal policies raised by the World Bank, the International Monetary Fund, and the WTO in the context of the Washington Consensus. This has stimulated great debates about the real benefits of free trade and the role of multilateral organizations.

The combination of these issues has brought about a strong reaction from North American TNCs that seek to secure their monopoly rents in products, activities, and/or services that incorporate high technology. In that sense, developed countries, guided by the United States, have promoted free trade agreements that go well beyond the WTO's regulations, with a view to eliminating the "hidden protectionism" mentioned. Bilateral agreements are more restrictive than those negotiated within the WTO. The goal of the so-called WTO-plus and WTO-extra free -trade agreements is to shrink even more the space for industrial policies, for the sake of leveling the play field. In particular, they target at public procurement, protectionist measures for manufactures (NAMA), licenses on hi-tech services related to software, internet and managing, environment and regulations on foreign investment. As Medeiros and Mazat state (on Chap. 5), this geopolitical strategy adopted by the United States is an attempt to reduce the influence of the peripheral countries, especially the BRICS, in the international sphere.

Several bilateral agreements including WTO-plus and WTO-extra have already been signed and the United States promoted, until not long ago, the deepening of the mega regional agreements TPP (Trans Pacific Partnership) and the creation of the agreement between the United States and the European Union, the TTIP (Transatlantic Trade and Investment Partnership). Certainly, both mega agreements are more focused on reducing non-tariff barriers to trade than on the traditional tariff reduction. In fact, the main discussion around the TTIP is the inclusion of an investor-state dispute settlement (ISDS). The obligation of ISDS implies a total loss of sovereignty since legal disputes between TNCs and States are resolved in international courts. This is a major gain for TNCs, since with an investment agreement any investor (without distinguishing between productive, portfolio or speculative origin of FDI) could take an ISDS case against the government. The motivation could be either that TNCs consider that investment was harmed either because it suffered discrimination with respect to a local competitor or because the government changed the macroeconomic conditions compromising its gains and profits. Therefore, ISDS have severe implications: (a) onerous implications, due to the costs of litigate in an international court; (b) discouraging effects on the government by applying new economic policies, since it never knows if the effects of these policies can lead to litigation; (c) loss of sovereignty (Khor 2015). To conclude, signing an investment treaty that includes ISDS implies handing over all power to the TNCs. In fact, instead of leveling the play field, TCNs would take advantage over their local competitors that cannot take ISDS cases against the government and would also benefit by dictating (indirectly) economic and social policies for the country hosting them.

The Policy Space Left and Some Concluding Remarks

The transformation of the productive structure remains one of the pillars for economic development. However, most of the policies followed by western developed countries and Asian countries[9] are no longer available, given the restrictive system of rules and regulations imposed by international trade. In this regard, it is necessary to rethink the recommendations and results of the structuralist theories.

As long as bilateral or multilateral agreements including ISDS, WTO-plus, and WTO-extra are not signed, there is some room for industrial policy within the framework of WTO regulations. In fact, the possibilities of indirect subsidies through investment policies in Science and Technology and through public procurement remained unrestricted, as well as the capacity of subsidizing industries or companies through services, including banking, insurance, and infrastructure. In view of this, the so-called new-developmentalist theories (e.g., Katz 2007; Rapetti 2013; Bresser-Pereira 2016) hold that the main way to boost economic development and deal with the external constrains is to stimulate the creation and consolidation of a domestic sector capable of being competitive at international scale. In order to do that, some policy interventions should be pursued. At a microeconomic level, the government should focus their efforts on the construction of a National Innovation System, aiming at creating the incentives for these tradable goods and services sectors. Some typical policies could be subsidies for research and development, creation of joint ventures between public and private institutions and government procurement, which are accepted by WTO. At a macroeconomic level, the agenda should focus on attaining competitive real exchange rates, fiscal stability, and conservative monetary policies that, according to their view, should enhance exports competitiveness (see Chap. 8).

As can be noted, this approach (followed by ECLAC after the nineties) opposes in so many ways to the traditional structuralist approach. While structuralists focus on domestic demand together with specific direct and sectoral policy intervention in order to boost industrialization, new developmentalists propose a strategy based on exports and international competitiveness. This shift in the growth strategy, from an inward-looking to an outward-looking scheme, has several implications on the economic system, income distribution, and the conditions for local producers in domestic markets.

In fact, it is hard to think through any development strategy based on promoting the creation or consolidation of one internationally competitive sector which does not belong to the handful of branches already enjoying comparative advantages. As stressed by the structuralist authors, peripheral economies are mainly characterized by having comparative advantages in the commodities and/or low-tech economic sectors. If we consider the actual Latin America participation in the GVCs, the results are not very promising regarding the possibilities of upgrading and creating spillover effects into the economy. As Medeiros & Trebat pointed out, "(d)espite a relatively low participation rate in GVCs compared to Southeast Asia, Latin America is characterized by significant levels of FDI in natural resource sectors and manufacturing activities oriented toward internal markets and for export processing. (…) Latin American countries participate in global trade mainly as raw materials producers and assemblers of manufactured goods with high levels of foreign value added. Generally speaking, South America falls into the first category, while Mexico and several Central American countries, such as Honduras, belong to the second" (Medeiros and Trebat 2017, 28–29).

To explore this path of development, the state should promote either wage reductions and flexible labor conditions or the development of commodities, which characterize themselves by having very few linkages within the domestic economy (see Olivera and Villani 2017). It is difficult to think that these policies could bring about a development process, since by shrinking the demand the outcome in terms of growth tend to be tiny and in terms of and income distribution tend to be harmful. The more so if Latin American goods should compete with Asian production, wages should be at minimum levels, considering the lack of technology and the regional productivity levels. At the same time, in the context of this specialization pattern, the possibilities for upgrading (as those suggested by Gereffi 2014) by participating in GVCs are extremely low, while the costs due to the openness required by the association with the TCNs are extremely high.

To conclude, to promote structural change leading to economic development in Latin America the options cannot be limited to choosing either for the closure of international markets (given by the international regulatory framework) or for participating in TCNs-controlled GVCs (since the long-run effects of bilateral agreements on investment and NAMA would condemn the future of the development process itself for the periphery). On the other hand, although not freed from potential problems and contradictions the only way-out which seems plausible is the Latin American regional association which could be based on their productive integration in order to increase the scales of production and consumption, as Prebisch and ECLAC recommended in the sixties and seventies (see Chap. 9). In fact, the levels of complementarity among the most dynamic Latin American countries are quite low (Olivera 2010), so that a way to induce intraregional productive linkages could be through the coordination of industrial policies at both micro- and meso-economic levels, as well as through regional policies aimed at enhancing the infrastructure. In this regard, the creation of regional value chains could be an interesting strategy to increase the value added in production, improve the economic activity levels, increase job-creation sectors, ease the external constraint and consolidate the autonomy of the region, which is today absolutely necessary in this multipolar world.

However, as mentioned by Fernández and Ormaechea (see Chap. 6), it is essential to note that the decision about what kind of strategy will be adopted in a peripheral economy in order to boost development depends on the class struggle, the question of power, and the domination that characterizes the economy. That is, the path of development is conditioned by the conflict between the different social classes, by the ability of one or another group to impose its political vision, and also by the geopolitics and geoeconomics (as was explained by Medeiros and Mazat in Chap. 5). These disputes end to determine the construction of the National State and the strategic capacity of the States to build a regional economic network capable of promoting industrialization beyond both, the WTO restrictions and the constraints and impositions of the GVCs.

Notes

1. See Lewis (1954), Rosenstein-Rodan (1943), Nurkse (1953), Hirshmnan (1958), Prebisch (1950), Singer (1950), Furtado (1959), among others.
2. Namely OECD countries.
3. The explanation for this difference in elasticity levels is intuitive. Unlike imported consumption goods from the center, imported capital goods from the periphery are fundamental to carrying out the productive process in these economies; then, due to the pressure exerted by this necessity even when income falls the purchase of this kind of goods by the periphery does not tend to decrease as much.
4. As documented in Nahón, Rodríguez Enríquez and Schorr (2006).
5. For more details on this topic, see Chap. 9.

6. In her own words: "A resistance mechanism may be defined as a policy that upholds the letter of the law but not necessarily its spirit. The letter, as written by a new World Trade Organization, supposedly abolished subsidies, freed trade, and deregulated competition. (...) It was within the relatively grey area of safeguards and selective subsidies that the neo-developmental state nested its new policy regime" (Amsden 2001, 268).
7. According to World Bank data, average World tariffs in 2014 was above 4%, while in 1996 was 35%. In peripheral countries, this average practically doubles.
8. Purchasing Power Parity.
9. The flying geese strategy that generate the Asian miracles (see Akamatsu 1962).

References

Akamatsu, Kaname. 1962. A Historical Pattern of Economic Growth in Developing Countries. *The Developing Economies* 1: 3–25.

Akyüz, Yilmaz. 2005. *The WTO Negotiations on Industrial Tariffs: What Is at Stake for Developing Countries?* TWN Trade & Development Series 24. Penang, Malaysia: Third World Network.

Amsden, Alice. 2001. *The Rise of 'the Rest': Challenges to the West from Late-Industrializing Economies.* New York: Oxford University Press.

Balassa, Bela. 1988. The Lessons of East Asian Development: An Overview. *Economic Development and Cultural Change* 36 (3): S273–S290.

Bhagwati, Jagdish. 2002. *Free Trade Today.* Princeton: Princeton University Press.

Bhagwati, Jagdish, and Anne Krueger. 1973. Exchange Control, Liberalization, and Economic Development. *The American Economic Review* 63 (2): 419–427.

Bianchi, Eduardo, and Carolina Szpak. 2013. *Cadenas globales de producción: implicancias para el comercio internacional y su gobernanza.* Serie Cátedra OMC 87. Buenos Aires: Red LATN.

Bresser-Pereira, Luiz Carlos. 2016. Reflecting on new developmentalism and classical developmentalism. *Brazilian Journal of Political Economy* 36 (2): 237–265.

Chang, Ha-Joon. 2003. Trade and Industrial Policy Issues. In *Rethinking Development Economics*, ed. Ha Joon Chang, 257–276. London: Anthem Press.

———. 2005. *Why Developing Countries Need Tariffs: How WTO NAMA Negotiations Could Deny Developing Countries Right to a Future.* Geneva: South Centre.

———. 2007. *Bad Samaritans. Rich Nations, Poor Policies & the Threat to the Developing World.* London: Random House Business Books.

Diamand, Marcelo. 1972. La Estructura Productiva Desequilibrada Argentina y el Tipo de Cambio. *Desarrollo Económico* 12 (45): 25–47.

Di Maio, Michelle. 2008. *Industrial Policy in Developing Countries: History and Perspectives*. Quaderno di Dipartimento n. 48. Macerata: Universita Degli Studi di Macerata.

Furtado, Celso. 1959. *Formação Econômica do Brasil*. Rio de Janeiro: Fundo de Cultura.

Gereffi, Gary. 2014. Global Value Chains in a Post-Washington Consensus World. *Review of International Political Economy* 21 (1): 9–37.

Gereffi, Gary, and Timothy Sturgeon. 2013. Global Value Chain-Oriented Industrial Policy: The Role of Emerging Economies. In *Global Value Chains in a Changing World*, ed. Deborah Elms and Patrick Low, 329–360. Geneva: World Trade Organization.

Herrera, Remmy. 2011. El 'Renacimiento' neoliberal de la Economía del Desarrollo. In *Globalización, dependencia y crisis económica – Análisis heterodoxos desde la economía del desarrollo*, ed. Juan Pablo Mateo, Ricardo Molero, and Rodrigo E. Santana, 13–25. Madrid: Fundación de Investigaciones Marxistas.

Hirschman, Albert. 1958. *The Strategy of Economic Development*. New Haven: Yale University Press.

Katz, Jorge. 2007. Cambios Estructurales y Desarrollo Económico. *Revista de Economía Política de Buenos Aires* 1: 71–92.

Khor, Martin. 2007. *The WTO's Doha Negotiations and Impasse: A Development Perspective*. TWN Trade & Development Series 32. Penang, Malaysia: Third World Network.

———. 2015. A Summary of Public Concerns on Investment Treaties and Investor-State Dispute Settlement. In *Investment Treaties: Views and Experiences from Developing Countries*, ed. Kinda Mohamadieh, Anna Bernardo, and Lean Ka-Min, 1–17. Geneva: South Centre.

Lewis, William Arthur. 1954. Economic Development with Unlimited Supplies of Labour. *Manchester School* 22: 139–191.

Medeiros, Carlos, and Franklin Serrano. 1999. Padrões Monetários Internacionais e Crescimento. In *Estados e Moedas no Desenvolvimento das Nações*, ed. Jose Luiz Fiori. Rio de Janeiro: Vozes.

Medeiros, Carlos, and Nicholas Trebat. 2017. *Finance, Trade, and Income Distribution in Global Value Chains: Implications for Developing Economies and Latin America*. Instituto de Economia, UFRJ, Discussion Paper 002/2017, Rio de Janeiro.

Moguillansky, Graciela, and Ricardo Bielschowsky. 2001. *Investment and Economic Reform in Latin America*. Santiago: ECLAC.

Nahón, Cecilia, Rodríguez Enríquez Corina, and Martin Schorr. 2006. El Pensamiento Latinoamericano en el Campo del Desarrollo del Subdesarrollo: Trayectoria, Rupturas y Continuidades. In *Crítica y Teoría en el Pensamiento*

Social Latinoamericano, ed. Fernanda Beigel, Nestor Kohan, and Martin Schorr, 327–388. Buenos Aires: Clacso.

Nayyar, Deepak. 2003. Globalization and Development. In *Rethinking Development Economics*, ed. Ha-Joon Chang, 61–82. London: Anthem Press.

———. 2013. *Catch Up: Developing Countries in the World Economy*. Oxford: Oxford University Press.

Nurkse, Ragnar. 1953. *Problems of Capital Formation in Underdeveloped Countries*. New York: Oxford University Press.

Olivera, Margarita. 2010. *Challenges to Regional Integration in Latin America*. Quaderni di Dipartimento 3. Università degli Studi di Pavia.

———. 2011. Las Teorías del Desarrollo desde la Posguerra al Nuevo Milenio: Un Recorrido Crítico. In *Globalización, dependencia y crisis económica – Análisis heterodoxos desde la economía del desarrollo*, ed. Juan Pablo Mateo, Ricardo Molero, and Rodrigo E. Santana, 26–48. Madrid: Fundación de Investigaciones Marxistas.

Olivera, Margarita, and Davide Villani. 2017. Potenciales impactos económicos en Argentina y Brasil del acuerdo de libre comercio entre el Mercosur y la Unión Europea. *Revista Ensayos de Economía* 50.

Prebisch, Raúl. 1950. *The Economic Development of Latin America and Its Principal Problems*. New York: United Nations Department of Social Affairs.

Rapetti, Martín. 2013. *The Real Exchange Rate and Economic Growth: Some Observations on the Possible Channels*. Working Paper 2013–11, Department of Economics, University of Massachusetts, Amherst.

Rodriguez, Francisco, and Dani Rodrik. 1999. *Trade Policy and Economic Growth: A Skeptic's Guide to Cross-National Evidence*. NBER Working Paper, 7081, National Bureau of Economic Research.

Rodrik, Dani. 1997. *Trade Policy and Economic Performance in Sub-Saharan Africa*. Paper Prepared for the Swedish Ministry for Foreign Affairs.

Rosenstein-Rodan, Paul. 1943. Problems of Industrialisation of Eastern and South-Eastern Europe. *The Economic Journal* 53 (210–211): 71–101.

Sargent, John, and Linda Matthews. 2008. China Versus Mexico in the Global EPZ Industry: Maquiladoras, FDI Quality, and Plant Mortality. *World Development* 37: 1069–1082.

Shafaeddin, Mehdi. 2011. *Trade Liberalization, Industrialization and Development: The Experience of Recent Decades*. TWN Trade & Development Series 40. Penang, Malaysia: Third World Network.

Singer, Hans. 1950. The Distribution of Gains Between Investing and Borrowing Countries. *American Economic Review* 40: 473–485.

Toye, John. 1993. *Dilemmas of Development: Reflections on the Counter-Revolution in Development Economics*. Oxford: Blackwell.

WTO. 2015. *Understanding the WTO*. 5th ed. Geneva: WTO Publications.

CHAPTER 8

Financing Development in the Financial Globalization: Revisiting Old Challenges in a New Context

Davide Villani and Nicolás Hernán Zeolla

Introduction

In the past years, the global economy witnessed a significant increase in financial markets complexity. This rise was reflected in the variety of financial assets, derivatives and hedge instruments, and growing international capital flows. These changes are often associated with the phenomenon of financialization. Many observers maintain that financialization contributed to short-termism of private investment, changed the wealth allocations, fueled debt-driven consumption of households, and determined a shift from banks to capital markets as the main source of financing investment and development of the public sector (Epstein 2005; Orhangazi 2008; Tori and Onaran 2017; Stockhammer 2012).

D. Villani (✉)
The Open University, Milton Keynes, UK
e-mail: davide.villani@open.ac.uk

N. H. Zeolla
Centre for Studies on Economics and Development/IDAES and CONICET, Buenos Aires, Argentina

V. R. Fernández, G. Brondino (eds.), *Development in Latin America*,
https://doi.org/10.1007/978-3-319-92183-9_8

The process of capital market development started in the mid-seventies after the end of the Bretton Woods regime (Eatwell and Taylor 2005). Before this period, international capital flows were strongly regulated and most of them were represented by foreign direct investment (FDI) and Official Development Assistance (ODA). These sources of capital were conceived as the most effective means to provide the needed amount of savings to end technical dependency from central economies. At the domestic level, interest rates control and credit allocation, together with the existence of development public banks, were common instruments to promote national development. In this context, Traditional Latin American Structuralism (LAS) approach emerged.

However, after the capital account deregulation process of the early seventies, the panorama changed considerably. Monetarism and neoliberalism spread worldwide. Latin American (LA) economies were not exempt from this process and promoted reforms more rapidly than other developing countries. According to the Chin & Ito Index of financial integration, from the seventies to the eighties, LA had lower capital controls than the largest Southern Asian economies such as South Korea and China.[1] One of the theoretical cornerstone of this reforms was the McKinnon-Shaw hypothesis. It holds that the elimination of government supervision on national interest rates and favoring the inflow of financial flows will promote growth (McKinnon 1973). However, contrarily to what was predicted by mainstream economic theory, the deregulation was not accompanied by economic development but greater financial instability, balance of payment, and public debt crises.

The aim of this chapter is to study how the growth of the financial sector influenced the literature on financing development in peripheral countries. Can the development of capital markets just be considered an "old game with new actors"? What is the qualitative difference between financing development through international institution or national developing banks and today's emerging economies bonds markets? And, in particular, how does the New Latin American Structuralist (NLAS) approach deal with the unexplored vulnerabilities that emerge from globalization? These are some of the questions that are addressed below.

The chapter is divided into three sections beside this introduction. In the next section, we analyze the LAS approach to financing development by differentiating between domestic and international aspects of financing development. We also briefly revise the determinants of development in some Asian countries, in order to establish the differences with LA experience. After this section we look at the role of international dimension instruments for promoting development in the post-Bretton Woods world and how these changes have been incorporated by NLAS thought. We revise the theoretical foundations that justified the use of foreign capital for development as well as the practical pros and cons of inflows of foreign capital. The section also focuses on the recent transformations of capital markets in the newly financialized world economy and the implications for public funding and firms' development strategies. Some final remarks concludes the chapter.

Traditional Structuralism View of Financing Development

Theoretical Aspects of Foreign Savings in LAS: FDI and International Aid

Finding a unified view of the role of foreign capital in LAS is not an easy task. Part of this difficulty lies in the fact that most structuralist authors treated the role of foreign capitals in relation to the structural conditions of peripheral economies as foreign currency net demanders, and rarely as an independent object of analysis.

To begin with, we need to have in mind the point of departure of structuralism thought and the condition of peripheral countries that determines the condition of dependency toward the center. Peripheral unbalanced productive structures are characterized by highly productive primary sectors able to compete internationally and by an industrial sector with lower productivity. The manufacturing sector is highly dependent on imported inputs of production which require a high amount of foreign currency but, on the other hand, is not able to generate it through exports since the output is sold in domestic markets. The high elasticity of imports in peripheral countries implies that in periods of economic growth imports grow at a faster pace than exports. This process will eventually erode the trade balance entering into a spiral of loss of foreign reserves, devaluation, and recession.

It is possible to divide our analysis between the international and domestic sphere.[2] The former sphere involves issues related to international capital flows, capital controls, FDI, and international grants, among others, while the latter is related to the supervision of the domestic interest rates, central banks operations, publicly owned banks for productive investment promotion, and domestic financial deepening. The two spheres of analysis have a close connection between them but, for the sake of clarity, it is worth distinguishing between them.

As to international aspects of analysis, LAS almost exclusively focused on FDI and international cooperation, in particular grants and loans. The main function of these instruments is to provide technical capabilities and additional savings, two factors that are strictly related. Dependency on central economies is considered to be principally technological and it is derived to the low level of domestic savings that impede genuine technological advances: "It is clear that if less developed countries would dispose of the required amount of savings needed to endorse their active population of the same capital intensity they could reach, [...] the same forms of production of central countries" (Prebisch 1973b, 9). Higher savings could contribute to the capital accumulation needed to transform the productive structure toward a less dependent one. In this context, FDI is useful to increase the level of savings to be channeled in the productive system.[3]

The inflow of FDI can contribute to providing the technical capabilities that are needed to fill the gap with developed countries, contributing to ameliorate the import coefficient of peripheral economies which would eventually reduce technical dependency (Prebisch 1969; Furtado 1970). Ultimately, structural change is the final goal of structuralist thinking.

However, FDI is not absent of drawbacks. First, some authors point out that FDI flows can be qualitatively different. FDI should be channeled in such a way that it could modify the causes at the origins of the external unbalances and should be focused on sectors that could potentially generate foreign currency, such as some manufactory and tourism, and could reduce import dependency. The peripheral state is expected to be involved in this decision and should be able to determine those sectors in which FDI is not desirable (Prebisch 1969).

Second, peripheral countries should be aware that with the increase in consumption, production becomes more sophisticated which makes increasingly more difficult to substitute imported inputs with locally produced ones. Therefore, they should be able to increase technological substitution at a faster pace as industrialization increase if the sustainability of the process should be maintained.

The third and final problem is profits remittances of foreign corporations. Profit remittances reduce the availability of foreign currency and the degrees of freedom of industrial policies available to peripheral countries (Prebisch 1969; Furtado 1970; Diamand 1973; Cardoso and Faletto 1979). To give an idea of the magnitude of the phenomenon, Furtado noted that American companies remitted 79% of their profits to the parent companies (Furtado 1970). Additional potential problems that can be associated with FDI are related to the influence that foreign companies may have on the decision-making process in peripheral countries. Most of structuralist authors were aware of this risk and maintained that foreign interests should not collide with national ones.

As previously mentioned, another possible channel to achieve the level of desired savings (and investment) is through financial aid or loans mostly provided through international cooperation and international institutions such as development banks. When referring to international cooperation, the main instrument considered by structuralism are loans that should be issued under favorable conditions in terms of interest rates and repayment conditions. As with FDI, these loans should be employed to promote structural change. Additional savings provided in this way would be ineffective if there is no corresponding shift toward an autonomous capitalization process (Prebisch 1963).

One of the benefits of these instruments (contrarily to FDI) is that, if they are of easy access and they exist in a broad amount, they are potentially not so dependent on cyclical downturns of the economy, providing an effective countercyclical instrument. Moreover, the activity of international institutions would also be able to consider possible shocks in domestic savings, so that the desired level of investments could be maintained independently of the domestic fluctuations of the saving rate.

As in the case of FDI, international aid is meant to cover only the difference between the desired levels of savings and the actual one in developing countries. International loans are not supposed to be a permanent instrument but should be employed only until the country has reached a level of economic development sufficient to generate autonomously the desired amount of savings (Prebisch 1973a, b, 23).

In spite of the benefits that could derive from this kind of instrument, also in this case there are political considerations related to the possibility of managing autonomously the process of development: "development would not be authentic, nor politically acceptable, if international cooperation contributed to perpetuating financial and technological dependency of Latin American countries" (Prebisch 1969). As mentioned above, development policy must aim toward the modification of the structural causes of dependency of peripheral countries. This approach is radically different from more recent view on development policies. As pointed out by Fisher (Fisher 2009), the structural problems of peripheral economies and "stop and go" dynamics are absent from contemporary international aid literature and policy. This change in view is also reflected in the development policies put forward by international organizations for development. The modification of the productive structure has disappeared from the operations of development organizations, underlying a change in the definition of development itself (Chang 2011).

In conclusion, it can be argued that for LAS FDI was considered an instrument to provide scarce means (savings and capital) that ideally would promote structural change. The degree of optimism toward foreign capitals varied among authors but there was a general agreement on the technical nature of the dependency. Regarding technological issues, in particular, foreign capital inflows, in the forms discussed above, posed some risks related to the incapacity for countries of moving out from the technological trap as well as political problems related to the autonomy in decision making. In this view, a genuine generation and access to technology would contribute to lower the import coefficient and contribute to reducing the duality of the productive structure. If these changes in the productive structure were realized, the biggest constraints to development would have been removed. This is not surprising in the light of the fact that Bretton Woods's system imposed limits to capital movements.

However, the collapse of Bretton Wood's regime made evident that the nature of dependency was not only technological but also financial (Vernengo 2005). The state was the main actor in charge of the development process and could directly lead the take-off process. Capital movements had to be kept under control, in order to avoid capital flights. FDI, international credits, and ODA had to be functional to national development and could be limited if it contrasted national interests.

National Development Banks and Interest Rates Supervisions

If we look at what we identified as domestic policies, we should mention the autonomy of monetary policy and the control of the domestic banking system, two key policies to promote financing of development within LAS thinking. During the second post-war, the international monetary system was ruled by Bretton Woods agreement. The three main pillars of the agreement were a fixed exchange rate of the dollar toward gold, controls of financial flows, and reserve accumulation/decumulation as the normal source to face current account surpluses and deficits (McKinnon 1993). In this context, capital controls had an important role in contrasting the full arbitrage between domestic and international financial markets.

This aspect was linked to the fact that, despite the limitation of allocation of domestic credit mentioned in the previous section, the government had a relative capacity to administrate the domestic financial system. Most countries could regulate the asset allocation of commercial private banks, allowing for a certain degree of control of the credit system. Following this idea, many countries created public national development banks to fuel structural change

> The state intervened actively providing fiscal incentives to new industries and in financing productive activities through state development banks such as BNDES in Brazil, CORFO in Chile, IFI in Colombia and NAFINSA in Mexico, and the establishment of directed credit to strategic sector. (Ocampo and Ros 2011, 7)

This mechanism was possible thanks to the conception of domestic savings that was in force at the time. Most of LAS authors considered that domestic savings were a surplus generated by national workers and firms and the financial system was only a tool to assign them (following market criteria) into most useful usages through the monitoring of the public sector.

In the more regulated financial systems, private banks were considered lenders on behalf of the national central bank. During regular operations, commercial banks made profits with the differential between active (borrower) and passive (depositor) interest rate. This implied that private banks should manage their balance sheets to fulfill the allocation credit priorities established by the public policy. Central banks operations also involved managing exchange rate that was realized in order to control inflationary pressures and shifts in income distribution (Furtado 1970, 98–99).

Some central banks were forged considering the peculiarities of peripheral countries, as in the case of Argentina under the direction of Raul Prebisch (1935–1943). The "stop and go" dynamics described in the previous section implied that during periods of growth the country would receive increasing flows of foreign capitals and increase the circulation of currency and imports. This situation would reverse during the downturn of the cycle implying convertibility problems. For this reason, it was important to set several anti-cyclical measures to contrast this tendency. Among these measures, we can find rediscount operations and sterilization to manage the supply of money (Samber 2012). Beside the orthodox flavor of some aspect of Prebisch thought, the set of measures put in place during this period could not be considered conventional

> Prebisch wanted to centralize several activities in the bank, including the management of the exchange control system, which allowed it to administer the exchange rate, to buy and sell bonds, and regulate import controls, and far reaching regulatory powers, in order not just to control inflation, but also manage the cycle. (Pérez Caldentey and Vernengo 2012, 12)

The anti-cyclical mechanism is clear in the words of Prebisch when cash increase during the expanding phase,

> [the central bank] should collect this cash to sterilize it, so that it could not be employed for the expansion of credit and, afterwards, when the situation reverses, give it back in order to avoid a contraction. (Prebisch 1991, 91; authors' translation)

What emerges is a continuity between the directioning of foreign capital (such as FDI, discussed above) and "domestically generated" funds. In both cases, the state had an active role in guiding the use of loans proceeding from domestic and foreign sources. In this sense, it is significant to note that Brazil's and Uruguay's central banks were governmental agencies until 1964 and 1967 (Torija Zane 2015, 155).

State and Foreign Capital Development Success: The Exceptional Case of Korea and Other East Asian Countries

The second post-war period was characterized by import substitution industrialization (ISI) policies. Meanwhile, other regions were beginning a process of take-off. Before moving to the evolution of the financial system, it is worth considering briefly the experience of some Asian countries, such as South Korea (Korea hereafter), that substantially managed to break their condition of peripheral countries.

Even though the discussion of the modalities of appropriation and implementation of new technologies is not the scope of this chapter, it is worth mentioning that, at least in principle, developing countries could fill the technological gap by appropriating foreign technology at a faster pace than that was needed in developing countries (Pasinetti 1981). Broadly speaking, this process of learning and appropriation of technology is the path followed by some developing countries in their early stages of development, opposed to the process of invention and innovation followed by European countries in their early phase of industrialization (Amsden 1987, 1989).

It would be inaccurate to state that all Asian countries followed the same pattern of development. The degree of public intervention was heterogeneous both qualitatively and quantitatively. However, many scholars maintain that, contrarily to mainstream beliefs, the state had a primary role in leading the development process (White and Wade 1988; Wade 1990; Yu 1997, among others), without pursuing the orthodox policy of productive specialization based on comparative advantages: "no developing [East Asian] country, apart from Hong Kong, followed comparative advantage at the outset of industrialization" (Riedel 1988, 6). To our purpose, Korea's process of development is relevant because of the role played by foreign capitals. Like the Plan Marshall, Korea received massive foreign aid, mainly from the United States. Foreign aid accounted for 15% of GNP between 1953 and 1958 (Amsden 1989). This amount exceeds by far what has been historically received by LA, but it is comparable to what is received nowadays by some least developed countries. However, one striking difference in the nature of international aid addressed to Korea and other more recent experiences of international aid is that in the case of Korea the flow of funds contributed to putting the basis for the industrial development and structural change of the subsequent years. Apart from the quantitative relevance of aid, Korea also accounted with technical assistance that helped to promote research centers (such as the Korean Institute of Science and Technology) and in some cases was backed American public procurement as in the case of the Vietnam war which contributed to boosting the military complex (Glassman 2011).

Moreover, economic policies were not based on the application of orthodox market practices. Investment was financed through concessional loans that were granted both through domestic and international sources. Korean commercial banks were nationalized by the Park's government and even after the liberalization of the eighties the government kept a tight control over the credit system (Amsden 1987). This regulation and control over the credit system contributed to the allocation of funds in strategic sectors (Rhee et al. 1984).[4]

In the early stage of industrialization, Korean manufactories were highly dependent on foreign inputs, similarly to LA countries. In order to facilitate foreign trade, intermediate inputs for the production of exports good had a zero-trade tariff. However, these benefits were limited to the number of imported inputs needed to produce a determined amount exports in order to prevent them to benefit from the domestic market (Rhee et al. 1984). Companies were pushed to achieve a certain amount of exports through a system of targets that were officially set by the government.

Moreover, during its industrialization process, capital flows were largely restricted. Inflows of foreign capitals were subject to a strict regulation that subordinated foreign action to government approval and quantitative limits to the purchase of foreign currency (Chang et al. 2001). This implied that the inflow of foreign investment was strictly regulated, sectoral allocation of funds and remittances profits were monitored. Until the economic reforms of the eighties, FDI was encouraged in those sectors devoted to exports but discouraged in those strategic sectors decided by the government (Kim and Hwang 2000). Although important, the amount of FDI received by South Korea was not exceptional if compared to other Asian experiences (Amsden 1989). The government maintained the ownership of different key industries, in line with the proposal of some structuralist authors. Outflows of capital and acquisition of foreign currency were also subject to strict controls (Chang et al. 1998) as well as remittances of money. The infringement of these norms could be prosecuted with years of imprisonment and a maximum sentence of death (Amsden 1989).

We do not have to forget the geopolitical circumstances that helped some of these processes to take place (see Chaps. 5 and 6). However, what is important to highlight here is the active role played by the state in these development processes and, in particular, the public control of the credit system and the allocation of productive investment. Korea's strategy of development was based on a combination of strong public control and intervention in the economy and a favorable international situation that backed external projection of the economy and provided concessional loans that were employed to implement a strong industrial strategy and contributed to the acquisition of technology. Foreign capitals had an important role but the state maintained large autonomy in the determination of economic policies (Castells 1992). From this review, it is necessary to ask how the new international economic architecture, and in particular with regard to the financial aspect, alters the possibility of intervention of the national state. Most experiences of the "Asian tigers" were at odds with recent vision and policies for external assistance promoted by international institutions whose policies do not aim at affecting the productive structure (Chang 2011).

Neo-Structuralism and the New Approach for Financing Development

Recent Transformation in the World Economy: The Rise of Finance

After analyzing the role of international capitals considered by LAS, we study the transformations in the world economy and how these were tackled by the NLAS. The NLAS approach emerges in the late eighties as an updated version of traditional LAS. The label NLAS indicates a link between the new perspective with the previous Economic Commission for Latin America and the Caribbean (ECLAC) tradition.[5]

As in the previous section, we will consider the distinction between the international and the domestic sphere of analysis. First, we will analyze how the recent transformations of the international capital markets impact on NLAS understanding of the benefits and risk on financing development. Second, we will analyze the NLAS approach to financing development in the domestic sphere.

Since the seventies, and with more strength at the beginning of the twenty-first century, the global economy witnessed a process of strong growth of international capital markets. This phenomenon is often associated with a more general process known as "financialization". Even if there is no unique definition, financialization can be defined as a process of growing importance of actors, institutions, motivations, and financial markets in shaping the general economic functioning (Epstein 2005).

This process was accompanied by substantial changes in the international monetary order and productive organization that, originating in the United States, created the conditions to expand the influence of the financial sector (Kindleberger 1973; Eatwell and Taylor 2005). Some of these transformations of the world economy are related with the emergence Global Value Chains (for a debate on GVC and development, see Chap. 7), capital account deregulations, and the growth of managed investment portfolio and money managers capitalism (Minsky 1990; Milberg 2008). Consequently, financial wealth expanded extraordinarily.

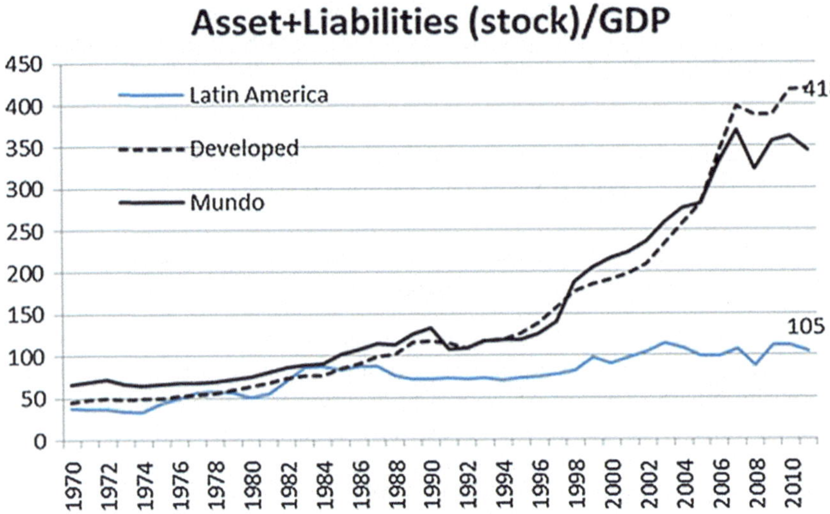

Fig. 8.1 Stock of financial wealth in the world economy. 1970–2010. Source: Authors' own elaboration based on Lane and Milesi-Ferreti (2007). Note: Latin America, 8 main economies, Argentina, Brazil, Chile, Mexico, Colombia, Peru, Venezuela, Uruguay. Developed: United States, United Kingdom, Germany, France, and Japan

As it is observed in Fig. 8.1, according to Lane and Milesi-Ferreti's (2007) dataset on external wealth, the world financial wealth, measured as the asset plus liabilities, has recorded a significant growth. As long as the financial wealth was 70% of gross domestic product (GDP) during the seventies, in the middle of nineties it increased to 130% and in the end of the two thousand's it records over 400% of GDP.

Similarly, there have been changes in the composition of the international flows with a significant growth of financial flows. As can be observed in Fig. 8.2, in the seventies the gross capital flows were 0.4% of the world GDP. After the beginning of the capital account deregulation, gross capital flows to GDP increased to 4% in the middle of the eighties. Gross capital flows rose to 9.7% of world GDP in the early of the two thousand, recording a maximum of 11% of world GDP in the years previous the world financial crises.

Figures 8.1 and 8.2 also show that the process of the growth of finance has not been homogeneous between countries. The financialization of international capital markets was predominantly led by central economies.

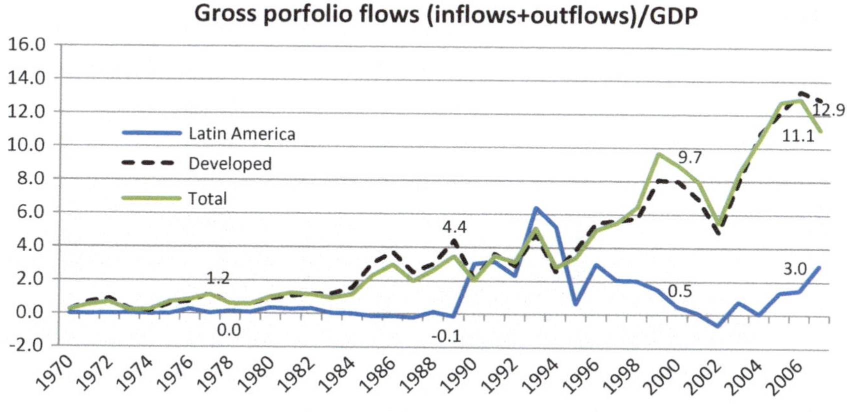

Fig. 8.2 Gross capital flows in the world economy. 1970–2007. Source: Authors' own elaboration based on Broner et al. (2013). Note: Latin America, 8 main economies, Argentina, Brazil, Chile, Mexico, Colombia, Peru, Venezuela, Uruguay. Developed: United States, United Kingdom, Germany, France, and Japan. Inflows are the net purchases of domestic assets by non-residents; Outflows are net purchases of foreign assets by domestic agents

In the case of financial wealth, the total accumulation in central economies is up to 60 times larger than peripheral economies. In the case of gross capital flows, the growth differential is three times larger in central economies compared to peripheral economies.

Because of this transformation, there was a surge of international flows of international. The process was accompanied by a deep redefinition of the institutional setting and peripheral countries were asked to deregulate the capital account and domestic financial markets. From the seventies, financialization of the world economy produced at least three large transformations in in LA. The first was the expansion of capital market-based loans for firms and countries. The second one is the reduction in instruments such as grants for development, also because of the shift that took place in the international ODA architecture. The third aspect is related to changes in the characteristics of FDI flows in the region. These aspects contributed to generating new vulnerabilities that were not present before.

As we mentioned, one of the major transformations related to financing development in LA is the substitution by non-financial corporations of bank-based liabilities to capital market bonds issuance. This process is led by large multinational corporations that actively participate in capital markets opera-

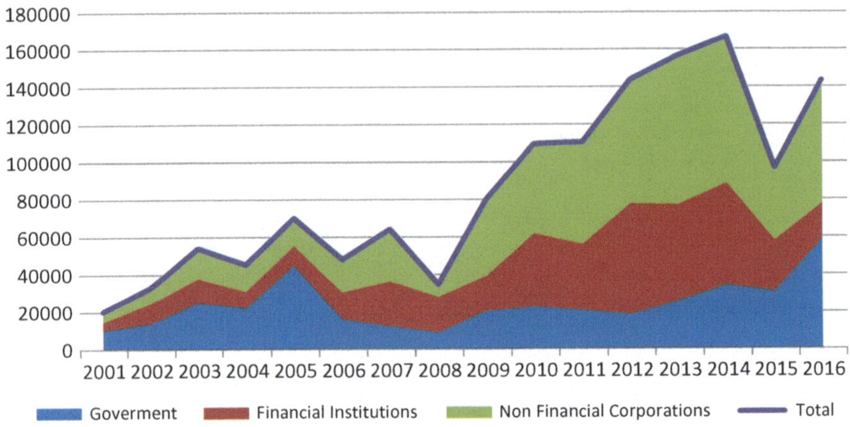

Fig. 8.3 Bond issuances in Latin American economies. 2001–2016. Source: Authors' own elaboration based on BIS debt statistics

tions. According to the Bank of International Settlements (BIS) statistics, total bond issuances of LA economies grew 600% between 2002 and 2016. This growth was very heterogeneous and it was mainly driven by non-financial corporations. To have an idea of the magnitude, Fig. 8.3 shows that, while in 2002 the issuances from Non-Financial Corporations (NFC) were 27% of total issuances, in 2017 they represented more than 47%.

This produced a large transformation in the modalities through which firms finance their operations. One of the main characteristics is the growth of offshore corporate bonds issuance, instead of domestic and international credit (Tarashev et al. 2016a, b). However, this shift was not directly traduced into productive investment. According to Rodrigues Bastos et al. (2015), the main destination for new bond issuances of NFC wasn't a productive investment surge but a strech in liabilities maturity profile and balance sheet cash-holdings and others short term liquid assets.

Capital Market Deregulation in Mainstream Economics and Their Link with the New Latin American Structuralism

Between the end of the seventies and the middle of the eighties, most of the LA countries removed state supervision on the national financial system, facilitating capital movements of large investment banks, eliminating exchange market and other capital market regulations (Taylor and Vos 2002).

For mainstream scholars, the new financial market exuberance implies the growth of a variety of financing windows for developing economies that will boost FDI and growth. As a pre-condition to taking advantage of this situation, underdeveloped economies would need to fit their institutional framework to the new monetary rules with a more deregulated capital account. From a general theoretical ground, the idea that larger financial market would promote development is deeply rooted in mainstream economics and the standard "loanable funds" theory. On the one hand, consumers would be able to smooth their budget constraints by borrowing from each other. On the other hand, firms would not be limited to self-finance out of past profits and expand their investment portfolio (Obstfeld et al. 1996).

It is possible to distinguish between direct and indirect benefits of financial deregulation. As to the former, the main channel is known as the relaxation of the "financial repression", originated in the strong interest rate supervision in a heavy state-related financial system (McKinnon 1973; Shaw 1973). Also in this case, the mechanism is based on the supply side drivers for growth and it is very schematic. Low interest rates discourage savings and, therefore, reduce resources to carry out investment, undermining growth and development.[6]

From mainstream approach indirect benefits from capital market deregulation can be divided between micro and macro benefits. At the micro level, capital markets growth is meant to help coordinating agents such as stockholders and managers. In a context of asymmetry of information, market demand to maximize the stock market price tied to larger dividends distribution produces a more efficient management into the firms by pursuing higher efficiency and lower costs (Ross 1973; Baker et al. 1988). At the macro level, it is believed that a deeper financial integration would lead to a more efficient international capital market allocation, by easing credit issuance and taking advantage of investment opportunities (Prasad et al. 2007). Larger and more liquid financial markets imply a greater variety of instruments through which it is possible to diversify idiosyncratic risk, smoothen family consumption cycles, and soften economic shocks (Summers 2000). Moreover, the mainstream approach also considers that capital markets could act as a persuasive tool to prevent "populist policies". This idea consists in the "dissuasive effects of globalization" for which international capital markets penalize (through higher interest rates) those governments that implement policies that are not in line with "healthy macroeconomic policies" (balanced public budget, low inflation, capital account deregulation, independent central bank, etc.) (Fischer 1998). Following this reasoning, domestic and international financial deregulations are directly associated with higher national growth. Consequently, policy recommendations aim at deregulating capital markets to prevent public deficit and achieve development more rapidly.

Despite this theoretical elaboration, there is little empirical evidence that supports both direct and indirect channels, even within mainstream literature. In the case of the direct channel, Rodrik (1998) maintains that none of the financial integration indexes is relevant in explaining growth. In the case of indirect channels, the debate is focused on the "thresholds" of institutional qualities from which the financial deregulation generates larger benefits than disadvantages (Kose et al. 2011). The evidence of indirect benefits from international financial integration is not robust to country and time length sample (Magud et al. 2011). For this reason, some authors support the idea that capital markets' deregulation generates larger disturbances than long-term benefits (Schmukler 2004).

NLAS view on deregulation of domestic financial markets and capital account is not straightforward. Even though there is a wide acceptance of the main foundation of mainstream economics, the main difference between NLAS and mainstream economics lies in the relevance of the "market failure" to understand LA economies, derived from structural heterogeneity of underdeveloped countries.

NLAS foundations emerged in the late eighties when Gert Rosenthal took over ECLAC's general secretary with Fernando Fajnzylber as its main economist. For LA, the eighties have been labeled as the "lost decade" because of the poor economic performance that was accompanied by public debt crises, hyperinflation, and null per capita GDP growth. In the view of Rosenthal and Fajnzylber, this was in part due to the failure of ISI policies. This puzzle in development was referred to as "the black box" of development. The main conclusion was that when compared with some Asian and European experiences LA countries were characterized by an "empty cell" which was connected to the poor export performance of manufacturing (Fajnzylber 1990, 18).

From this critical assessment to traditional LAS, the new ECLAC generation of economists was labeled NLAS (see Chap. 2). NLAS thought derives from Fajnzylber contributions and, although with different emphasis, take on board different mainstream aspects. These aspects will be clearer in the next section, where we will analyze in detail the approach of NLAS for financial markets distinguishing between international and domestic spheres of analysis.

"Boost" and "Booms" of Foreign Capital Flows and Development: The Role of Real Exchange Rate

As LAS, NLAS considers foreign saving as an additional driver to promote development. As in the traditional view, not all types of flows have the same impact nor are beneficial for the economy. For instance, portfolio and other short-term capital flows are considered a disruptive feature of financial integration. This aspect leads NLAS to move away from the adoption of the "financial repression" thesis and (in some cases) support capital controls in order to moderate the consequences of the financial cycle after the last international crises. However, as we will see below, other supply-oriented policies trace a continuity with mainstream approaches.

In the case of the exchange rate, some of NLAS authors advocate for the existence of a unique, stable, high, and competitive real exchange rate (RER) to encourage competitiveness for non-traditional exports, especially in the industrial natural resource-based industries or other industrial branches that would promote higher economic growth (Bresser-Pereira 2009; Frenkel and Rapetti 2008).

In this view, the achievement of this target exchange rate level is considered one of the most effective mechanisms for development. Although there is no agreement on the theoretical foundations that links higher exchange rate and development, it is suggested that a higher (more competitive) exchange rate would encourage exports diversification and promote structural change in a simultaneous double way. The first reason is that high exchange rates act as a barrier for imports of more dynamic foreign competitors and, at the same time, promote higher exports. A competitive exchange rate guarantees an export-led strategy providing foreign currency needed to avoid a balance of payment crisis. Following Bresser-Pereira:

> an overvalued exchange rate prevents modern and efficient enterprises in a developing country from having access to the international market ... In this case we have an export-led growth strategy supported by the country's ability to rely on a reasonable number of enterprises using the most modern technology, and by the government's ability to keep the exchange rate 'competitive' or at the 'industrial equilibrium' level—which is defined as the exchange rate that favors enterprises using worldwide state-of-the-art technology. (Bresser-Pereira 2012, 351)

The same position is shared by Roberto Frenkel. In the view of Frenkel and Rapetti (Frenkel and Rapetti 2008, 2014), there is a productivity gap between tradable activities in developing and developed economies, as the first ones are less profitable under market (over-valuated) RER, a higher exchange rate will improve profitability and growth. For this reason, "rapid capital accumulation requires a sufficiently competitive high RER to compensate for the market failures caused by the increasing returns" (Frenkel and Rapetti 2014, 85).

Second, RER plays also an active role as a stabilizer of the financially driven balance of payment crises. In fact, the high-RER development strategy theory is subsequent of the financial stability and short-term capital inflows. For NLAS, the main benefit from having an over-depreciated RER is to avoid the pro-cyclical tendency of private and public consumption. RER appreciation reduces domestic prices, raises real wages, downsizes domestic risk and boosts financial wealth. This increase in financial wealth expands both public and private sectors by easing domestic and international credit, under a misperception that this transitory new income is permanent but creating unsustainable long-term asset positions. The upswing in consumption may be reinforced by promoting short-term capital inflows to finance the trade balance deficit. The crisis spurs when it is impossible to satisfy the demand of foreign currency; interest rate and the domestic risk rises, currency devaluates and private balance sheet deteriorates, investment falls, triggering a crisis (Frenkel 1983; Neftci 1998).

In this reasoning there is implicit assumption of the existence of a GDP natural growth rate. In LA, the exchange rate overvaluations generate a pro-cyclical tendency in public and private consumption besides the maximum capacity of the economies. This over-expenditure manifest itself in the balance of payment deficit or in higher imports over exports. The maintenance of a competitive RER would prevent the economy to have "boom-bust financial cycle" dynamics while it would promote exports-led growth and development.

In the case of financial integration, NLAS authors are very pessimistic about the benefits of capital account deregulation on development. As LAS, NLAS accepts the existence of an "original sin", that is, the inability for peripheral countries to issue debt on its own currency. This implies that, in order to finance the balance of payments deficit, developing countries have to promote international capital flows, including foreign debt. But, contrarily to LAS center-periphery asymmetrical relationship, in the NLAS approach, the origin of this weakness is related to "market failure" rather than a permanent characteristic of the world economy that determines the status of dependency. This lack of theory behind the asymmetry of international traces a connection between NLAS and mainstream theory.

The market failure that gives birth to the LA "original sin" is based on a misperception of risks due to the incompleteness of information in both international and domestic capital markets that could trigger balance sheet crises. As Ocampo stresses:

> domestic financial markets in the developing world are significantly more 'incomplete' than those in the industrial world, and thus that some financial intermediation must necessarily be conducted through international markets. As a result, developing countries are plagued by variable mixes of currency and maturity mismatches in the balance sheets of their economic agents. This also implies that integration into international financial markets is an integration between unequal partners. (Ocampo 2003, 68)

For this reason, NLAS considers that full capital account deregulation is an undesirable macroeconomic policy for development because it promotes short-term financial flows that can be very disruptive. Hence, in order to avoid the desirable effects of short-term capital flows the NLAS designated a series of policies under the label of capital flow management measures (CFM). These policies include both capital account controls and macroprudential policy regulations such as official reserve accumulation, limitations to currency denominated debt for residents, taxes and non-remunerated mandatory reserve for short-term capital flows, among other measures (Ocampo et al. 2008; Ocampo 2010).[7]. This position is based on some wide accepted empirical evidence that considers that capitals controls are ineffective to manage the volume of capital flows (level) but very efficient to modify their composition (from short term-financial to commercial-productive flows) (Ostry et al. 2010).

Another main difference between NLAS and LAS is related to the degree of public intervention of the of capital outflows. NLAS supports capital controls for administrate inflows, but rejects capital regulation on outflows during the capital bust phase (quantitative restrictions in the money market to buy currency for non-productive ends, utility remittances, imports, etc. are not desirable). As Ocampo (2012) stresses: "finally, and perhaps most importantly, regulations are a complement to sound macroeconomic policies, not a substitute for them" (Ocampo 2012, 16–17).

According to this aspect, CFM measures are understood as a "leaning against the wind" type of policy, mainly collaborating in generating larger space for monetary policy:

> capital account regulations potentially have a dual role: as a macroeconomic policy tool, which provides some room for countercyclical monetary policies that smooth out spending and avoid excessive debt ratios, and as a 'liability policy' (...) will provide some room to 'lean against the wind' during periods of financial euphoria, through the adoption of a contractionary monetary policy and/or reduced appreciation pressures.

Finally, for the NLAS approach a low financial integration may also contribute to promoting productive investment and structural change. This is ought to, first, the volatile nature or financial flows, and, second, the short-termism that governs capital markets and financial business. Both effects could reinforce each other affecting capital formation and employment.

> Financial market overly dominated by agents specializing in the short term rather than in long-term productive investment. Consequently, only a small share of capital inflows financed productive investment, a shortcoming aggravated by the financial and currency crises that increased their volatility, and whose recessive effects have weighed down on capital formation by local companies and employment. (Ffrench-Davis 2010, 20)

Financing Development from Financial Domestic Markets: The "Inclusive Finance" Approach

As mentioned at the beginning of this chapter, given the highly regulated Bretton Woods monetary order, traditional LAS devoted little attention to the disruptive effects of international financial flows on peripheral countries for development and growth. Contrarily, NLAS puts much interest into the study of the vulnerabilities created by the international financial system. As mentioned in the previous section, there is a broad literature on financial flows as a cause of balance of payment crises and on the role of macroprudential policy and capital controls.

LA countries have a lower degree of development of their financial system and capital markets compared to other developing regions. According to the World Bank, in 2016, the ratio credit/GDP for LA was 49%. For the same year, the world's credit to GDP was 131.4% while for Asia and the Pacific was 143%. Even among LA countries there is a high heterogeneity. The credit to GDP ratio was 62% for Brazil and 14% for Argentina. The same is true for national capital markets development. According to the World Bank, in 2016, Brazil, Colombia, México, and Peru have a capital market to GDP ratio between 37 and 44%, while Argentina, Costa Rica and Ecuador this ratio is below 10%.

Another structural characteristic of LA economies is that domestic financial flows are very volatile. This could explain the fact that recessions are deeper and more persistent compared to other regions. As long as credit contraction during recessions in advanced economies is on average around 60% from the peak of the credit cycle, credit contractions in emerging market economies are on average around 120% and include the transition from positive to negative growth rates, which imply nominal credit cuts (Claessens et al. 2010). As the recession deepens, the larger risk aversion of domestic banks cuts credit supply and makes it more difficult to counteract the downside phase of the cycle. Consequently, the contraction lasts longer (Pérez Caldentey and Titelman 2014).

Along with traditional LAS, NLAS also accept that peripheral economies have a low level of international currency hierarchy, with periods of large and persistent capital outflows and, (deepened by the commodity specialization) are more frequently exposed to larger terms of trade swings (Ocampo 2013).

In the view of NLAS, shadow banking and the higher volatility of capital flows contributed the belief that a more developed financial system was needed in order to reduce the constraints for development. Both NLAS and mainstream economics consider that financial markets are a significant tool to smooth the impact of exogenous economic cycle shocks on firms and households (Allen and Gale 1997). The more inclusive and developed the financial system is, the more efficient a country is to smooth and reduce the undesirable effects recession.

However, contrarily to the mainstream, NLAS considers that structural heterogeneity is a factor that makes LA a special case within conventional theory. Therefore, this establishes a tension in NLAS theory between domestic financial deepening and international financial capital markets integration.

In order to deepen the domestic financial system, the NLAS subscribes to the "inclusive finance" view. This approach is defined as the facilitation of access to financial services for those companies that do not have access (or only a limited access) to formal financial systems.[8] Financial access of effective policy evaluation focuses on three spheres: *access*, *usage*, and *quality*. *Access* refers to the supply availability, the existence of the financial service, or financial instrument and usage to the coverage and uses of financial services. In between the two spheres, there is *quality*, a characteristic related to accuracy between the financial service supply and users need (Ferraz and Ramos 2017).

A key component of this strategy is technology and innovation in the financial sector. From the firms' perspective, it is maintained that the main constraints are due to the excess of formal requirements and guarantees such as investment plans, tax and balance sheet statement, time delay for approval, or the lack of knowledge of special financing programs. As to the banking sector, it is believed that the difficulties to expand credit services are related to geographic factors such as distance from enterprises to bank offices, the informality of the accounting statements of the firms, and the lack of credit records to monitor firm's payment capacity, among others. As a result, technology innovations would help to diminish adverse selection in the financial system. As the financing development program of ECLAC stresses, "financial innovation can serve as a catalyst for financial inclusion of households and businesses through greater densification of the financial system" (ECLAC 2017).

Even though both households and large firms are a target for financial services expansion policy, the "financial inclusion approach" is mainly conceived as a productive policy, especially aiming at financial inclusion of small and medium enterprises (SME). SME have a high demand for financial products and services that account for their specificities. These policies would favor also family-based and micro-entrepreneurship projects that contrarily to large firms have limited access to the credit system.

In theoretical terms, note that the main policy recommendation from the inclusive finance perspective is supply-side oriented. It is conceived that technological improvements could help to improve firms' access to financial resources as a tool to boost investment by relaxing the firm's budget constraint. For NLAS approach, capital market incompleteness imposes a large constraint to improvements in productivity and growth (Neira Burneo 2016). According to the World Bank, empirical evidence for LAC shows that only around 45% of small enterprises have access to credit from official financial institutions, while this percentage is 67.8% for larger enterprises. This aspect implies that the access to official funding for bigger enterprises is 1.5 times easier than for smaller firms. This asymmetry could be even larger if other financial sources, like stock and bond issuances channels were considered. For NLAS, the origin of this difference is due to incompleteness of information and higher monitoring costs for smaller enterprises that often have incomplete formal tax statements and do not meet other formal requirements (ECLAC 2017).

Having these aspects in mind, we can now comment some differences between new and traditional structuralism approach on domestic financing development. The most important difference lies in the deepening of state intervention and guidance of financial supply. Excluding some exceptions,[9] many NLAS authors consider that there is no need for a direct state intervention on bank asset allocation or a strong monetary authority mandate to assign credit as it was maintained by traditional LAS. Moreover, NLAS rarely mentions a public owned bank (or the public control on credit) as a desirable tool for development. On the contrary, the excess of state participation in the domestic financial system competes with the private sector for the domestic savings usage.

Regarding debt securities, they are dominated by public sector bonds, while the corporate bonds are not common instruments to finance investment in most countries. For this reason, private bonds markets are less developed in relative terms and less illiquid (Vera and Titelman Kardonsky 2013, 8). These elements are in line with the supply-side orientation of the approach. Moreover, even when NLAS mentions the role of public banks in inclusive finance promotion, these banks should be guided by a profit market criterion as any other private bank, even though public banks count with a number of benefits such as an agiler economic policy execution and a long-term perspective of operations (Ferraz and Ramos 2017).

Multilateral Development Banks and Official Development Assistance Under Financialization

As mentioned in the second section of this chapter, LAS considered ODA from international development banks as a potential source of political inference. Many of the successful development processes (Europe in the aftermath of the Second World War, South Korea or Israel, as some examples) accounted with a large amount of ODA. LAS conceived ODA as a very desirable source of foreign savings since it can help to promote

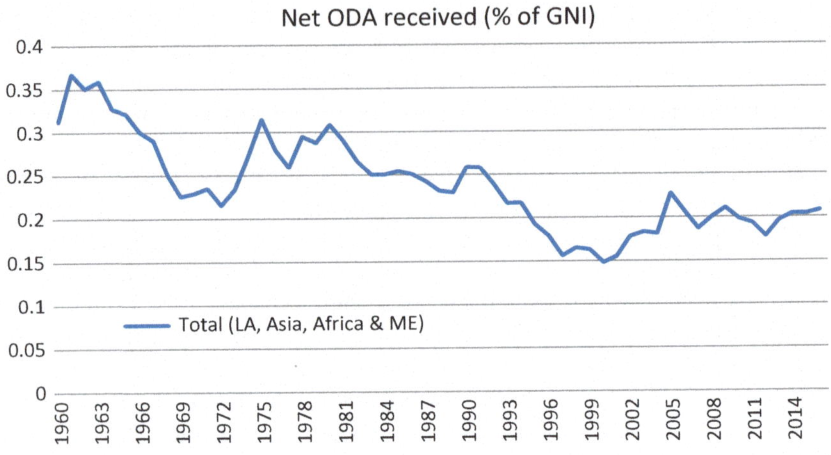

Fig. 8.4 World net Official Development Assistance received as % of GNI by Region. Source: Authors' own elaboration based on OECD data

domestic credit and because they are foreign currency nominated, relaxing the balance of payment constraint.

In recent years, ODA continued the diminishing trend registered since its peak in the sixties. As we can see in Fig. 8.4, according to the Organisation for Economic Co-operation and Development (OECD) (2018) the world ODA in terms of gross national income (GNI) was 0.3% in the sixties, 0.26% in the seventies, and 0.25% in the eighties. From this moment, the diminishing tendency is even more evident. During the nineties, it was 0.20%, and since the two thousand it stabilized around 0.19%.

The distribution of ODA between regions has not been homogeneous. As we can see in Fig. 8.5, during the sixties Asia was the most beneficiated region with ODA as a percentage of GNI, followed by Africa and the Middle East (AME), and finally, LA. During these years stands out the Korean case that received 6.13% of GNI of ODA. From the seventies, the most beneficiated region was AME followed by Asia and then LAC. During this decade, the ODA to Korea reduced significantly from 3% of GNI in the seventies to 0.2% of GNI in 1979, while the ODA to Israel increases from 0.9% of GNI in 1970 to 5.7% in 1979. For the next decades, AME remains at the top of ODA significance in GNI. In the case of LA, none of the top six richest economies ever received more than 3% of GNI of ODA.

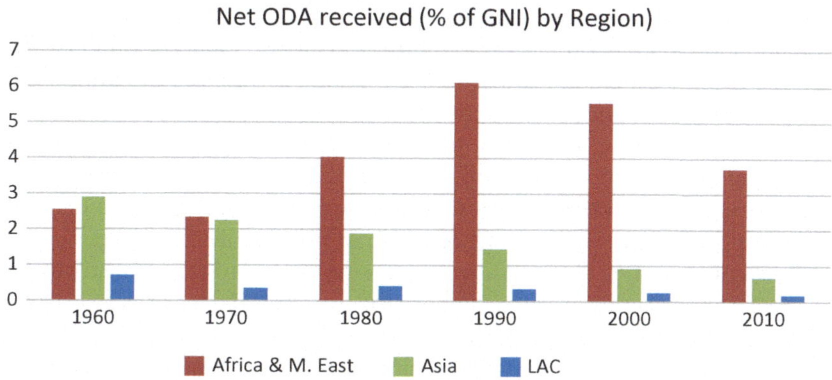

Fig. 8.5 World net Official Development Assistance received as % of GNI by Region. Source: Authors' own elaboration based on OECD data

If apart from ODA flows we consider also other financing sources for development, one of the most important institutions for development financing in LA is the Corporacion Andina de Fomento (CAF). The CAF is a development bank that was founded in 1968 by six countries (Bolivia, Chile, Colombia, Ecuador, Peru, and Venezuela) and has subsequently included most of LA countries and Spain. The CAF has the capacity of raising funds in the capital markets at more favorable conditions than the single countries would be able to do. This allows the institution to lend money to member countries at more favorable interest rates. Moreover, the CAF accounts with several aspects that make it more attractive, such as quicker decisions and less binding activities compared to other international development banks. In the last years, the role of development banks has increased in magnitude and counts with relevant experiences promoted by peripheral economies. To have an idea of the increasing importance of this regional bank consider that, in the decade between 1995 and 2005, the loans emitted together by the Inter-American Development Bank (IABD) and the World Bank were lower compared to those of the CAF alone (Titelman 2006).[10] In 2006 half of the loans approved were destined to infrastructure and 22% of this amount to regional integration infrastructure (Griffith-Jones et al. 2008, 7).[11] Non-tradable sectors have a strong role in increasing the productivity of the economy as a whole. However, it is clear the limited financial effort that is directly allocated to structural change.

In relation to this aspect, the literature often ignores the fact that the modalities of realization of infrastructural projects not irrelevant. In the extreme case in which an infrastructure is realized with a high component of imported goods and services, the outcome of the project may be of difficult evaluation. The loan, contracted in foreign currency, may affect its repayment capacity in case the infrastructure has not an appreciable impact on imports and exports elasticities in the short run. Therefore, the benefits of the improvement in infrastructure may potentially be offset by the external constraint.[12] This consideration is important to remark the importance of the direction of investment policies and the need to consider productive heterogeneity, as remarked by LAS.

With the decreasing flows of ODA, financialization of the world economy has largely contributed in providing supply in capital markets, especially for large corporations (see Fig. 8.3). This generated a number of new vulnerabilities and challenges in the international sphere of financing development. Access to private capital markets funding imposes a multiplicity of requirements and conditionalities, mostly associated with short-term profitability criteria. These requirements can undermine the capacity of developing a structural approach to financing and reliable financial resources for development (ECLAC 2015, 7). Private financial flows, however, tend to be more volatile and asymmetric than ODA flows. This aspect is associated with a marked pro-cyclical tendency in capital flows: they increase during booms and stop during recessions. Contrarily, ODA and developing banks financing could have an important anti-cyclical role (Griffith-Jones and Cozzi 2016). As Cavallo et al. (2016) show, based on a dataset for 24 advanced and 121 developing (27 of them from LA) for the period 1970–2013, countries with "large and persistent current account deficit" (more than 4% GDP in current account deficit for 10 years) experiment abrupt crises, with GDP loss, large devaluation and slowdown in investment, except those who obtained substantial amounts of official aid and grants.

In conclusion, despite some encouraging signals the total amount of funding for development is still insufficient to meet the needs, especially in regions like LA. Moreover, it is not uniquely a matter of the amount of funding. Ideally, development institutions could have an important role in promoting structural change considering the role of external constraints. As we argued, changes in the development agenda (at the national and international level) modified the modalities of intervention of these institutions, taking distance from a development strategy aimed at the modification of the productive structure as advocated by traditional LAS.

Concluding Remarks

This chapter is an explorative attempt to account for the recent transformation of international capital markets and the sources for financing development in LA economies.

We showed how traditional LAS analyzed the role of foreign capital in relation to the strategy of structural change that was needed in order to break the relation of technological dependence and ultimately achieve development, emphasizing the pros and cons of FDI and other foreign flows of capital. The relationship between the peripheral state and foreign capital was not necessarily harmonious. In this context, the public sector had a strong role in regulating and shaping the development process. Public intervention involved the creation of state-owned development banks, the establishment of capital controls to short-term capitals, and the supervision over domestic interest rates to promote to facilitate productive credit.

The fall of the Bretton Woods system brought to the reconsideration of the domestic market industrialization strategies in favor of liberalization policies of capital flows as means to finance economic growth. In LA, in particular, financialization of the world economy can be characterized by two aspects. The first one is the increase in magnitude and volatility of financial flows (both banking and capital markets). The second one is the expansion of the capital market-based instruments to finance firms. On the other hand, ODA decreased its importance in the region. These aspects contributed to making both firms and governments more dependent on capital markets as a source of foreign currency supply in order to face the always present balance of payment constraint.

From a political economy perspective, markets cannot be considered neutral instruments. Development policies should aim at modifying the productive structure which could imply picking the recipients of intervention policies, the redistribution of natural resources' extraordinary rents, and heavy state intervention (and regulation) of key industries. This set of policies cannot be implemented through international markets alone, because of the "short-termism" that governs shareholder value strategy or because of the political interest linked to the current *status quo*.

In the case of the transformation of the financial system and ECLAC economic though, there are some points to stress. NLAS includes a number of aspects and differentiates itself from the mainstream, in particular with regard to the relevance of market failures and specificities of peripheral economies. By supporting the "inclusive finance approach" NLAS supports the idea that peripheral economies need financial markets growth to promote development. However, this process does not lack of potential risks. It is recognised that financial deepening and international financial capital markets integration is not a win-win game. Contrarily to the mainstream, NLAS is concerned about exchange rate regime, overvaluations, discourages short-term capital inflows and balance sheet crises. On the other hand, similarly to the mainstream, NLAS advocates for a deepening in capital markets with the objective of relaxing financial constraints and enables to smooth cyclical fluctuations in consumption, in order to boost investment and growth.

Lastly, an additional element emerges when comparing NLAS with traditional LAS. While for the latter center-periphery is conceived as a political asymmetrical relationship, in the NLAS approach the origin of this debility is fundamentally related to market failures rather than to a permanent characteristic of the world economy that determines the status of dependency. In spite of the fact that both NLAS and traditional LAS are aware of the risks associated with short-term capital inflows (and on the need of capital controls), NLAS embraces the "healthy macroeconomics fundamentals first" view over other monetary autonomy policy. As a result, NLAS seems to have a less radical critique to the new international capital reconfiguration, as advocated by a considerable part of the financialization literature.

Notes

1. From 1970 to 1984 Brazil, Chile, Argentina, Venezuela, Peru and Uruguay (in average) were more financially open (1970 = 0.34/1984 = 0.10 in KOPEN index) than China (1984 = 0.16 in KOPEN index) or South Korea (1970 = 0.16/1984 = 0.16 in KOPEN index). Higher values of the index mean more financially open.
2. This distinction that we are using is closely related with that of Chenery and Bruno (1962), Chenert and Strout (1966), and McKinnon (1964), among others. It also has a long tradition in LAS growth and balance of payment constraint modeling. See Diamand and Crovetto (1988).
3. Note that for many structuralists thinkers the causality runs from savings to investment, in line with the orthodox view of validation of Say's law. Within this view, foreign capital is in charge to fill the gap between required investment and the saving rate domestically available. Some authors, like Prebisch, point out that if the saving gap cannot be filled with foreign sav-

ings, the private sector would satisfy its demand for additional savings recurring to bank credit. Hence, banks have the capacity to create credit endogenously. However, newly created bank credit would have inflationary movements since the additional demand that it caused would not be matched by a sufficiently rapid expansion of supply (Prebisch 1973a).

4. Also in Taiwan virtually the entirety of the credit system was publicly owned (Wade 1988).
5. According to Bielschowsky (1998) and the official ECLAC perspective, the main links between the old LAS and the NLAS approach is methodological. But some relevant disagreements as the rejection for state direct production of goods and services, the absence of class struggle in the inequality and the absence of recognition of political conflict in the international relationship made the methodological approach the main difference and not the main link. See Telechea and Zeolla (2014).
6. This is also strongly related to the deep neoclassical Solow "convergence theory" on development. Consider a world of free capital markets, if capitals move internationally chasing profit differentials, the inverse relation between physical capital stocks and their returns (interest rates) implies that for less capitalized economies free capital movements would determine the inflow to investment from high capitalized economies. The foreign savings inflows will boost investment and the country will grow at a faster pace than developed countries. In the long run this process will produce a convergence in the income per capita between the two countries.
7. "There is overwhelming evidence that capital flows to developing countries are pro-cyclical and have become one of the major determinants (and perhaps the major determinant) of business cycles in emerging economies" (Ocampo 2012, 13).
8. The "Financial inclusion" ECLAC program is devote to study the best financial inclusion instrument for development. It has start with a series of workin paper document about national level which include in Argentina, Brazil, Colombia, Costa Rica, Ecuador, Mexico and Peru, and thereafter, built a regional perspective, that will be forthcoming document.
9. "Economic development should be financed essentially with domestic savings. In order to achieve this goal, the creation of public financial institutions to ensure full utilization of domestic resources, in particular labor, finance innovation and support investment is required" (Sao Paolo School of Economics 2010, 2). "Secondly, and depending of the planning scale in financial leverage subject, it is important to know if it would be decided to go forward to the institutionalization of an organization (new or existent) or it would look forward to increase the efforts of deepening and coordina-

tion between different state agencies and organization that today act as development banks" (Woyecheszen 2017; [authors translation]).

10. From a broader perspective, Culpeper et al. (2016) show that both commitments and disbursements of loans from development banks increased considerably during the global downturn of the economy, mostly due to the public sector.
11. Even though the increase in the resources reflects a general trend, they seem still far from satisfying regional needs. Bhattacharya et al. (2012) estimate that the global investment required in infrastructure is the double of that currently available. Among the actual expenditure in infrastructure only a small minority can be imputed to international aid and development banks, which denotes the reduced role of these institution on a global-scale perspective.
12. Broadly speaking, this path reflects the experience followed by the European Investment Bank (EIB). One of the main focus of the EIB was infrastructure and it contributed to reduce the gap between European countries. In spite of the strong reduction in the infrastructural gap between countries, the difference in terms of structural productive differences is still great which was evidenced during the recent crisis.

References

Allen, F., and D. Gale. 1997. Financial Markets, Intermediaries, and Intertemporal Smoothing. *Journal of Political Economy* 105 (*3*): 523–546.

Amsden, Alice H. 1987. The Paradigm of Late Industrialisation. *Political Economy. Studies in the Surplus Approach* 3 (2): 133–159.

———. 1989. *Asia's Next Giant*. New York: Oxford University Press.

Baker, G.P., M.C. Jensen, and K.J. Murphy. 1988. Compensation and Incentives: Practice vs. Theory. *The Journal of Finance 43* (*3*): 593–616.

Bhattacharya, Amar, Mattia Romani, and Nicholas Stern. 2012. *Infrastructure for Development: Meeting the Challenge*. Centre for Climate Change Economics and Policy Grantham Research Institute on Climate Change and the Environment Policy Paper.

Bielschowsky, R. 1998. *Cincuenta años del pensamiento de la CEPAL: textos seleccionados*. Santiago: Fondo de Cultura Económica/CEPAL. Vol. I, introducción.

Bresser-Pereira, L.C. 2009. From Old to New Developmentalism in Latin America. In *The Handbook of Latin America Economics*, ed. J.A. Ocampo and J. Ros. Oxford, UK: Oxford University Press.

———. 2012. Structuralist Macroeconomics and the New Developmentalism. *Revista de Economia Política* 32 (3): 347–366.

Broner, F., T. Didier, A. Erce, and S.L. Schmukler. 2013. Gross Capital Flows: Dynamics and Crises. *Journal of Monetary Economics* 60 (1): 113–133.

Cardoso, Fernando H., and Enzo Faletto. 1979. *Dependency and Development in Latin America*. Berkeley: University of California Press.

Castells, Manuel. 1992. Four Asian Tigers with a Dragon Head: A Comparative Analysis of the State, Economy and Society in the Asian Pacific Rim. In *State and Society in the Pacific Rim*, ed. Richard Appelbaum and Jeff Henderson. London: Sage Publications.

Cavallo, E., B. Eichengreen, and U. Panizza. 2016. Can Countries Rely on Foreign Saving for Investment and Economic Development? *Review of World Economics* 51: 1–30.

Chang, Ha Joon. 2011. Hamlet Without the Prince of Denmark: How Development Has Disappeared from Today's 'Development' Discourse. In *Towards New Developmentalism: Market as Means Rather Than Master*, ed. Shahrukh Rafi Kahn and Jens Christiansen. Oxon: Routledge.

Chang, H.-J., H.-J. Park, and C.G. Yoo. 2001. Interpreting the Korean Crisis: Financial Liberalization, Industrial. Policy and Corporate Governance. In *Financial Liberalization and the Asian Crisis*, ed. H.-J. Chang, G. Palma, and D.H. Whittake. Basingstoke: Palgrave Macmillan.

Chang, Ha Joon, Hong Jae Park, and Chul Gyue Yoo. 1998. Interpreting the Korean Crisis: Financial Liberalisation, Industrial Policy and Corporate Governance. *Cambridge Journal of Economics* 22 (6): 735–746.

Chenert, H.B., and C. Strout. 1966. Foreign Assistance and Economic Development. *American Economic Review* 56: 679–733.

Chenery, H.C., and M. Bruno. 1962. Development Alternatives in an Open Economy: The Case of Israel. *Economic Journal* 72: 79–103.

Claessens, S., M.A. Kose, and M. Terrones. 2010. *Business and Financial Cycles in Emerging Markets*. IMF Working Paper.

Culpeper, Roy, Stephany Griffith-Jones, and Daniel Titelman. 2016. Multilateral Development Banks. In *Global Governance and Development*, ed. Jose A. Ocampo. Oxford: Oxford University Press.

Diamand, Marcelo. 1973. *Doctrinas Economicas, Desarrollo E Independencia*. Buenos Aires: Paidos.

Diamand, M., and N. Crovetto. 1988. *La estructura productiva desequilibrada y la dobre brecha*. Buenos Aires: Instituto Torcuato Di Tella Centro de Investigaciones Económicas.

Eatwell, J., and L. Taylor. 2005. *Finanzas globales en riesgo. Un análisis a favor de la regulación internacional*. Buenos Aires, Argentina: Siglo xxi.

ECLAC. 2015. *Financing for Development in Latin America and the Caribbean: A Strategic Analysis from a Middle-Income Country Perspective*. Santiago, Chile: United Nations, ECLAC.

———. 2017. *Inclusion Financiera PyMES*, Noviembre 8. https://www.cepal.org/es/inclusion-financiera-pymes/antecedentes.

Epstein, G. 2005. *Financialization and the World Economy*. Northampton, MA: Edward Elgar Publishing.

Fajnzylber, F. 1990. *Industrialización en América Latina: de la 'caja negra' al 'casillero vacío': Comparación de patrones contemporáneos de industrialización.* Cuadernos de la CEPAL, no. 60, Santiago de Chile.

Ferraz, J.C., and L. Ramos. 2017. *Promovendo inclusão financeira através práticas inovadoras de bancos de desenvolvimento para apoiar a desenvolvimento social e produtivo e a mudança estrutural com ênfase especial nas empresas de menor porte da América Latina*. Rio de Janeiro: CEPAL, Divisão de Desenvolvimento Econômico.

Fischer, Stanley. 1998. Capital Account Liberalization and the Role of the IMF. *Should the IMF Pursue Capital-Account Convertibility?* (No. 207). International Economics Section, Department of Economics Princeton University, 1–10.

Fisher, Andrew M. 2009. Putting Aid in Its Place: Insights from Early Structuralists on Aid and Balance of Payments and Lessons for Contemporary Aid Debates. *Journal of International Development* 21: 856–867.

Frenkel, R. 1983. Mercado financiero, expectativas cambiarias y movimientos de capital. *El trimestre económico* 50: 2041–2076.

Ffrench-Davis, R. 2010. Macroeconomics for Development: From "Financierism" to "Productivism". *Cepal Review* 2010 (102): 7–26.

Frenkel, R., and M. Rapetti. 2008. Five Years of Competitive and Stable Real Exchange Rate in Argentina, 2002–2007. *International Review of Applied Economics* 22 (2): 215–226.

———. 2014. *The Real Exchange Rate as a Target of Macroeconomic Policy.* Rethinking Development Strategies after the Financial Crisis – Volume I: Making the Case for Policy Space.

Furtado, Celso. 1970. *Economic Development of Latin America*. Cambridge: Cambridge University Press.

Glassman, Jim. 2011. The Geo-Political Economy of Global Production Networks. *Geography Compass* 5 (4): 154–164.

Griffith-Jones, S., and G. Cozzi. 2016. The Roles of Development Banks. In Efficiency, Finance, and Varieties of Industrial Policy, ed. Noman A and Stiglitz J. E. New York: Columbia University Press.

Griffith-Jones, Stephany, David Griffith-Jones, and Dagmar Hertova. 2008. Enhancing the Role of Regional Development Banks. *G24 Discussion Paper Series* 50.

Kim, June-Dong, and Sang-In Hwang. 2000. The Role of Foreign Direct Investment in Korean Economic Development: Productivity Effects and Implications for the Currency Crisis. In *The Role of Foreign Direct Investment in East Asian Economic Development*, ed. Takatoshi Ito and Anne O. Krueger. Chicago: University of Chicago Press.

Kindleberger, C.P. 1973. *The Formation of Financial Centers: A Study in Comparative Economic History*. Massachusetts, MA: MIT Press.

Kose, M.A., E.S. Prasad, and A.D. Taylor. 2011. Thresholds in the Process of International Financial Integration. *Journal of International Money and Finance* 30 (1): 147–179.

Lane, P.R., and G.M. Milesi-Ferretti. 2007. The External Wealth of Nations Mark II: Revised and Extended Estimates of Foreign Assets and Liabilities, 1970–2004. *Journal of International Economics* 73 (2): 223–250.

Magud, N.E., C.M. Reinhart, and K.S. Rogoff. 2011. *Capital Controls: Myth and Reality – A Portfolio Balance Approach*. National Bureau of Economic Research (No. w16805). Cambridge, MA: National Bureau of Economic Research.

McKinnon, R.I. 1964. Foreign Exchange Constraints in Economic Development and Efficient Aid Allocation. *The Economic Journal* 74 (294): 388–409.

———. 1973. *Money and Capital in Economic Development*. Washington, DC: Brookings Institution Press.

———. 1993. The Rules of the Game: International Money in Historical Perspective. *Journal of Economic Literature* 31: 1–44.

Milberg, W. 2008. Shifting Sources and Uses of Profits: Sustaining US Financialization with Global Value Chains. *Economy and Society* 37 (3): 420–451.

Minsky, H.P. 1990. Money Manager Capitalism, Fiscal Independence and International Monetary Reconstruction. *The Future of the Global Economic and Monetary System*, 209–218. Budapest: Institute for World Economics of the Hungarian Academy of Sciences.

Neftci, S.N. 1998. *FX Short Positions, Balance Sheets and Financial Turbulence: An Interpretation of the Asian Financial Crisis*. SCEPA Working Papers 1998–18, Schwartz Center for Economic Policy Analysis (SCEPA), The New School.

Neira Burneo, S. 2016. *Inclusión financiera de las pymes en el Ecuador*. Santiago: CEPAL, Oficina de Financiamiento para el Desarrollo.

Obstfeld, M., K.S. Rogoff, and S. Wren-lewis. 1996. *Foundations of International Macroeconomics*. Cambridge, MA: MIT Press.

Ocampo, J.A. 2003. Capital Account and Countercyclical Prudential Regulations in Developing Countries. In *From Capital Surges to Drought*, ed. R.F.-D.-J. En, 217–244. London: Palgrave Macmillan.

———. 2010. Time for Global Capital Account Regulations. *Economic and Political Weekly* 45: 32–35.

———. 2012. The Case for and Experience with Capital Account Regulations. In *Capital Account Regulations for Stability and Development: A New Approach*, ed. K. Gallagher, S. Griffith-Jones, and J.A. Ocampo.

———. 2013. *Balance of Payments Dominance: Its Implications for Macroeconomic Policy*. Initiative for Policy Dialogue Working Paper Series. New York: Columbia University.

Ocampo, J.A., and J. Ros. 2011. *The Oxford Handbook of Latin American Economics*. Oxford: Oxford University Press.

Ocampo, J.A., S. Spiegel, and J.E. Stiglitz. 2008. Capital Market Liberalization and Development. In *Capital Market Liberalization and Development*, comp. J.A. Ocampo and J.E. Stiglitz, 1–48. Nueva York, EEUU: Oxford University Press on Demand.

Orhangazi, Ozgur. 2008. Financialisation and Capital Accumulation in the Non-Financial Corporate Sector: A Theoretical and Empirical Investigation on the US Economy: 1973–2003. *Cambridge Journal of Economics* 32: 863–886.

Ostry, M.J.D., M.S. Qureshi, M.K.F. Habermeier, D.B. Reinhardt, M.M. Chamon, and M.A.R. Ghosh. 2010. *Capital Inflows: The Role of Controls*. Washington, DC: International Monetary Fund.

Pasinetti, Luigi L. 1981. *Structural Change and Economic Growth: A Theoretical Essay on the Dynamics of the Wealth of Nations*. Cambridge: Cambridge University Press.

Pérez Caldentey, E., and D. Titelman. 2014. Macroeconomics for Development in Latin America and the Caribbean. *International Journal of Political Economy* 43 (1): 65–91.

Pérez Caldentey, Esteban, and Matias Vernengo. 2012. *Heterodox Central Bankers: Eccles, Prebisch and Financial Reform in 1930s*. University of Utah Department of Economics, Working Paper No: 2012–04.

Prasad, E.S., R.G. Rajan, and A. Subramanian. 2007. *Foreign Capital and Economic Growth*. Cambridge, MA: National Bureau of Economic Research (WP 13619).

Prebisch, Raul. 1963. *Hacia Una Dinamica Del Desarrollo Latinoamericano*. Mexico City: Fondo de Cultura Economica.

———. 1969. *La Inversion Privada Extranjera En Desarrollo Latinoamericano*. Washington, DC: Unión Panamericana.

———. 1973a. *La Cooperacion Internacional En La Politica de Desarrollo Latinoamericana*. Santiago de Chile: ECLAC.

———. 1973b. *Problemas Teoricos Del Desarrollo*. ECLAC.

———. 1991. *Raul Prebisch. Obras 1919 – 1948. Vol. II*. Buenos Aires: Fundacion Raul Prebisch.

Rhee, Young Whee, Bruce Ross-Larson, and Garry Pursell. 1984. *Korea's Competitive Edge: Managing the Entry into World Markets*. Baltimore: Johns Hopkins University Press.

Riedel, James. 1988. Economic Development in East Asia: Doing What Comes Naturally? In *Achieving Industrialization in East Asia*, ed. Helen Hughes. Cambridge: Columbia University Press.

Rodrigues Bastos, F., H. Kamil, and B. Sutton. 2015. *Corporate Financing Trends and Balance Sheet Risks in Latin America (n. 10/15)*. Washington, DC: International Monetary Fund.

Rodrik, D. 1998. Who Needs Capital-Account Convertibility? *Essays in International Finance* 207: 55–65.

Ross, S.A. 1973. The Economic Theory of Agency: The Principal's Problem. *The American Economic Review* 63 (2): 134–139.

Samber, Florencia. 2012. El Papel de Raúl Prebisch En La Creación Del Banco Central de La República Argentina. *Estudios Criticos Del Desarrollo* 2 (3): 133–157.

Sao Paolo School of Economics. 2010. *Ten Theses on New Developmentalism*. Sao Paolo: Getulio Vargas Foundation. Available at http://blogs.bu.edu/cban/files/2012/12/brazil-final-proofs_oct-20n-2012.pdf.

Shaw, E. 1973. *Financial Deepening in Economic Development*. New York: Oxford University Press.

Stockhammer, E. 2012. Financialization, Income Distribution and the Crisis. *Investigación económica (Investigación económica)* 71: 39–70.

Summers, Lawrence H. 2000. International Financial Crises: Causes, Prevention, and Cures. *American Economic Review* 90 (2): 1–16.

Tarashev, N., S. Avdjiev, and B. Cohen. 2016a. *International Capital Flows and Financial Vulnerabilities in Emerging Market Economies: Analysis and Data Gaps*. Note Submitted to the G20 International Financial Architecture Working Group, August, BIS.

———. 2016b. *International Capital Flows and Financial Vulnerabilities in Emerging Market Economies: Analysis and Data Gaps*. Note Submitted to the G20 International Financial Architecture Working Group, BIS.

Taylor, L., and R. Vos. 2002. *Balance of Payments Liberalization in Latin America: Effects on Growth, Distribution and Poverty. Economic Liberalization, Distribution and Poverty: Latin America in the 1990s*. Cheltenham, UK; Northampton, MA: Edward Elgar Pub.

Telechea, J.M., and N. Zeolla. 2014. *El pensamiento económico latinoamericano del desarrollo y la industrialización: estructuralistas y neoestructuralistas ¿giro o actualización?* Revista del CCC, Nro. 21. Available at http://www.centrocultural.coop/revista/21/el-pensamiento-economico-latinoamericano-del-desarrollo-y-la-industrializacion.

Titelman, Daniel. 2006. Subregional Financial Cooperation: The Experiences of Latin America and the Caribbean. In *Regional Financial Cooperation*, ed. Jose A. Ocampo. Baltimore, MD: Brookings Institution Press.

Tori, D., and Ö. Onaran. 2017. *The Effects of Financialisation and Financial Development on Investment: Evidence from Firm-Level Data in Europe (No. 16089)*. Greenwich, UK: University of Greenwich, Greenwich Political Economy Research Centre.

Torija Zane, Edgardo. 2015. Bancos Centrales 'periféricos': El Caso de América Latina. In *Estructura Productiva Y Política Macroeconómica*, ed. Alicia Bárcena, Antonio Prado, and Martín Abeles. Santiago de Chile: ECLAC.

Vera, C., and D. Titelman Kardonsky. 2013. *El sistema financiero en América Latina y el Caribe: una caracterización*. Series de proyecto: financiamiento desarrollo. Santiago, Chile: Comision Económica para América Latina (CEPAL).

Vernengo, M. 2005. Technology, Finance, and Dependency: Latin American Radical Political Economy in Retrospect. *Review of Radical Political Economics* 38 (4): 551–568.

Wade, Robert. 1988. The Role of Government in Overcoming Market Failure: Taiwan, Republic of Korea and Japan. In *Achieving Industrialization in East Asia*, ed. Helen Hughes. Cambridge: Cambridge University Press.

———. 1990. *Governing the Market: Economic Theory and the Role of Government in East Asia Industrialization*. Princeton: Princeton University Press.

White, Gordon, and Robert Wade. 1988. Developmental States and Markets in East Asia: An Introduction. In *Developmental States in East Asia*, ed. Gordon White. Basingstoke: Palgrave Macmillan.

Woyecheszen, S. 2017. *Inclusión financiera de la pequeña y mediana empresa en Argentina*. Series de proyecto: financiamiento del desarrollo. Santiago, Chile: Comisión Económica para América Latina y el Caribe (CEPAL).

Yu, Tony F. 1997. Entrepreneurial State: The Role of Government in the Economic Development of the Asian Newly Industrialising Economies. *Development Policy Review* 15: 47–64.

CHAPTER 9

The Structuralism of Prebisch and the Integration of Latin America

Armando Di Filippo

The Meaning of Industrialization and Regional Integration for Structuralist Thinkers

The historical events studied and experienced by Latin American structuralist thinkers have been and continue to be the ontological source from which the epistemological framework that gives its identity to Latin American Structuralism has emerged until today.

The structuralist view of history is, above all, global in the sense of planetary. It is also systemic, first addressing the capitalist system as a referential axis, and then becoming multidimensional as it revalues the political and cultural aspects of the social systems involved. It dynamically examines social structures starting with the technological change that has induced the transformation of contemporary societies since the British Industrial Revolution.

The introductory chapter, written by Prebisch, of the Economic Survey for Latin America of 1949 (which was considered the Latin American manifesto that supported the later development of structuralist thought), begins with these three paragraphs:

A. Di Filippo (✉)
Alberto Hurtado University, Santiago, Chile

V. R. Fernández, G. Brondino (eds.), *Development in Latin America*,
https://doi.org/10.1007/978-3-319-92183-9_9

> The spread of technical progress from the countries where it had its source to the rest of the world has, from the point of view of each generation, been relatively slow and irregular. During the long period which elapsed between the industrial revolution and the First World War, the new methods of production in which technique has constantly found its expression have reached only a small proportion of the world's population.
>
> The movement began in the United Kingdom, continued in varying degrees of intensity in Europe, received an extraordinary impulse in the United States and finally reached Japan, which strove rapidly to assimilate Western methods of production. Thus the great industrial centers of the world grew up, while the vast and heterogeneous peripheral areas of the new system shared only to a slight extent in the improvement of productivity.
>
> In these peripheral areas, technical progress only affected small sectors of the vast population as it usually only penetrated where it was needed to produce foodstuffs and raw materials at low cost for deliver to the great industrial centres. (UN ECLAC 1951, 3)

It was in this historical framework that Latin American Structuralism, in examining the capitalism of the centers, proposed the objective of industrialization, not as a mere growth of the manufacturing branch but as an authentic expression of productive power based on its scientific-technical sources. Societies that managed to assimilate and expand this productive power achieved the conditions to reach processes of integral national development. The recent examples of East Asia (EA) and especially China are the strongest historical evidence of this assertion (see Chaps. 6 and 7).

It could be suggested, nevertheless, that despite the enormous proliferation of recent economic literature on this subject, some aspects have been underestimated that may be worth highlighting. From a historical and structural point of view, two important long-term differences have characterized the industrial development of EA, as opposed to the historical experience of Latin America: First, the scarcity of exploitable natural resources together with the high population density led the EA nations to a type of industrialization based on the import of primary products and the export of manufactured goods; and, second, the secular existence of solidly pre-established civilizations (in terms of languages, and of ethical and religious values such as Confucianism, Taoism, or Buddhism) gave these societies a strong national identity in spite of the successive invasions and colonization exerted by Western invaders during different periods of the modern era. These specific historical conditions in the EA countries (including China) that have remained beyond the capitalist or socialist character of the industrial development processes granted them a social discipline, facilitated by their ancient cultural structures.

On the other hand, the Latin American historical reality was radically different: First, the formation of Latin American Societies implied the collapse of pre-Columbian cultures, the internment of African slaves, and the irreversible super-imposition of Western culture (Iberian languages, Catholic values, and, since the nineteenth century, the impact of Anglo Saxon modernity) that led to peripheral forms of republicanism and democracy. Second, enormous wealth of exploitable natural resources with low population density subject to servitude and slavery during four centuries of Western colonialism led to a foreign trade based on the export of primary products and the import of manufactured goods. The process of industrialization by import substitution in Latin America is a historical derivation of the previous primary export position of this region in the international economic order under conditions very different from those of Asia-Pacific. Additionally, the process of political independence implied the fragmentation into multiple small and medium nations by the Spanish American colonies lacking, in many cases, sufficient scale to undertake a comprehensive and relatively autonomous industrialization.

A third essential political difference is that, in the "Asian tigers" from the seventies of the twentieth century, their strong states relied on authoritarian governments that autonomously promoted the industrial productive power oriented to compete in world markets, while in Latin America, military coups that interrupted their fragile democracies were generally at the service of oligarchies contrary to the industrialist ideology and favoring the export of primary products. To avoid voluntarist approaches, it must be remembered that the room of maneuver of states is, in part, a long-term historical product of specific, not only economic but also cultural and political circumstances. These long-term economic, cultural, and political differences cannot be neglected in order to fully understand the industrial development of Latin America compared with the EA experience.

It should be underlined that from its origins linked to the values of the United Nations, the industrial development process promoted by Latin American Structuralism included the strong defense of democracy and human rights, rejecting coercive forms of promotion of industrial development.

In this respect, Prebisch wrote in the sixties:

> It would be a tragedy if in order to free man from want we had to sacrifice other values and subject him to the demands of an arbitrary power. The very idea is fundamentally incompatible with the genius of the Latin American peoples, with their latent urge to shake off the trammels of poverty in order to liberate the human personality and give full rein, by means of economic development, to democracy and human rights, especially as regards the underprivileged half of the population of Latin America. (Prebisch 1963, 20)

The ideal of Latin American unity was not reduced in Prebisch to the economic sphere. In the same cited text, he also observed:

> The creative aptitude of Latin America cannot be exercised fully in the microcosm of national life. It also requires a large space for scientific activity, to overcome our technological inferiority and take advantage of talents that are now wasted. If there are privileged brains that tend to go beyond narrow confines, offer them the wide soil of all Latin America.
>
> The cultural space is also very fragmented, despite common roots that are deep. There is not enough communication. The spirit of each man of letters, of each artist of merit, can be better projected in a Latin American context and acquire more vigor and fruitfulness in a process of reciprocal stimulation of creative aptitude. (Prebisch 1970, 244; translated directly from the original)

In short, not only Prebisch but all the pioneers of the structuralist approach, applying their historical-structural perspective, considered the common economic, political, and cultural traits that unite Latin American countries from the moment of conquest and colonization. In this sense, they have issued a nationalist message. This form of *Latin American nationalism* that transcends the borders of each Latin American nation could be called "Latin Americanism". From this perspective, the study of each nation refers only to a component of that totality that we call Latin America. The effort to convert these fragments into a unified whole can be called Latin American integration.

The Sixties: Latin American Regional Integration

Already from the "Economic development of Latin America and its principal problems" explicit connections with an integrationist strategy were left:

> no systematic study of productivity and its relation to the optimum size of the establishment and the industry has yet been made in these countries. Depressive examples are quoted, however, of the sub-division of industry into an excessive number of inefficient undertakings within one country or of the multiplication of comparatively small enterprises in countries which, by combining their markets for a number of products, could reach a higher degree of productivity. The present division of markets, with its consequent inefficiency, constitutes another limitation of industrial growth, in this case one which could be overcome by the combined efforts of countries which, by reason of their geographical position and economic features, would be able to undertake it to their general advantage. (Prebisch 1962, 18)

The idea of reciprocal advantages is associated with what Prebisch (1963) called the principle of reciprocity:

> The effectiveness of the [industrial complementarity] agreements and of the whole [integration] regime... depends on the application of the principle of reciprocity. The interpretation of this principle, enshrined in the Montevideo Treaty, must be crystal clear. No member country can expect to derive from the Area more benefits than it offers. But the Treaty does not stipulate what measures will have to be adopted to correct a persistent inequality of benefits in its application. (Prebisch 1963, 97)

In terms of reciprocal trade among member states, this issue refers to countries that, given their productive weaknesses, suffer from structural deficits in their trade with other partners with greater productive and market powers. The principle of reciprocity expresses, ultimately, a principle of solidarity, that if necessary, it is imposed on the forces of the market. It means helping chronically weaker and deficit countries through special treatments. Thus, Prebisch continues:

> A clear definition of the principle of reciprocity will help to dispel the misgivings entertained in some circles regarding complementarity agreements. It will not always be possible to work out absolutely equal levels of trade benefits in every agreement or set of agreements. Hence equality will have to be sought through the medium of other activities. If this had to be done in every instance, the conclusion of complementarity agreements might become lengthy and complicated, when it should be precisely the opposite. Herein lies the significance of the following principle: each member country should be given an assurance that if the agreements and the reduction or abolition of duties do not provide equality of benefits, other measures will

> be taken to achieve it. This must be a binding obligation on all the countries concerned, and particularly those which regularly export more then they import. (Prebisch 1963, 98)

The issue of regional integration was not deepened in the "manifesto" of 1949, but very soon there was a languishing of industrial growth due to a lack of sufficient domestic demand (smallness and fragmentation of national markets) and "external asphyxia" caused by trade deficits that limited the capacity to import the materials required by the industrialist project. A fundamental option to overcome this trend was the promotion of Latin American integration to expand markets and generate economies of scale that favored the industrialization under the technology of those times. More than a hundred years before, similar integrationist strategies had been proposed by Alexander Hamilton, Henry Carey, and Friedrich List for North America and Germany, leading to the formation of two new nation-states that became powerful industrial nations.

In 1958, Raul Prebisch took up this central issue and began institutional efforts to move toward a common market. This obviously Latin-Americanist initiative openly confronted with the Pan-Americanism originated in the strategies of the United States toward Latin America. The project to create a common market despite having been proposed as a long-term objective immediately won the opposition of the General Agreement on Trade and Tariffs (GATT) and the International Monetary Fund (IMF) that advocated unrestricted multilateralism. Nor did the Frondizi government, at the time president of Argentina, supported the idea since its interest was in obtaining the technical and financial contribution of large oil transnationals to sustain its "developmentalist" project on a national scale. Even so, after long negotiations, the project was accepted in its "lightest" version and was born with the name of the Latin American Free Trade Association (LAFTA). This agreement had to adapt to GATT regulations, which as a rule prohibited these preferential treaties and accepted them only under certain conditions. Take this brief reminder to highlight the institutional power struggles that always underlie any integrationist project in Latin America.

LAFTA and the Central American Common Market, aimed at reducing reciprocal tariffs and maintaining protection against third-party competitors, constituted the first major post-war effort in favor of Latin American integration. However, already in the sixties, protectionism, combined with integrating mechanisms, began to be used for their own benefit by transnational corporations (TCs), which were already installed within the main economies of Latin America. TCs also benefited from the protection of external trade barriers and the preferences that had been established in LAFTA. The TCs were becoming, even in the manufacturing branches, the personification of the power of the hegemonic centers over the Latin American productive apparatus. The "official" position of Comisión Económica para América Latina y El Caribe (CEPAL) on TCs was ambivalent, because on the one hand the TCs were carriers of productive capital and technical progress, but on the other hand they made a closed appropriation of productivity gains, repatriating profits and accentuating the asymmetries of the productive structures without contributing to reciprocal regional trade. In addition, the presence of TCs presented a bias aimed at repatriating the productivity gains thus obtained. In this way, one of the main sources of capital accumulation was beginning to be outside the control of the national economic authorities.

The Emergence of Dependency Theory at the End of the Sixties

In this hectic historical conjuncture, and in parallel with the contributions of Latin American Structuralism, the dependency theory began to emerge as a more radically critical interpretation of the conditions of underdevelopment in Latin America promoted by political scientists and sociologists. The most important work within CEPAL was prepared by Cardoso and Faletto who explicitly subjected to analysis the positions of subordination (dependence) of the peripheral economies. This "dependency" movement counted both inside and outside CEPAL with Latin American thinkers of clearly Marxist affiliation (Theotonio Dos Santos, Rui Mauro Marini, Vania Bambirra, etc.). It should be noted, however, that the so-called theory of dependence, despite its criticisms of the work of CEPAL, took advantage to a high degree of the interpretations of peripheral capitalism previously elaborated by the institution. Reciprocally, several leading structuralist thinkers such as Celso Furtado and Osvaldo Sunkel began to use the language of dependency but without fully subscribing to what was called dependency theory. Thus, taken together the structuralist and "dependentist" paradigms contributed to the creation of a critical theory that could be grouped under the name of Latin American School of Development (Di Filippo 2007).

Cardoso and Faletto published *Dependence and Development in Latin America* in 1969, and that work had special influence on the use of that concept by Latin American Structuralism. In this book, the authors outlined a typology of two basic situations in strategic export activities: on one side those where the ownership of strategic resources was national, and, on the other, those where said property was held by foreign corporations. From this fundamental distinction, the book obtains important differentiating consequences in the political-social sphere.

The influence of the dependence movement strengthened three essential characteristics of structuralist thinking: First, the central role of the notions of power and domination in the interpretation of the Latin American Structuralism regarding such important categories as, among others, the center-periphery relationship or the structural heterogeneity. Second, the multidimensional nature (not only economic but also political and cultural) of the structuralist approach that Latin American Structuralism without losing the central axis of the economic dimension was gradually introducing. And third, the anticipation of the role of TCs in the growing cooptation and manipulation of Latin American integration. Currently, it is possible to distinguish with maximum clarity between markets integration only (free trade agreements [FTAs]) highly controlled by the interests of TCs under the rules of Washington Consensus on the one hand, and the most comprehensive regional integration treaties with economic, cultural, and political clauses, on the other (Mercado Común del Sur (MERCOSUR), Unión de Naciones Suramericanas (UNASUR), Comunidad de Estados Latinoamericanos y Caribeños etc. (CELAC)).

The Seventies: Military Dictatorships

After the assassination of John Kennedy and his brother Robert, the republican government of Nixon, advised by H. Kissinger, reinstated the policy of the "big stick", and in the early seventies, a new era of military governments that practiced state terrorism began to replace the cooperative and integrative efforts of the previous decade. Latin American military trained in the School of the Americas (Panama) collaborated in these concerted repressive tasks. There emerged, then, a sui generis species of "cooperation" between military dictatorships (Plan Condor) with the objective of coordinating repression on a South American scale.

Under these new historical conditions, regional integration as an instrument of industrial development and Latin American unity entered a state of hibernation. In 1980, Latin American Integration Association (Treaty of Montevideo of 1980) was created, which abandoned the original objective of moving toward a Latin American common market and opened the game to a variety of preferential agreements between Latin American countries, giving rise to something like a "menu" of options "a la carte" in terms of agreements.

The Eighties: Dramatic Ideological Changes in the Centers

Meanwhile, throughout the eighties both the power structures and the ideological framework were radically transformed in the centers. Keynesianism had proved ineffective in combating the "stagflation" situations experienced in the United States and Western Europe, and monetarist policies were beginning to dominate the scene. The rise to power of Ronald Reagan in the United States, Margaret Thatcher in Britain and Helmut Kohl in Germany, began the so-called Conservative Revolution. On the East-West axis at the end of the decade, there was the collapse of the Soviet bloc and the unification of Germany.

ECLAC, as a UN agency, received the directives from the governments that were its constituents through its biennial meetings. During the seventies, the oil crisis had generated an abundance of Eurodollars that led to credit permissiveness on behalf of private banks. The resulting Latin American indebtedness during that decade precipitated a crisis aggravated by the acute world recession of the eighties. Latin American countries, to comply with the financial commitments acquired, accepted the conditionalities imposed on them by the IMF and the World Bank. The pressures of these organizations contributed decisively to the imposition of the neoliberal model that ended up being fully installed on a Latin American scale at the beginning of the nineties.

The Ideas of the "Last" Prebisch: A New Point of Departure for Latin American Structuralism?

Raul Prebisch retired from his official duties and in parallel to these events, began to publish in the CEPAL Review (of which he was founder and director), a series of interpretative essays in the same structuralist line of which, 30 years earlier, he had been inspirational father. These reflections led to the publication of his last book *Peripheral Capitalism, Crisis and Transformation* (1981). It was an effort to bequeath a last set of ideas of their own that also tried to assimilate 30 years of Latin American Structuralism thinking, considering the dramatic changes that took place in the international order.

In these essays and in the aforementioned book, Prebisch's ideas were radicalized in a direction contrary to the orientations that neo-structuralism took, and explicitly and systematically incorporated the notion of power, including a typology of the main forms of power that operate in the social structure of the periphery. Prebisch spoke frankly and directly of the "hegemony of the centers" and of the forms of peripheral dependence, to culminate with his proposal on the social use of the surplus (SUS) considered by himself as a hybrid between socialism and liberalism.

It should be underlined again that in his last book Prebisch rescues with great force the notion of power (already used by him on previous books), distinguishing between different types of power (economic, social, political, etc.) that integrate the social structure. It thus transcends the conventional limits of economic thought resorting to its notion of social structure capable of including the multidimensional (institutional and technological) forms of Latin American societies, both the historically inherited and those that continue to be transferred from the hegemonic centers.

Prebisch's diagnosis is clearly different from the conciliatory vision oriented toward the self-regulation of market forces in the global era. By opposition, its interpretation presupposes an internally conflicting process inherent in the dynamics of peripheral capitalism, which inevitably leads to situations of crisis. This presentation of his arguments is already synthesized in the very title of his book that anticipates both the social struggle that leads to the crisis and the outline of an alternative path.

The notion of power is not an empty abstraction in Prebisch thought. It includes economic power (productive power and market power), social power (control of the means of information, communication and knowledge), and political power (institutions and mechanisms that condition the management of the state).

This position also implies a revolutionary rethinking, at least for Latin American countries, of the predominant economic theory in the hegemonic centers, when it affirms that the dynamics of the markets is an expression of deeper forces underlying in the dynamics of the social structure. This perspective, shared to some degree by other representatives of "classical" institutionalism (Veblen, Commons, Mitchel), rethinks the fundamentals that regulate the formation of market prices. Prebisch not only questions the notion of stable general equilibrium but also distances himself from the theories of labor value (in the Ricardian and Marxist versions), as well as from the neoclassical marginalists (of "utility value") opening the doors to a new and multidimensional theory of value (Di Filippo 2013).

Prebisch says:

> As a first approximation to reality we could consider peripheral development as a phenomenon of penetration of the technique of the centers, accompanied by transformations in the structure of society. This changing structure in turn affects the kind of technology and the intensiveness and extensiveness with which they are adopted.
>
> The structural transformation is varied and complex. The changes which occur in the income strata as technological penetration brings about a rise in productivity are of great importance for our analysis.
>
> The strata change according to the rate at which productivity increases and the way in which its effects are distributed. But as this happens, changes also take place in the social political and organized labour power of the different strata and, consequently, in the relations between them.
>
> Now, the power relations that derive from the structure of society ultimately determine the distribution of income, and the pattern of this distribution, conditions the penetration of technology and the ensuing rise in productivity.
>
> This influence of distribution (and therefore the structure of society) on technological penetration is discernible mainly in the capital accumulation the latter requires, in the kinds of technology adopted and in the patterns of consumption. All this acts in turn upon the social structure. (Prebisch 1976, 21)

In connection with his proposals about the SUS, Prebisch pointed out that a systemic transformation of such magnitude could only be carried out at a Latin American, or, at least South American level, but that is hardly feasible at national scales. The role of integration and cooperation, or, more broadly, of the search for Latin American unity, becomes crucial to undertake the paths that Prebisch's inspiring utopia shows us. Finally, Prebisch himself was responsible for clarifying that his proposals were only a constructive intellectual provocation to continue thinking and, in this task, it will be very necessary to rescue with energy the ideal of Latin American integration.

The Nineties: The United States Begins to Play the Integration Game

Beginning the nineties, the United States, for the first time since the postwar period, broke into the issue of regional integration, proposing the Initiative for the Americas in which it offered favorable treatment to the indebted Latin American countries that signed investment agreements and facilitated the penetration of TCs through FTAs. At the same time, it negotiated the North American FTA, with Canada and Mexico, and launched the negotiation proposal for the creation of the FTA of the Americas.

To counteract these tendencies and create a "South Americanist" bloc, presidents Raul Alfonsin of Argentina and José Sarney of Brazil, (with the accession of Uruguay and Paraguay) gave life to the Common Market of the South. Despite having recovered the ideal of a common market, the ideological turn that Latin America was experiencing quickly influenced the implementation of MERCOSUR when Carlos Menem and Fernando Collor took over after the presidential replacements. Even so, MERCOSUR (together with the Andean Community of Nations [CAN]) continued to be a benchmark for multidimensional integration (with not only economic, but also political and cultural objectives), as opposed to the type of one-dimensional integration (market integration only) of the FTAs. The irruption of United States in the integration treaties at the beginning of the nineties formed part of the transition to a new power structure linked to the new neoliberal rules of the game.

The Nineties: From the Latin American Structuralism to the Latin American Neo-Structuralism Integrationist Approach

Latin American Neo-Structuralism for its part (connected with the more "politically correct" postulates of CEPAL) refocused on the short and medium term on macroeconomic aspects without major incorporation of power relations. More precisely, Latin American Neo-Structuralism has undoubtedly privileged the macroeconomic-financial approach, returning to a greater disciplinary compartmentalization. Thus, its main contributions of the eighties were linked to the studies on the fiscal adjustments required for the payment of the debt, or to the macroeconomic balances on the short and medium term.

Departing from *Changing production patterns with social equity* (1990), the industrialist proposal was replaced by the new axis of international competitiveness in a clear return to the consideration of the forces of the world market as guides without major counterweights to the Latin American development process. This reorientation in favor of market self-regulation is even clearer in the document on *Open Regionalism*, coordinated by Gert Rosenthal and published in 1994 also as a conference document where it can be read:

> This document calls "open regionalism" the process that arises when reconciling both phenomena described in preceding paragraphs: the interdependence born of special agreements of a preferential nature and that driven basically by market signals resulting from trade liberalization in general. What is pursued with open regionalism is that explicit policies of integration are compatible with policies aimed at raising international competitiveness, and that they complement them.
>
> What differentiates open regionalism from the opening and non-discriminatory promotion of exports is that it includes a preferential ingredient, reflected in the integration agreements and reinforced by the geographical proximity and cultural affinity of the countries of the region. (ECLAC 1998, 911)

In short, the original integrationist ideal proposed by CEPAL is reduced in the new proposal to a "complement" of policies aimed at raising international competitiveness, and an "ingredient" of non-discriminatory promotion (that is, exclusively oriented by market signals) of exports. These brief paragraphs eloquently reflect the enormous theoretical and ideological contrast between the structuralist approach and the neo-structuralist one.

In the two documents aforementioned, the interpretative terminology of Latin American Neo-Structuralism changed. Any reference to the debates on *styles of development* of the previous decade disappeared, and the notions of hegemonic centers and of dependent peripheries were completely eliminated, there was no longer any further deepening of the notion of structural heterogeneity that could imply a critical analysis of the role played by TC. And CEPAL assumed in a very conventional way the notions of international competitiveness guided by market forces. In the background of these new proposals, the "new invisible hand" of TCs favored by the new integrationist strategy of the United States was superimposed on the "old invisible hand" of the market.

Twenty-First Century: The Irruption of China and the Protectionist Answer of Trump

While this process took place at the hemispheric level, the rapid economic expansion of the Asia-Pacific countries, which had already begun in the seventies with the Japanese economy and had continued throughout the eighties and nineties with the so-called Asian tigers (Korea, Taiwan,

Singapore, Thailand, etc.), acquired a new and enormous momentum with the emergence of China, which began to grow at double-digit rates starting in the nineties, unprecedented in the previous history of the capitalism. This emerging parallel process of the Asia-Pacific and of China in particular is fundamental to understanding the mega-agreements signed in connection with the Economic Association strategies on a world scale that began to take place throughout this century.

For the first time since the origins and consolidation of industrial capitalism and Western democracies, the economic development of the Asia-Pacific and of China in particular emerged with enough force to configure a new pole or center of development, able to counterbalance and even surpass the Western powers. This data is central to understanding the strategic realignments that are taking place in international economic relations. The foundation of APEC (Asia-Pacific Economic Cooperation), and, later, of the TPP (Trans-Pacific Partnership) with the active incorporation of the United States until the arrival of Trump to the Oval Office, was intended to participate in this new international playing field, helping to define its rules.

The TPP initially had the explicit goal of supporting the process to achieve "free trade" of goods, services, and investments within the APEC in 2020, as agreed by the leaders of this forum in 1994 in Bogor, Indonesia (the so-called Bogor Goals). For this, the preamble of the TPP affirms the commitment of the member countries to promote the adhesion of other economies to the agreement. Likewise, Article 20.6 established that both members and non-members of APEC can join the TPP.

In South America, the creation of the *Alianza del Pacífico* (Pacific Alliance) took place in 2011. It was integrated by Mexico, Peru, Chile, Colombia as full members, and Panama, Costa Rica as observers. Mexico, Peru, and Chile had joined the Trans-Pacific Partnership Agreement (Trans-Pacific Partnership). However, there was still a lack of approval from the respective national congresses.

The TPP established a free trade area without product exclusions (except a few for Brunei). It also included chapters on trade in services, public procurement, intellectual property, competition policy, and disputes resolution, among other matters, as well as an Environmental Cooperation Agreement and a Memorandum of Understanding on Labor Cooperation. The issues of investments and financial services were incorporated into the current expansion negotiations. In this sense, its norms followed the model previously established in other agreements such as the

North American Free Trade Agreement (NAFTA) or the frustrated Free Trade Agreement of the Americas.

In 2016, Donald Trump was elected president of the United States and raised a vision of the international order that means the deepest transformation of the international economy since the end of the Second World War. As soon as he took office, Trump withdrew the United States from the TPP, and reconsidered a deep renegotiation of NAFTA.

Although surprising and unexpected, this strategic reversal of the United States toward nationalist and protectionist positions is an expression of the loss of participation of this country in trade and production on a world scale. As it loses its industrial leadership, the United States becomes protectionist as an attempt to recover the positions of its country. The counterpart or "mirror" of this strategic shift has been the defense of free international trade on the part of China, which not only assumes the leadership in the world economic dynamism but also begins to decisively influence the orientations of the world development, not only through its direct investments but also through the constitution of the Brazil, Russia, India, China, and South Africa (BRICS) with its cooperation policy that includes the creation of a new world bank (Shanghai 2014). China has not only become a global player but, in addition, also bets to become the new hegemonic center of capitalism on a planetary scale.

Twenty-First Century: The "Pink Tide" and Its Weaknesses

A new wave (so-called the pink tide) appeared at the beginning of the twenty-first century giving place to the birth of UNASUR, CELAC, and ALBA, where it was recovered a multidimensional interpretation of integration and cooperation as mechanisms not only economic but also political and social in defense of Latin American interests and human rights.

On one hand, the "rebellious" governments that emerged in South America at the beginning of the twenty-first century (Chavez in Venezuela, Correa in Ecuador, Evo Morales in Bolivia, etc.) carried out a redistributive strategy (known as *inclusive neo-extractivism* and sometimes *twenty-first century socialism*) taking advantage of high prices of the basic products derived from the demand coming from China.

On the other hand, Argentina (under the government of the Kirchner couple), and Brazil (ruled first by Luis Ignacio Da Silva (Lula) and afterwards by Dilma Roussef) tried to deepen their industrial structures relying in their internal integrated markets. But, unfortunately their fiscal policies could not hold their redistributive efforts to develop a strong enough concerted productive strategy in the line originally proposed by Prebisch and CEPAL on the fifties. When the decline of commodity prices occurred again, the proverbial productive weaknesses already recorded in the Latin American Manifesto of 1949 arose once more.

The two major causes that led to the failure of the "pink tide" were first a redistributive voluntarism not sufficiently sustained on a solid and dynamic productive base; and, second, a wave of transversal corruption propagated from the advent of neoliberal capitalism that affected governments of all ideological colors (including the "pink" ones) with special virulence from the twenty-first century. Latin America was affected by this deep moral crisis, associated with the cultural impact of the market fundamentalism under the rules of the game of neoliberal financialization.

Regarding the first point, the profound structural cause that affected the redistributive measures in favor of the majorities was the weakness of the primary-exporting economies that supported this strategy. Hence, when China and the rest of Asia-Pacific began to reduce the intense pace of demand for food and raw materials, the prices of primary products began to fall, in the same way as the diagnostics of CEPAL had explained since the fifties. The mechanisms of integration and cooperation established during the period (UNASUR, CELAC, ALBA) remained since 2017, (as had happened in previous historical opportunities with other agreements) in a state of "hibernation".

Latin American Regional Integration: Notes for an Agenda

The role that Latin American integration can achieve in the twenty-first century will be linked to the deepening and updating of the structuralist approach formulated by Prebisch and CEPAL in the late forties and early fifties.

Among the topics to be developed or deepened are (a) the way in which space is introduced in development studies, (b) the insufficient and precarious form in which foundational structuralism dealt with the functions of a democratic state committed to the objective of development, and (c) the conflicts and forms of power that are articulated around the central role of the state (see Chap. 2).

With this objective, a way of conceiving integration (whether at the regional or sub-regional level) is here suggested in accordance with the structuralist approach and the Bolivarian tradition originated in the birth of Latin American nations. This way must be clearly distinguished from the way in which neoliberalism has conceived and implemented the theme of integration (through the FTAs mechanisms) since the nineties (Di Filippo 2013).

On the one hand, we can distinguish the (multidimensional) integration of nations whose natural limit is full political unity and the formation of supranational forms of democracy; and, on the other side, the (one-dimensional) integration of markets that leads to the transnational control of economic processes and, through this control, to the manipulation of political and cultural institutions by the hegemonic centers. It is obvious that the conflicts and power relations that permanently energize the social structures of Latin American nations are underlying in these two alternative approaches.

The distinctive role played by the territory in the definition of state and the legitimate use of physical violence emphatically highlights the geopolitical dimension without which it is not possible to speak of nation-states. This political dimension not only involves the notion of sovereignty but also the central role of citizenship as an essential and primary component of the state that was already highlighted more than 2000 years ago in Aristotle's *Politics*. In the political sphere, the process of supra-nationalization implies a growing sharing of sovereignties based on the installation of common regulations applicable directly in all the member countries of an integration bloc. In democratic regimes that compartment of sovereignties expresses a previous consultation to the will of the citizens of those countries.

The center-periphery relationship in its strict and original structuralist sense is a relationship between central national states on the one hand and peripheral states on the other. In the legal sphere, the state is the space of formal political power where the economic magnitudes that make possible the existence of balance of payments or calculations about the deterioration of the terms of exchange come to life. The state is also the legal sphere in which customs regulations are determined or tax regimes are applied, or expenditure budgets are calculated.

The multidimensional integration of national states is, in addition a multi-scalar process that supports political-administrative stratifications such as, for example, the local-municipal, the provincial-state (sub-national), the national, and the regional (supranational). In the case of the peripheral nations that address a process of multidimensional integration, common regulations may arise, referring, for example, to customs laws, military defense of borders, diplomatic representation activities, common agricultural policies, and so on. A reference source with rich experiences to be exploited refers, as is obvious, to the history of the European Union. The development of this topic puts us immediately in the field of geopolitics.

Two particularly sensitive issues in this area are those related to industrial policy and financing for development. In the one-dimensional market conception of integration that now predominates, it is easy to identify the leading role that TCs are fulfilling in both topics. By opposition in the multidimensional vision (integration of nation-states), it is possible to imagine common rules that allow the creation of strategies destined to regulate the productive and financial behavior of the TC. The issue directly affects the new versions of the economic interdependence that has been imposed by the globalization of capitalism. In particular, it affects the formation of global value chains that refer not to complete productive branches but rather to more specific products (or groups of products).

Regarding the issue of productive global chains (or global value chains), Raúl Prebisch observed (explicitly agreeing with previous opinions of Aldo Ferrer):

> Although it is seen, the strong industrial exchange of the centers is not based on the specialization of industrial sectors but of goods of such sectors under the powerful influence of the advancement of technology. In other words, the process of industrialization is characterized by industrial integration, that is, the combination of a wide range of sectors, without excluding agricultural production. In my opinion, nothing indicates that the centers are willing to dismantle sectors of their productive apparatus so that the periphery can increase their exports. The solution is not in this but in the specialization of products.
>
> And this is where the possibilities of reciprocal exchange, that is, the possibilities of joint import substitution, are also enormous, especially in the regional sphere and also in the global scope of the periphery. Reciprocal exchange to encourage internal integration and not to dismantle it. (Prebisch 1981, 239; Translation from the original)

In the other aforementioned subject, closely connected with the previous one, the issue of financing for productive activities originating in private transnational banking within the peripheries, exercised mainly to favor the management of TCs that operate in the production of goods, must be distinguished from other issues like public-state banking controlled by the peripheral states or from that of multilateral international organizations like World Bank or Inter-American Development Bank. In any case, the multidimensional blocks of Latin American integration (such as MERCOSUR or CAN) together with cooperation agencies for the defense of common interests within the framework of democratic ideals (as in the case of UNASUR, Comunidad Andina de Naciones (CAN), Alianza Bolivariana para los Pueblos de Nuestra América (ALBA), and CELAC) must play a decisive role. It is up to them to create the mechanisms to deal in a concerted manner with the productive or financial TCs, or to create shared and common regulations among them that are different from the rules and conditionalities emanating from the IMF or the World Bank.

The issue of economies of scale was central to ECLAC's argument for promoting regional integration to increase the size of the markets required for the expansion of certain manufacturing branches in accordance with the technological conditions of the fifties and the sixties. Today, in the second decade of the twenty-first century, the importance of mega markets belonging to giant nations such as China and India, as well as those derived from the inclusive integration agreements (like Transatlantic Trade and Investment Partnership [TTIP] or the aforementioned TPP) currently being negotiated, not only respond so much to the old industrialist concept of economies of scale but also take into account geopolitical and geoeconomic reasons in this particularly turbulent period in the history of capitalism. The increasing role of global markets refers not so much to the trends of trade itself but to the field of capital accumulation on the side of (financial and goods-producing) TNCs that increasingly influence the productive allocations at a planetary scale.

The subordination of international markets to the hegemony of global TCs with parent houses located in the Western world (including others originated in Japan and the southeastern Asian "tigers") lasted during the last 30 years of the twentieth century but is increasingly challenged by the BRICS since the beginning of this century.

The geopolitical dimension of regional integration and of world cooperation is also evident in the current struggle between the multilateral credit agencies of the Western World on the one hand, and the new financial institutions created within the BRICS under the undisputed leadership of China on the other hand. In the present conjuncture, these forms of competition between emerging hegemonic centers and preexisting ones can be strategically beneficial for Latin America and other peripheral regions of the world.

Concluding Remarks

The issue of regional integration in Latin America is at the heart of the productivist and industrializing message propagated by ECLAC and its main representatives of Latin American Structuralism since the fifties. The historical conditions have changed profoundly during the last 70 years, but Latin America has not been able to transform its productive structures and the nations that compose it continue to depend on the production and export of food and raw materials with relatively low levels of processing.

It is a significant fact that the low percentages of manufactures exported by the most industrialized countries of South America (such as Brazil or Argentina) are directed to a high degree to reciprocal trade. The liberalization of the exchange promoted by the integration agreements, with reduction in tariffs, improvement in transport, and communications infrastructures together with other forms of territorial connection and trade facilitation, has been of great help in this process. But the interconnection between the productive structures themselves and their mechanisms of capital accumulation is controlled to a high degree by the TCs.

Beyond the liberalization promoted through the FTAs, the formation of common markets and other more complete forms of socio-economic and political union requires coordination, harmonization, and, if such a thing is possible, also the unification of norms related to the labor and migratory legislation, with access to pension and health systems, and so on. All these aspects are essential to achieve a unification of labor markets (Di Filippo and Franco 2000).

In the same way, in the business world, coordination, harmonization, and eventual unification of tax, health, environmental, credit norms, and so on will be required, both for companies with headquarters in Latin America and for TCs. Obviously, the treatment of TCs, many of whose subsidiaries operate simultaneously in several Latin American countries, should be the subject of special coordination. The size and economic weight of these corporations, some of which have amounts of capital and sales that are long over the gross product of some Latin American countries, require concerted negotiation strategies in relation to tax issues, reinvestment of capital, remittance of utilities to parent companies, and so on. This aspect concerns not only the manufacturing and commercial companies but especially the TCs that operate in the mining-extractive industries and in the banking and financial areas. This regulatory and negotiating convergence does not ipso facto imply a hostile treatment before these companies but rather the assumption of concerted Latin

American positions that allow to improve their negotiating power. The important thing is to achieve regulatory convergences and highly concerted negotiating powers from Latin America.

Then, a multidimensional and profound integration such as that required to increase the productive interdependence of our nations is, above all, a geopolitical and geoeconomic process. It not only involves the structures of power but also the functioning of legal systems at the service of the nation-states with sufficient support to converge on these joint actions, whose final limit (located for now in the confines of utopia) would be the political union of Latin America, or, at least of South America, which is more viable. The world view of Latin American Structuralism can contribute to the achievement of these objectives (Di Filippo 2013).

References

Di Filippo, Armando. 2007. *La Escuela Latinoamericana del Desarrollo, Revista Electrónica de Moebio*, Número 29. Universidad de Chile.

———. 2013. *Poder Capitalismo y Democracia*. Santiago de Chile: RIL editores.

Di Filippo, Armando, and Rolando Franco. 2000. *Integración regional desarrollo y equidad*. Mexico: Siglo XXI editores.

ECLAC. 1998. *La Visión Centro Periferia Hoy, Revista de la CEPAL, número extraordinario para el 50 aniversario*, páginas 175–186.

Prebisch, Raúl. 1962. The Economic Development of Latin America and Its Principal Problems. *Economic Bulletin for Latin America* VII (1): 1–22.

———. 1963. *Towards a Dynamic Development Policy for Latin America*. New York: United Nations. https://repositorio.cepal.org/handle/11362/14892.

———. 1970. *Transformación Y Desarrollo: La Gran Tarea de América Latina*. Sección de Obras de Economía. México, D.F.: Fondo de Cultura Económica.

———. 1976. A Critique of Peripheral Capitalism. *CEPAL Review* (1): 9–76. http://repositorio.cepal.org/handle/11362/12273.

———. 1981. *El Capitalismo Periférico: Crisis y Transformación*. México, D.F.: Fondo de Cultura Económica.

UN ECLAC. 1951. *Estudio Económico de América Latina 1949*. Naciones Unidas Departamento de Asuntos Económicos E/CN.12/164/Rev.1, página 3.

Index[1]

[1] Note: Page numbers followed by 'n' refer to notes.

V. R. Fernández, G. Brondino (eds.), *Development in Latin America*,
https://doi.org/10.1007/978-3-319-92183-9

The manufacturer's authorised representative in the EU is Springer Nature Customer Service Centre GmbH, Europaplatz 3, 69115 Heidelberg, Germany. If you have any concerns regarding our products, please contact ProductSafety@springernature.com

Printed and bound by CPI Group (UK) Ltd, Croydon, CR0 4YY
25/09/2026
02222850-0001

This edited volume discusses the development theory advanced by the Economic Commission for Latin America and the Caribbean (ECLAC) in the 1940s, and its transformations through the second half of the twentieth century. In this time frame, the authors identify two approaches: structuralism (1950–1980) and neo-structuralism (1980-onwards). The contributors describe the transition in terms of economic theory and policy; the conceptualization of the State; and the consideration of space on regional and global scales. They argue that structuralism is still relevant for understanding the current problems of development if a careful and appropriate recovery and update of its main ideas and concepts is made in relation to the current context of globalization and internationalization of production and finance.

Víctor Ramiro Fernández is Professor at the National University of Litoral (UNL), Researcher of the National Scientific and Technical Research Council (CONICET), and Director of the Institute of Humanities and Social Sciences (UNL and CONICET), Argentina.

Gabriel Brondino is Lecturer at the National University of Litoral (UNL) and Doctoral Fellow of the National Scientific and Technical Research Council (CONICET), Argentina.

palgrave
macmillan

ISBN 978-3-030-06380-1

9 783030 063801

www.palgrave.com